The Puritan Way of Death

The Puritan Way of Death

A STUDY IN RELIGION, CULTURE, AND SOCIAL CHANGE

DAVID E. STANNARD

OXFORD UNIVERSITY PRESS
Oxford   New York   Toronto   Melbourne

Oxford London Glasgow
New York Toronto Melbourne Wellington
Ibadan Nairobi Dar es Salaam Cape Town
Kuala Lumpur Singapore Jakarta Hong Kong Tokyo
Delhi Bombay Calcutta Madras Karachi

Copyright © 1977 by Oxford University Press, Inc.
First published by Oxford University Press, New York, 1977
First issued as an Oxford University Press paperback, 1979
Library of Congress Cataloging in Publication Data
Stannard, David E
The Puritan way of death.
Includes bibliographical references and index.
1. Death. 2. Puritans—New England. I. Title.
BT825.S76   230′.5′9   76-42647
ISBN 0-19-502226-2
ISBN 0-19-502521-0 pbk.

Printed in the United States of America

To my parents
—who have always understood

And yet—in fact you need only draw a single thread at any point you choose out of the fabric of life and the run will make a pathway across the whole, and down that wider pathway each of the other threads will become successively visible, one by one.

HEIMITO VON DODERER
The Demons

Preface

An essay, wrote Dr. Johnson, is "a loose sally of the mind; an irregular undigested piece." Now that is not the sort of definition designed to encourage a modern scholar to refer to his or her work as an essay. Still, what follows *is* an essay—but I beg for a newer definition. "A rank of spotlights" is what Perry Miller once called a collection of his essays, and that seems good enough for me. Thus, what follows is a tentative, occasionally frankly speculative effort to shine a spotlight that it is hoped will illuminate some portions of a neglected area of study at the same time that it may make more comprehensible certain problems that continue to loom large in the modern consciousness. This is a work designed, then, to open a field of inquiry to questions rather than one claiming to dictate answers. The focus is on the human concern with death. The Puritans of New England are the people chosen to serve as exemplars of this concern.

Almost a century and a half has now passed since Alexis de Tocqueville began his monumental work on the state of American civilization by observing: "If we were able to go back to the elements of states and to examine the oldest monuments of their history, I doubt not that we should discover in them the primal cause of the prejudices, the habits, the ruling passions, and, in short, all that constitutes what is called the national character."[1] Historians today are generally more skeptical of such implied determinism than were Tocqueville and his contemporaries, but it may well be that something of an intuitive sense of agreement with Tocqueville on this matter is at least in part responsible for the fact that America's Puritans are today the objects of so much intensive historical study; indeed, considering their limited numbers in the population of American history, probably no other group of individuals has received as much historical attention in the past few decades.

There is, of course, another possible explanation for this interest. After he had been warned away from Puritanism as an object of study because "that field," his instructors noted, "was exhausted, all that wheat had long since been winnowed, there was nothing but chaff remaining," Perry Miller proceeded with his work anyway, largely because, as he was later to recall, the relative isolation and homogeneity of Puritan society afforded him what he called "an ideal laboratory."[2] It has become fashionable in recent years to criticize Miller's work for precisely this assumption: scores of books and articles have appeared during the past two decades that have taken as their primary purpose the undoing of Miller's vision of Puritan homogeneity. Most of these works have been detailed community studies, and many of them have been of exceptional quality and value. Whether they have seriously compromised Miller's work is still a question for debate; but it seems not at all improbable that their motivation has in large measure been similar to Miller's—that is, they have seen in Puritan culture and society the lineaments of numerous matters that transcend the world of those earliest New England settlers.

I should confess here that, while I do not literally regard early

1. Alexis de Tocqueville, *Democracy in America,* ed. by Phillips Bradley (New York: Alfred A. Knopf, 1945), Vol. I, p. 28.
2. Perry Miller, *Errand into the Wilderness* (Cambridge: Harvard University Press, 1956), p. viii; Miller, *The New England Mind: From Colony to Province* (Cambridge: Harvard University Press, 1953), Foreword.

New England as either the seedbed of American national character
or as a laboratory for controlled research, I have in subtler ways
been influenced in this study by the motivating ideas that under-
girded the work of both Tocqueville and Miller. The Puritans of
New England lived life and, as this book attempts to show, faced
death with an intensity virtually unknown in modern American life.
As a result, I believe that much of importance in subsequent
American history can be better understood by closely examining
the ideas and actions of the Puritans; I believe that Puritan culture—though not the whole of early New England society—was
sufficiently homogeneous for an extended period of time to permit
perhaps more responsible generalization than would be possible in
most other American cultural settings; and I believe that by focusing on a single critical thread of that culture—in this case the problem of death—"other threads," as Heimito von Doderer puts it in
the words chosen to serve as the epigraph for this study, "will become successively visible, one by one."

In this endeavor I have been greatly assisted by several persons.
Their number is not large, but my indebtedness to them is enormous. Sydney E. Ahlstrom, William A. Clebsch, David Brion
Davis, Bruce Kuklick, and Michael McGiffert all read and com-
mented helpfully on earlier drafts of portions of the manuscript.
Kai T. Erikson, Stephen Foster, and Richard Warch have provided
insightful criticism and advice concerning the entire study. But it is
to Edmund S. Morgan, for his criticism, his guidance, and most of
all his warm personal support, and to Valerie M. Stannard, for her
assistance with interpreting French and German language materials, for ironing out faulty logic and cumbersome prose in certain troublesome passages, and for always being there when it
counted, that I owe my greatest personal and intellectual debts.

Another debt of another kind should at least be acknowledged here.
It is to Ezra Pound for writing, many years ago, some words that
are relevant to every work of history that has ever been produced:

> And even I can remember
> A day when the historians left blanks in their writings,
> I mean for things they didn't know.

The day Pound envisioned has not yet come to pass, so the reader is advised against searching for blank spaces in the pages that follow, though no doubt more than a few should exist. It is hoped, however, that some of the missing answers, and some of the missing questions, will surface in a larger book on changing perceptions of the life cycle in American culture that I am now in the process of researching. In a sense, then, as many a Puritan would have agreed, death is only a beginning.

Acknowledgments

Grateful acknowledgment is made to *The American Historical Review* and *American Quarterly* for permission to include, in Chapters 2 and 3, revised versions of work previously published in their pages. *Frontispiece.* Photograph by Daniel Farber, printed with permission.

Fig. 7. *Top,* Courtesy of Yale University Art Gallery, The Mabel Brady Garvan Collection; *bottom left,* Courtesy of Essex Institute, Salem, Massachusetts; *bottom right,* Courtesy of Yale University Art Gallery, gift of Mrs. Charles Seymour in memory of Charles Seymour.

Fig. 8. Photographs by Daniel Farber, printed with permission.

Fig. 9. Photographs by Daniel Farber, printed with permission.

Fig. 10. Photographs by Daniel Farber, printed with permission.

Fig. 11. *Opposite page, top and bottom,* Reprinted, by permission, from Dickran and Ann Tashjian, *Memorials for Children of Change.* Middletown, Conn.: Wesleyan University Press, 1974; *this page,* Reprinted, by permission, from Edmund V. Gillon, Jr., *Victorian Cemetery Art.* New York: Dover Publications, 1972.

Fig. 12. Reprinted, by permission, from Edmund V. Gillon, Jr., *Victorian Cemetery Art.* New York: Dover Publications, 1972.

Fig. 13. Reprinted, by permission, from Edmund V. Gillon, Jr., *Victorian Cemetery Art.* New York: Dover Publications, 1972.

Contents

I

Introduction

1

Death in the Western Tradition

Religion, marriage, and burial of the dead—in these three institutions "all men agree and always have agreed." So wrote Giambattista Vico more than two and a half centuries ago. Indeed, "these institutions," he asserted, "will be able to give us the universal and eternal principles . . . on which all nations were founded and still preserve themselves." Vico thought he had reduced human culture to a hard and irresistible core, and it was from these three "eternal and universal customs" that he proposed to derive his New Science.[1]

Today we live in a time when the first two of Vico's first principles are loudly being called into question. But death and burial remain. They comprise perhaps the only constant. For death, unlike any other adventure or trial humans must experience, is a phenomenon marked by inevitable conceptual inconsistency. All the senses of the living agree in their perception of the death of another as the cessation of being; but to conceive of the cessation of self is quite another matter, requiring as it does the imaginative reconstitution of the self as a perceiving agent in order for the very conception of nonbeing to exist. "It is indeed impossible to imagine our own death," wrote Freud, reflecting on the aftermath of the First World War, "and whenever we attempt to do so we can perceive that we are in fact still present as spectators. Hence . . .

3

at bottom no one believes in his own death, or, to put the same thing in another way, in the unconscious every one of us is convinced of his own immortality." Writing at almost precisely the same time, the Spanish philosopher Miguel de Unamuno put it even more concisely: "It is impossible for us, in effect, to conceive of ourselves as not existing, and no effort is capable of enabling consciousness to realize absolute unconsciousness, its own annihilation."[2] Freud and Unamuno would have been among the first to agree that other poets and prophets had long preceded them in this observation; indeed, as one psychoanalyst has more recently noted, perhaps the psalmist David said it best: "A thousand shall fall at thy right hand and ten thousand at thy left, but it shall not come nigh thee."[3]

In facing this dilemma we are driven to resolve it. Man has never been able to live comfortably with the awareness of contradiction and uncertainty. And if a certainty of man's imagination points to his own individual immortality, resolution of the attendant conflict has always seemed to demand the sharing of that immortality at least with one's recognized peers. It is this fundamental dilemma imposed by the existence of death, and the limited knowledge that men necessarily have of it, that Malinowski and other early anthropologists saw as the primary source of religion. And it is this same fundamental dilemma, coupled with the various forms of its imaginative resolution, that is the cornerstone of this book on Puritan America. But first it is necessary to undertake a brief, necessarily schematic review of the long human traditions the Puritans, and all of us, have inherited. We must begin at the beginning.

The dawn of the human era has recently been placed at roughly four million years B.C., with the Australopithecine discoveries in southern and eastern Africa, though with each new archaeological finding that dawn seems to be ever receding. Still, it is with Peking man (ca. 500,000 B.C.) that we continue to find the first clear signs of culture and ritual. The specific content and purpose of this ritual remains unclear. Some archaeologists, viewing the evidence, regard it as indicative of no more than Peking man's participation in cannibalistic feasts. Others argue that the prehistoric data suggest Peking man's involvement in a fairly complex burial ritual through which, as one scholar has put it, "the memory of the departed was cherished and their help and protection sought for the tribe."[4] But whatever the tribal intent of this, man's earliest ritual behavior, one point remains unchallenged: the occasion and motivation for that activity was death.

When turning to the Upper Pleistocene Period (ca. 50,000–60,000 B.C.), scholars no longer have any doubt that man was engaging in purposeful and elaborate funeral ritual and almost certainly believed in a postmortem existence. Bodies were placed in graves filled with shells and bone and ivory ornaments, and the flesh or bones of the corpses were often coated with a red ocher substance, the red tint probably suggesting the color of life. Prior to burial, the body was often bound into a fetal position, a practice whose symbolic significance has stimulated widespread debate among anthropologists.[5] To some observers, this practice suggests a prehistoric belief in rebirth; others have interpreted it as an attempt by the living to restrict the movement of the dead—more specifically, as a device to prevent the dead from returning to the world of the living. Either way, the idea that the dead lived on either in a spiritual or material sense was almost surely present.

To appreciate the early state of man's development at the time when such relatively sophisticated ideas emerged, it is worth noting here that these rituals probably took place before man had developed the skills to express even the most minimally abstract ideas in language and well over twenty-five thousand years before the appearance of the most primitive forms of cave art.[6] During these hundreds of intervening centuries, no substantive conceptual elaboration of man's vision of a postmortem existence can be demonstrated. To be sure, there appear to be many variations and changes in the ritual treatment of the dead, but there is no evidence that prior to the middle of the third millennium B.C. there existed any widespread consensus as to the specific nature of an afterlife state. It is true, for instance, that as early as 7000 B.C. there apparently existed ancestor cults in the Jordan Valley and elsewhere, cults that used clay to remodel the features of the dead around the shape of the skull.[7] But the earliest clear signs of a culturally consistent picture of the afterlife must be found in written records, and for them, we must look to Ancient Mesopotamia and Egypt.

The Epic of Gilgamesh, compiled from various Mesopotamian texts apparently independently created, is generally dated around 2000 B.C., although as individual works these writings are surely much older.[8] An afterlife is clearly presented in this tale of a man's quest for immortality, and the presentation is a grim one. The dwelling place of the dead is described as "the house of darkness . . . the house whose occupants are bereft of light; where dust is their food and clay their sustenance." Further, this dank, dark underworld—believed to exist not much more than a few feet beneath the earth's crust—is the unpleasant end for all, "the common lot of mankind," regardless of one's earthly station or behavior. We have here, then, perhaps the first portrayal of death in the eventually archetypal role of the great leveler—stripping all equally not only of life but of earthly accomplishments and pretensions, treating alike those who had achieved distinction in life and those who had not.[9] Small wonder, then, that the most potent advice offered the young seeker of eternal life was that of Siduri, the wine maiden:

> Gilgamesh, whither runnest thou?
> The life which thou seekest thou will not find;
> [For] when the gods created mankind,
> They allotted death to mankind,
> [But] life they retained in their keeping.
> Thou, O Gilgamesh, let thy belly be full;

Day and night be thou merry;
Make every day [a day of] rejoicing.
Day and night do thou dance and play.
Let thy raiment be clean,
Thy head be washed, and thyself be bathed in water.
Cherish the little one holding thy hand,
[And] let thy wife rejoice in thy bosom.
This is the lot of [mankind . . .][10]

Even older than the Gilgamesh epic are the Pyramid Texts of Egypt, which take their name from the fact that they are inscribed on the walls of the five pyramids at Sakkarah built in the middle of the third millennium B.C. Along with the later Coffin Texts and the still later papyrus inscriptions of the eighteenth dynasty, the Pyramid Texts make up what is today known as the Egyptian Book of the Dead; but as with the Gilgamesh epic, it is evident that the Pyramid Texts arise out of religious and funerary beliefs dating back to a much earlier period.[11] The Egyptians of this period, like the Mesopotamians, had a definite picture of the afterlife. And, also like the Mesopotamians, they were generally in no hurry to accomplish that final passage. With the Egyptians, however, this reluctance was not based on a fear of a universal and common postmortem fate; rather, it was at least in part due to the Egyptian belief that different fates awaited different individuals. For as best we can tell, it was in Egypt that the idea of divine judgment after death made its first appearance in human society.[12] Although it is now impossible to assign specific conscious motives to those who developed and popularized the idea of a postmortem judgment, the proposition that this concept emerged in response to the anxieties evident in the Gilgamesh epic concerning the psychic emptiness of death seems plausible if not likely.

Premised on the resurrection-based religion of Osiris, which had dominated most of Egypt by the time of the sixth dynasty, the Pyramid Texts deal primarily with the problem of how to determine the legitimacy of divine lineage for deceased pharaohs seeking their rightful place in the afterlife. Yet from this narrow cultural base, the fundamental principles were established on which later, more elaborate, and more socially inclusive ideas of postmortem judgment would be founded. And by the time of the Coffin Texts (ca. 2000 B.C.) the belief in a *general* postmortem judgment—a judgment based on an evaluation of the individual's morally upright earthly behavior—was held widely. An elaborate procedure designed to facilitate the rendering of a favorable decision by Osiris began with the deceased proclaiming his innocence of a long list of sins to which mortals are susceptible and concluded with the god Osiris rendering his judgment based on the outcome of the "weighing of the heart," at which time the deceased's heart was required to be so pure that it perfectly counterbalanced the Feather of Truth.[13]

The details of Egyptian belief and ritual are of less concern to us, however, than is the historical importance of this early conception of a postmortem judgment. Not only is it true, as S. G. F. Brandon has observed, that "no other people were to achieve a comparable view of the eternal significance of a morally good life until many long centuries had passed,"[14] but it is also noteworthy that when such a view did begin to spread, it would leave few corners of the habitable Western world untouched by its influence.

But if the idea of a postmortem existence and judgment addressed the fundamental problems of death as the simple cessation of self, it brought with it anxieties of a different kind. For it was not without some apprehension that Egyptians viewed the trial awaiting them before the shrine of Osiris. Whether or not the ultimate conscious rationale for the idea of judgment can be seen—as Hannah Arendt has said of the Platonic vision of Hell—as "an ingenious device to enforce obedience upon those who are not subject to the compelling power of reason, without actually using external violence,"[15] the end result was the same. Death came to be feared and often to be viewed as an enemy despite—indeed, as a direct result of—the apparent Egyptian attempt to deal with the terrifying threat of death as simply the cessation of self. This new fear, of course, was based on the problematic nature of the fate that lay on the other side of the chasm of death; but as such, that fate could at least be influenced by evidence of one's goodness in life. In this, and especially in view of the fact that most Egyptians apparently were judged favorably in the Osirian presence, the judgment-based apprehension of death was perhaps something of a psychic improvement over the response to the great gray fate described in Mesopotamian legend. But psychic improvement or not, in either case the cultural response to death—from the prescribed quasi-hedonism of the Gilgamesh epic to the elaborate funerary ritual of the Egyptians—was directly related to the vision of death's meaning.

And so it is with all cultures. Whether, as with hunting and gathering communities, where, as Joseph Campbell puts it, people "live in a world of animals that kill and are killed and hardly know the organic experience of a natural death," and thus regard death as an externally caused phenomenon to be strenuously resisted by magic, or, as in ancient Taoist China, where death was given its place in the "general attitude toward the universal laws of nature, which is one not merely of resignation nor even of acquiescence, but a lyrical, almost ecstatic acceptance," the behavior of a people in the face of dying is the result of their attitude toward, and their vision of, death.[16]

In a more generalized sense, as Clifford Geertz has written, the *ethos*—"the tone, character, and quality of . . . life, its moral and aesthetic style and mood"—grows out of the *world view,* that is, the "picture of the way things, in sheer actuality are, [the] concept of nature, of self, of society." The influence is of course two-directional; the two elements are, as Geertz puts it, "reflexes of one another." Suggesting a certain synonymity between these terms and religious "belief" (world view) and "ritual" (ethos), Geertz goes on:

> Religious belief and ritual confront and mutually confirm
> one another; the ethos is made intellectually reasonable by
> being shown to represent a way of life implied by the actual
> state of affairs which the world-view describes, and the world-
> view is made emotionally acceptable by being presented as
> an image of an actual state of affairs of which such a way of
> life is an authentic expression.[17]

In short, the two phenomena, ethos (in the present case, the prescribed "way" of dying) and world view (the vision or concept of
death) reinforce one another, and thus fused, give meaning, order,
and stability to their cultural source. Men of all times may well
fear death, as Bacon wrote, "as children fear to go in the dark."[18]
But they deal with that fear first by imagining something existing
in the darkness, and then by acting accordingly.

So it was with those members of prehistoric cultures who imagined a life beyond death and who thus applied cosmetic coloring to
the bodies of the deceased, bound them, and buried them with
tokens of their earthly goods. So it was with the Mesopotamians of
antiquity, who imagined that the life awaiting them beyond the
grave was one of universal wretchedness, and who thus urged upon
themselves a philosophy of life characterized by self-indulgence.
So it was with the Ancient Egyptians, who imagined an awesome
face-to-face judgment following their death, and who thus composed long prayers denying culpability in sin and put to use all
the artistic and literary powers at their command to ward off an
unfavorable verdict. And so it was, two millennia later, with the
early Christians.

Prior to the Christian era the Homeric Greeks had devised the
concept of the soul, an idea that grew out of a common earlier belief that the dead continued to live under the earth. This later
vision of the disembodied spirit seems to have opened the way to
the practice of cremation. But it was not until the worship of Dio-
nysius, and in the writing of Heraclitus, that the belief in the soul's
immortality attained explicit and clear expression. This spiritual

answer to the fear of cessation became part of one of the central tenets of Christian doctrine in the idea of the resurrection. "I am the Resurrection and the life," Christ had said, "he that believeth in Me, although he be dead shall live: and everyone that liveth and believeth in Me shall not die for ever." Thus, in the fourth century, Augustine could say of the death of his mother, "we thought it not fitting to solemnise that funeral with tearful lament, and groanings; for thereby do they for the most part express grief for the departed, as though unhappy, or altogether dead; whereas she was neither unhappy in her death, nor altogether dead." And Saint Ambrose, in his oration at the funeral of Valentinian, says: "But if the gentiles, who have no hope of resurrection, are consoled by this alone, in that they say that after death the departed have no life and consequently no sense of pain remains, how much the more should we receive consolation because death is not to be feared, since it is the end of sin, and that life is not to be despaired of which is restored by the resurrection?"[19]

Yet if Christianity was successful in combating the fear of death as cessation of self, it retained at its philosophical center the source of anxiety that had afflicted the Ancient Egyptian—the concept of divine wrath, of punishment for sin; for along with the doctrine of immortality, Christianity devised and elaborated various places of bliss and misery as the potential residences of the soul. For the saved there was Heaven, for the unrepentant Hell, and for the great masses, who had not yet been thoroughly cleansed of minor sins, there developed in later centuries the idea of Purgatory. As Aquinas was to observe in the thirteenth century, "since a place is assigned to souls in keeping with their reward or punishment, as soon as the soul is set free from the body it is either plunged into hell or soars to heaven, unless it be held back by some debt, for which its flight must needs be delayed until the soul is first of all cleansed."[20]

While Hell was clearly a place to be avoided, and although the temptations of Satan were many and great, the sinful were afforded a variety of ways through which they might avoid Hell. Baptism cleansed the soul of original sin; confession and the administration of the Eucharist throughout life prepared the soul for Heaven; the sacrament of extreme unction and the viaticum at death further cleared the way; and even while the imperfect but uncondemned soul lingered in Purgatory, indulgences, requiem masses, and the prayers of the living helped improve the likelihood of imminent removal to Heaven. For those who would not repent, Christianity evolved through a literary and artistic tradition a vision of Hell that surpassed virtually all other cultures in literal, horrific depictions of the fate awaiting the sinful, depictions most often accompanied by a warning such as that bordering the Last Judgment tympanum of Conques (ca. 1130): "Sinners, if you do not mend your ways, know that a heavy judgment awaits you." The consequences of sin were clearly terrifying, but the critical point not to be missed was that the fate of the Christian individual was largely in his own hands. The sinner did not have to sin, and having sinned, might still at any later time be able to mend his ways and thereby avoid Hell. Though it was a fearsome end for the soul, Hell was an end that could, though admittedly with a good deal of work, be avoided.

In Ancient Egypt one of the most common symbols on funerary art had been the scale of judgment, whereon the individual's soul was to be so totally without sin that it perfectly counterbalanced the Feather of Truth. In Christendom that same symbol appears and reappears, with one fundamental difference: now the good of the soul must outweigh the evil. In both instances, however, the depicted result is almost always favorable—and in much medieval art this is also true despite the wily but vain attempts of devils to tip the scales in their favor. It is not surprising, then, to find the early Christian attitude toward the death of a believer reflecting a certain similarity with that of the Egyptian *Migratio ad Dominum,* an optimistic and joyous journey home.[21]

But if, in at least certain respects, there was a similarity between

the Egyptian and Christian ideals, when compared with the Mesopotamian view of mortal and postmortal existence the Christian
vision provides a vivid and critically important reversal. Instead of
clinging to the world of the living, of making the most of mortal
pleasures before succumbing to the wretchedness of death and the
afterlife, the Christian was urged to forgo earthly pleasure for the
greater peace of salvation. Again and again in the writings of
the early Christians, reference is made to the passage in 1 John
2:15–16 to "love not the world, neither the things that are in the
world. If any man love the world, the love of the Father is not in
him. For all that is in the world, the lust of the flesh, and the lust of
the eyes, and the pride of life, is not of the Father, but is of the
world."

   Taken to its logical and literal extreme this and other early doctrines could and did cause problems in the first few centuries of the
Christian era, problems that were destined to remain at least latent
in the church's belief system for many centuries to come—and problems that this study will be returning to in subsequent chapters.
The early Christian emphasis on predestination is one of these concerns, as is the tendency found in the earliest of the church's leaders to stress the literal imminency of Christ's Second Coming. As
for the ascetic and otherworldly bias built into the theme to "love
not the world, neither the things that are in the world," one extreme affective response during the first few centuries of Christendom was what can only be described as a suicidal lust for martyr-
dom. From the zealousness of Saint Ignatius's "passion for death"
and his longing to "be fodder for wild beasts" expressed in his de-
fiant letter to the Romans, to the suicidal "daily sport" (to quote
Saint Augustine) of the Donatists of the fourth and fifth centuries,
early Christianity was beset with inner tensions and contradictions
that demanded resolution if the faith were ever to exist with even a
modicum of internal equilibrium. In time, most notably behind the
force of Augustine's powerful writings, most of these tensions and
contradictions were subdued, if not resolved.[22] In short, to return

to the terms employed earlier, Christian world view (belief) and ethos (ritual) successfully fused. Thus, for example, supramundane existence was seen to be made up of God; of Heaven, Hell, and eventually Purgatory; and of the souls of men assigned their place principally on the basis of their earthly behavior. At the same time, the institutions—from baptism to the requiem mass—had been created to make such a world view emotionally and intellectually acceptable. In theory at least, a believing and practicing Christian was armed against fear when death approached. A culturally functional concept of death had been constructed and made viable; now it had only to be maintained.

Fear, of course, still plagued men, even Christians. In Europe during the late Middle Ages it appears to have reached a peak of intensity, probably due in large measure to the devastating plagues that wracked western Europe during the fourteenth and fifteenth centuries, though other possible explanations have been offered.[23] During this period the *danse macabre* and *Ars Moriendi* traditions developed and flourished. Tomb sculpture turned toward literal representations of the deceased in advanced stages of decomposition; life-size images of the naked dead were sculpted, with great care taken to depict such details as the abdomen stitches of the embalmers and the decayed and vermin-infested flesh of the corpse. And it was during this period that, as Theodore Spencer has put it, "a great poet, like Villon, had nothing but death to write about." "It is hardly an exaggeration," Spencer writes, "to say that in Northern Europe the whole fifteenth century was frenzied about death."[24]

Frenzied, perhaps, but a confined frenzy, a frenzy that operated

---

Fig. 1. *Opposite page, top,* Ancient Egyptian weighing of the heart of the scribe Ani; the classic scene of the judgment of the dead in the Hall of Maati; *bottom,* Thirteenth century depiction, from a Catalan altar, of the weighing of the soul by Saint Michael.

Fig. 2. An example, from the tomb of Francois de Sarra (ca. 1400), of the late medieval preoccupation with bodily decomposition and the physical horrors of death.

within the parameters of the Christian scheme and the ecclesiastical system. The primary medieval concern was with the physical horrors of deterioration and death. The *danse macabre,* Johan Huizinga has noted, "is a dance of the dead and not of Death." Its principal purpose was to "remind the spectators of the frailty and the vanity of earthly things . . . while at the same time [it] preached social equality as the Middle Ages understand it, Death levelling the various ranks and professions."[25] Similarly, the poetry of Villon and others, whether focusing on life or death, was typically rendered in such passages as

> My forehead's wrinkled, my hair grey,
> my eyebrows thin, and sight grown dim
> whose eyes once glanced and led my way
> so many men. My ears once trim
> hang down like moss, my face is grim,
> colourless, dead, with furrowed chin,
> nose far from beauty bent, a rim
> of lips, fleshless as trod grapeskin.
>
> So this is human beauty's end:
> arms writhed, crazed hands too weak to lift,
> back hunched until the shoulders bend.
> My breasts? No tits to nudge a shift;
> my tail the same, skin all adrift.
> My quim, for Christ's sake! And thighs?
> No more than hafts, skin, bone and rift,
> all blotched like sausages. Some Prize!

and

> Death trembles him and bleeds him pale,
> the nostrils pinch, the veins distend,
> the neck is gorged, skin limp and frail.
> Joints knot and sinews draw and rend.
> O Woman's body, so suave and tender,
> so trim and dear, must you arrive
> at such an agony in the end?
> Oh yes, or rise to Heaven live.[26]

Even when the subject of the Resurrection was addressed, there was an intense emphasis placed on the problems thus posed for the disintegrated corpse. In *La Lumiere as lais,* for instance, as in the relevant sections of Aquinas's *Summa Theologica,* much of the catechismal interrogation explicitly demonstrates a deep concern for the eventual physical condition of both condemned sinners and the resurrected elect. A popular belief of the period, now re-

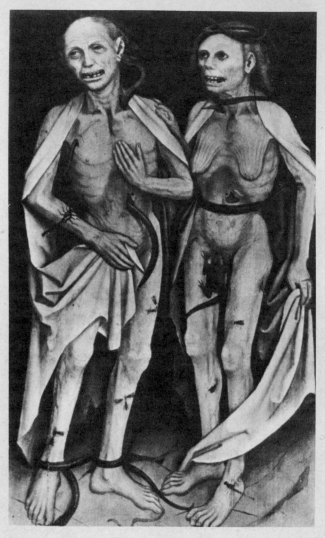

Fig. 3. Another example of the "preoccupation with putrefaction" of the late Middle Ages. From Mathias Grunewald's "The Damnation of Lovers," Strasbourg Cathedral Museum, 15th century.

ferred to as the "myth of Lazarus," claimed that, following his resurrection, Lazarus lived in constant torment with the knowledge that he would have to endure the physical act of dying a second time. And little wonder, when it was believed that the most excruciating mortal torment imaginable occurred at the very moment of death. As one popular fourteenth-century manuscript advised, that terrifying moment could best be understood if one "lykend mans lyf til a tre"—a tree with roots stretching into and fastened onto every part of the body, from the tips of the fingers and toes, through the veins and joints and sinews, and finally wrapping tightly about the heart. At the moment of death the pain experienced was like the violent wrenching of that tree and its grasping roots from the crumbling bodily "soil" in which it was imbedded.[27]

But whatever the particular source of irresistible horror, and such sources abounded in most of Europe throughout the late Middle Ages, it was invariably the physical quality of death and dying which elicited that response. Even the *Ars Moriendi,* "in spite of its purpose," as Mary C. O'Connor notes, "is not a doleful book—no clarion call to repentance. There is little stress upon hell, only hope of heaven. Always is Moriens encouraged and consoled."[28] Death in the late Middle Ages was a ghastly visitation upon the *body* of man, but fear of the soul's fate—as can be clearly seen in the final line of the verse quoted from Villon above—remained blunted by the Christian tradition. As Huizinga observes: "The dominant thought, as expressed in the literature, both ecclesiastical and lay, of that period, hardly knew anything with regard to death but these two extremes: lamentation about the briefness of all earthly glory, and jubilation over the salvation of the soul."[29]

In short, Christian optimism, the principal weapon against the fear of death, was not shaken by the morbidity of the Middle Ages. This was true largely because of the closely contemporaneous development of the two themes. Paralleling the medieval fascination with the physical texture of death was the Christian tradition of the *contemptus mundi,* which opened in full flower midway through

Fig. 4. The concluding scene in the *Ars Moriendi* (ca. 1450): The dying man has resisted the temptations of the demons depicted in disarray in the foreground and has died peacefully. His soul is shown issuing from his mouth and being received by a company of angels.

the medieval period. Although preceded by a good many other writings on the same theme (and of course deeply indebted to the ascetic impulse of the early church fathers), the *De Contemptu Mundi* of Pope Innocent III, written at the turn of the thirteenth century, was for several centuries regarded as the seminal statement on the subject of man's relation to the world and the afterlife. During the following three hundred years Innocent's work was translated and reprinted time and time again—in London, Cologne, Paris, Lyons, Barcelona, and elsewhere—though more often than not under the work's even more revealing subtitle, *Liber de Miseria Humanae Conditionis.*

Innocent's message, though elaborately argued, was in fact quite direct and seemingly elemental in purpose. It was, as Donald R. Howard has aptly remarked, "a kind of ascetical *summa.*"[30] All the pains of mankind as well as all the vanities were valued less than nothing in the scale of things. In Innocent's work, and perhaps even more openly in the work of those many writers who were for centuries to follow in his footsteps, earthly corruption, vileness, and depravity were natural to the state of man; only by turning away from earthly fears and desires, only by pursuing an ascetic and celibate ideal, only by renouncing mortal passions and concentrating solely on the spiritual glories of God and Heaven—only then could true humility and salvation be found.

Whatever the reasons for the obsessive concern with death in the late Middle Ages, the most striking legacy of that era is that in the face of such an enormous challenge, the dominant belief system of the age—Christianity—remained essentially intact. At the same time that it doubtless contributed to what T. S. R. Boase has recently termed this "strange preoccupation with putrefaction,"[31] the ascetic bias of traditional Christianity, as expressed (in mediated form) in the *contemptus mundi,* served as a release for the tremendous inner tensions such a direct and graphic confrontation with death must have wrought. And when this intense preoccupation finally began fading at the close of the Middle Ages, the immemorial

Christian answers to the fear of death remained secure. Moreover, with the growth and acceptance of the idea of Purgatory, men's minds seem to have become increasingly less concerned with the awesomeness of judgment and damnation.[32] Thus, Edelgard Dubruck observes, Renaissance poetry on the theme of death

> stressed immortality and the afterlife. The word "death" was often avoided and replaced by euphemisms . . . [and] depiction of the realistic aspects of death was carefully suppressed. . . . In the early sixteenth century, poets dwelt upon fame and immortality rather than death, and in the Reformation writings death had at least lost its sting, and both Lutherans and Calvinists insisted that death was at long last vanquished with the help of Christ.[33]

Indeed, more than vanquished, there is every indication that in the early stages of the Reformation death—linked with repentance and conversion—took on a renewed sense of optimism. The death-bed torments and fears preceding the peaceful death depicted in the *Ars Moriendi* became anachronistic as the power of good works waned; but the *contemptus mundi* theme held sway. "Yearning for death," as Luise Klein has noted, became "the center of belief, for it [meant] the rejection of the world—sin—and the affirmation of God." The horrors of the physical texture of death—the horrors that had so dominated art and literature in the Middle Ages—were thus diminished and, indeed, transformed. This is not to say that literal artistic depictions of the dead were no longer created (though never again would they be so pervasive as they were in the late Middle Ages), but when they did appear—as in the powerful sixteenth-century image of the corpse of René of Chalons offering his heart to Heaven—the terrible tension between earthly and heavenly existence had been clearly resolved in Heaven's favor. Once again, as Klein observes, "contempt for the world, contempt for death, and yearning for it," totally dominated the Christian confrontation with death.[34]

It is not at all surprising, then, to find John Harington, for example, writing in 1554:

> Death is a porte whereby we pass to joye;
> Lyfe is a lake that drowneth all in payne;
> Death is so dear, it killeth all annoye;
> Lyfe is so lewd, that all it yields is veyne.
> For, as by lyfe to bondage man was brought,
> Even so by deathe all freedom too was wrought.[35]

And by the time the seventeenth century was underway, among the more typical responses to death were those of William Drummond, who saw it as "but a short, nay, sweet sigh; and . . . not worthy the remembrance," of Jeremy Taylor, who wrote that "it is so harmless a thing, that no good man was ever thought the more miserable for dying, but much the happier," or of Sir Thomas Browne, who because of the expected negative reactions of others—even "the Birds and Beasts of the field"—to his physical remains, was "not so much afraid of death, as ashamed thereof."[36]

If this common seventeenth-century attitude can be traced, at least in part, to the *contemptus mundi* theme, it is also crucial to note that the idea of contempt for the world had begun to encounter serious resistance in some quarters in the late fifteenth and sixteenth centuries. Few examples of this resistance are more informative than that of the famous Erasmus of Rotterdam.

In 1488 or 1489, when Erasmus was a twenty-year-old monk, he wrote a treatise on the contempt of the world. This was a common enough activity by this time for a young monk to engage in, what was not common happened some thirty years later. Having been made aware that copies of this youthful document were being circulated, Erasmus supported publication of the work, but only after he added a preface and a new final chapter. In the preface he referred to the treatise as but a "trifling piece with which I amused myself while a mere boy in practicing the art of composition." Erasmus's uncharacteristic modesty here is made more understand-

able when the new last chapter is examined. In it Erasmus attacks the monasteries of the day (in the earlier-written chapters he had praised the silent, celibate monastic life and attacked marriage and the pleasures of the flesh) and argues that life in the world can be at least as pure as that in the monk's retreat.[37]

Now, to be sure, the direct impact of Erasmus on popular religious thought of sixteenth-century Europe was certainly limited. But his impact on several religious innovators of the time—most notably John Calvin—was little short of profound. It may be going too far to say, as H. R. Trevor-Roper has, that Calvin was in fact "the heir of Erasmus,"[38] but the fact does remain that there are clear connections between certain ideas of the two men. And unlike those of Erasmus, the ideas of Calvin ignited a popular religious upheaval throughout sixteenth-century Europe.

The world to Calvin's mind was not at all a thing from which the godly should withdraw. On the contrary, it was the handiwork of God, and men, as part of that world, were urged to engage fully in it—though not, it must be emphasized, to partake fully *of* it. Indeed, to Calvin the Pauline denunciation of "disorderly persons" applied "not to those that are of a dissolute life, or to those whose characters are stained by flagrant crimes, but to indolent and worthless persons, who employ themselves in no honourable and useful occupation."[39] To many reformers reading these words a better description of the monastic life could not have been penned.

For centuries throughout Christendom the idea had been com-

Fig. 5. *Opposite page,* The Sixteenth century tomb of René of Chalons. Depicted as it was conjectured he would have looked three years after his death in 1544, the image of René is as gruesome as any earlier representations of the dead—but the outstretched arm containing the young man's heart (his actual heart was supposedly sealed inside the statue) is powerfully suggestive of the transcendent glory of salvation. "And though after my skin, worms destroy this body," reads the tomb's inscription, "yet in my flesh shall I see God."

mon that monks and priests were led to their holy station in response to a special "calling" they had received from God. To Calvin and other reformers, including the English Puritans, the concept of "calling" had a very different meaning. It was simply, wrote the Puritan divine William Perkins, "a certain kind of life, ordained and imposed on man by God, for the common good." But specifically excluded under Perkins's conditions were those who had traditionally assumed exclusive right to it. Immediately following a passage on the lack of calling to be found among "rogues, beggars, [and] vagabonds . . . [who] are as rotten legges, and armes that drop from the body," Perkins turned to the similarly un-Christian "condition of Monks and Friars"

> who challenge to themselves that they live in a state of perfection, because they live apart from the societies of men in fasting and prayer: but contrariwise, this Monkish kind of living is damnable; for besides the generall duties of fasting and praier, which appertaine to al Christians, every man must have a particular & personal calling, that he may bee a good and profitable member of some society and body. And the auncient Church condemned all Monkes for theeves and robbers, that besides the generall duties of prayer and fasting, did not withal imploy themselves in some other calling for their better maintenance.[40]

In a striking rejection of the *contemptus mundi* tradition, Puritan after Puritan would write, as did Richard Sibbes in 1637, that "worldly things are good in themselves, and given to sweeten our passage to Heaven . . . [since] this world and the things thereof are all good, and were all made of God, for the benefit of his creature."[41] To be sure, "excesses," or as at least one English Puritan put it, "carnal fancies," were not to be tolerated;[42] but in death, as well as in life, the message was clear. "He who is not happy before death in worldly things," wrote John Robinson, "cannot be happy in them, by it. . . . The godly are truly happy both in life and death: the wicked in neither."[43]

In turning against Catholic monasticism and otherworldliness—against extreme, if traditional, expressions of the *contemptus mundi* theme—the Puritans did not, of course, cease to yearn for Heaven. Nor did they question the inferiority of mortal existence or the matter of man's innate depravity; if anything, in many ways they greatly intensified this vision. But God had created the world and it was their duty to live in it and to work in it, among sinful as well as saintly men and women, and to live and work with a zeal possible only for those who are convinced they are embarked on a divine mission. However, in addition to this aspect of the reformist drive—indeed, intertwined with it—was another major shift of emphasis: the Puritans drew heavily in their theological expositions on the Calvinistic renewal of the early Christian dogma of predestination, of salvation for a very few based not on good works or on ritualistic expressions of penance, but as a free gift of an inscrutable God—a gift that had been bestowed on some since the very beginning of time, and a gift that was theirs and theirs alone. To the Puritan, a man could no more choose to be among the elect than he could choose to be human, insect or animal: such choices belonged only to God.

The effects of this combination of forces on the mind of the Puritan has been the subject of seemingly endless historical debate, most of it focused on the controversial idea of the "Protestant ethic." As Ernst Troeltsch has summed it up, "this peculiar combination of ideas . . . produces active industry within the economic sphere, but not for the sake of wealth; it produces an eager social organization, but its aim is not material happiness; it produces unceasing labor, ever disciplining the senses, but none of this effort is for the sake of the object of all this industry."[44] It is the burden of much of the argument that follows to show how these and other forces, including a revived sense of the imminence of Christ's Second Coming, within a particular social context, worked as well to create a distinctive Puritan way of death.

In much of England and Europe throughout the seventeenth

century the vision of death and dying maintained the form expressed in the earlier quoted words of William Drummond, Jeremy Taylor, and Sir Thomas Browne. But the seventeenth century did not belong entirely to the Drummonds, the Taylors, and the Brownes; it was also the century of the Mathers, the Hookers, and the Willards—the century of New England Puritanism. The Puritans, though heirs to the Christian and Reformed traditions, sought to purify those traditions as they had evolved in their time, to cut through the extraneous trappings of the formal church and revive the spirit of the earliest Christians. As Thomas Cartwright put it as early as 1572, theirs was not a mission of "innovation but a renovation, and the doctrine not new but renewed."[45] With this in mind, they closely examined the teachings of the church of which they were a part, the Anglican, and challenged many of those teachings. In the end some of them sought a richer ground for their work of renewal in the rocky soil of New England.

II

The Puritan Way of Death

2

The World of the Puritan

Before turning to the specific ways in which New England's Puritan communities approached the problem of death, it is important to have a look at their confrontation with life. For only when viewed in the context of their world view and the consequent realities of their perceived cosmological and physical environment does the Puritans' handling of death take on understandable meaning.

Because the previous few pages have not attempted to provide more than an admittedly purposeful and highly selective outline of the general contours of traditional Western attitudes toward death, it is easy—far too easy—for both writer and reader alike to treat the subject of this study as abstract ideology and to ignore the human realities of the problem. The Puritans themselves did not possess this luxury. To be sure, death had for them enormously complex metaphysical meaning; but it was also shaped by the physical texture of their everyday, ever-present reality. And that reality greatly differed from our own.

Puritanism was a reform movement within a reform movement. When in the 1530s, Henry VIII broke away from the direct influence of Rome, thereby establishing the English or Anglican Church, he opened the door to other changes in the church far greater than any he could have foreseen or desired. Henry's action was in many respects at least as politically and personally motivated as it was

31

ecclesiastical in impulse, but it was an action that took place at a time when the continent was alive with anti-Catholic sentiment of a far more idealist bent. It was not long before that sentiment took hold in England and spread throughout the country, leaving a good deal of political and religious turmoil in its wake. The story of the Reformation in England is too well known to require retelling here, but it is worth noting that out of the English Reformation there emerged a large and varied collection of religious idealists who were deeply dissatisfied with what they considered to be the incomplete break with Rome that the Anglican Church of the sixteenth century had effected. The term "Puritan" was attached to some of these groups by the orthodoxy of the Church of England and was intended as an epithet. Although they never formally adopted it, in time many of these reformers of reform accepted it as, in the words of one of them, "the honourable nickname of the best and holiest men."[1]

These self-styled best and holiest of men differed sharply among themselves over many matters of doctrine and reform tactics, but they were as one at least in their determination to rid England of the residue of papism. Thus, in the same way that the Puritans' enemies did in sixteenth- and seventeenth-century England, most modern historians have come to concede the Puritans' diversity while still treating them as a group. This study follows that lead: "It is unnecessary to posit a unity in all Puritan thought," wrote A. S. P. Woodhouse nearly forty years ago, "it is sufficient to recognise a continuity."[2]

But if there was a continuity or commonality in the thought of many otherwise diverse and opposing groups of Puritans, there was also a good deal of agreement among them and the most non-Puritan of men. This was especially so when it came to matters of the most profound significance, matters focusing on the nature and order of the universe. In this respect Englishmen of the sixteenth and seventeenth centuries—a time long recognized as one of enormous scientific achievement—were probably closer to the Middle Ages than they are to us today.

Today we live not only in a post-Puritan world, but in a post-Einsteinian, post-Darwinian, post-Freudian world. It is a world that in conquering the ignorance and stripping the supernaturalism from man's vision of his universe, his species, and his self has uncovered new mysteries of an even more troubling nature. Thus, in the melodramatic language of youthful recognition, at the turn of the twentieth century Bertrand Russell addressed the fears and anxieties of many in our own time when he wrote: "Brief and powerless is man's life; on him and all his race the slow, sure doom falls pitiless and dark. Blind to good and evil, reckless of destruction, omnipotent matter rolls on its relentless way."[3]

No Englishman of the seventeenth century would have understood such language. Even the most "atheistical" and worldly of men at that time would not have thought to question the divinely inspired, perfect order of things. Sir Walter Raleigh spoke for virtually all his contemporaries, including the most skeptical among them, when he described

> that infinite wisdom of God, which hath distinguished his angels by degrees, which hath given greater and less light and beauty to heavenly bodies, which hath made differences between beasts and birds, created the eagle and the fly, the cedar and the shrub, and among stones given the fairest tincture to the ruby and the quickest light to the diamond, [and] hath also ordained kings, dukes or leaders of the people, magistrates, judges, and other degrees among men.[4]

For the Englishman of the seventeenth century, as for his predecessors of the Middle Ages, there was simply no such thing as accident—as something happening or existing without divine purpose. Everything in this perfectly systematic and meaningful universe was at once intimately related to, and yet a distinctive part of, God's grand synthetic scheme. Thus, for example, when on one occasion in the Middle Ages a question arose at the University of Paris as to whether examination fees should be levied for intermediate degrees, the debate that emerged was waged not on matters of human law or tradition or financial necessity—but on the question of whether or not such a practice would be contrary to divine laws regarding covetousness and greed. On another occasion, when Margaret of Scotland, queen of France, was found kissing the poet Alain Chartier, she successfully exculpated herself in a manner that, if spurious, was perfectly in tune with the medieval view of divine order and minute design; she pointed out: "I did not kiss the man, but the precious mouth whence have issued and gone forth so many good words and virtuous sayings." As Johan Huizinga has observed, it was this tendency to eternally divide, subdivide, and subordinate concepts of divine origin that could permit, in theological speculation, the idea of God's "antecedent will," desiring the salvation of all, and his "consequent will," extending it only to the elect.[5]

If in many details the life of the seventeenth-century Englishman was very different from that of the man of the Middle Ages, at least in broad outline both held views of the universe and the world that were remarkably similar. It is true, of course, that standing between these two epochs was the revolutionary work of Copernicus, later elaborated on and extended by such men as Brahe, Kepler, and Galileo. And it is undeniable that the seventeenth century was the seedbed for the rise of experimental science and that the Puritans of Old and New England were remarkably hospitable to many of the scientific advances of their time. Still, it would be a mistake to assume that the Copernican revolution, or most of the other great discoveries of the time, met anything but popular resistance until well after the world of the Puritans had passed into history. Brahe and Kepler may well have further developed the insight of Copernicus, but as Thomas S. Kuhn has noted, they were able to do so only because of financial and intellectual support based on their abilities to cast superior horoscopes.[6] And in 1635 an English encyclopedia of "rare and excellent matters"—not written by a man of Puritan leanings—expressed the conventional wisdom on the subject this way:

> Next unto this, I subjoyne the franticke and strange opinion of *Copernicus,* who taketh on him to demonstrate, speaking of the worlds frame, that the Sunne is immoveable and placed in the Center of the World, and that the Globe of the Earth is moveable, rolling and wheeling about, admitting the change of States to depend upon the Eccentrick of the Earth; so that hee giveth not onely to the said Earth a daily running about the Sunne in 24 houres, in the space of the day and night, but likewise an annual revolution; which opinion how absurd it is, as Nature convinceth it of errour, so authorities of the Learned shall confound it: for besides that, in Scripture we have warrant, that the Earth is stablished sure.[7]

Apart from the reference to scripture—the most powerful support the man of the seventeenth century could muster—the author's subsequent appeal to classical learning epitomizes a good deal of the structure of logical argument then common. Turning to Archimedes, Person writes that this "rarest Mathematician"

> granted to King *Hieron* of *Siracusa,* that there was no weight which he could not move; And that if there were any other earth beside this whereon he might establish his Machin, and Mathematical Instruments, he durst undertake to move this out of its place, whereon we dwell; By which he would have us know, that the earth budged nor moved not, much lesse in such celeritie to compasse the Sunne, as *Copernicke* esteemed.[8]

This was a view held even by members of the Royal Society well after the Restoration of the 1660s. "The view of the world which had been fashioned in the early centuries of the Christian era and reduced to perfect logical precision by the great schoolmen was still widely current," G. R. Cragg has observed. "It was natural that the findings of the new science should seem to threaten the security of people who had imagined that they inhabited the centre of the universe, and equally natural that they should attack those who disturbed their peace of mind."[9]

But if to the man of the seventeenth century the earth retained its position of honor in the center of God's perfectly designed and ordered universe, all the doings of the creatures on that earth were hardly a symphony of bliss. It was, of course, all part of God's plan; but also part of God's plan was his titanic struggle with the Devil. And if evidences of God's will were everywhere to be found, so too were the earthly manifestations of Satan's plan. Witches and demons infested the world of man, luring him and tricking him into cooperation with their evil designs. It was man's duty—indeed, one of his tests—to resist such evil spirits whenever and wherever they might appear. And appear they did. Between 1560 and 1680 in England's Essex County it is estimated that at least 400 individuals were accused of over 1,500 witchcraft-related crimes. If this seems high, it is worth remembering that on the continent there were towns and villages that suffered witchcraft accusations numbering up to one-third of their resident populations and that executed, in less than a year, close to 10 percent of their own people. In one small canton in Switzerland between 1611 and 1660 alone, 2,500 people were accused of having made pacts with the Devil. All were executed.[10]

The earth, then, was God's temporal kingdom—placed squarely in the middle of his magnificent universe. And on that earth all things were arranged in a hierarchy of importance; man stood at the top of that hierarchy, the individuals within the species making up a divinely ordered hierarchy of their own. But the kingdom was not a paradise and had not been one since Adam and Eve had rejected God four thousand years before the birth of Christ. It was a kingdom under siege by the forces of infinite evil. And those who succumbed to the Devil could expect their just reward. Hell not only unquestionably existed, but was situated, many believed, very close to home—close enough, in fact, that the cries and laments of the damned might even be heard by the living. As that sober encyclopedist David Person noted, the belief was widespread that Hell was located in the center of the earth, because of reports from *"Aetna* in *Italy, Hecla* in *Island,* Saint *Patriks* hole in *Ireland,* or that formidably burning Mountayne by the *American Mexico* . . . [that] there are plaints and mourning voices to bee heard through by the vents and Chimneyes of hell, as they give out."[11]

It was a world of perfection in a universe of perfection, but a world at the same time preoccupied with witches and ghosts, with good and evil spirits, with such portents of God's displeasure as comets, earthquakes, droughts, and plagues, and with an incredible assortment of magical and astrological answers to the spiritual forces at large in the land.[12] But as eyes turned heavenward or searched about for evidence of spiritual evils, the day-to-day world that could not be overlooked was often one of unrelenting and devastating physical hardship. Doubtless the reaction to deprivation and pain of men and women who had known nothing else was quite different than ours today would be; doubtless such people would not respond with alarm to conditions they and their families had come to expect as their natural lot; but if they were not always alarmed, they were certainly aware of the poverty and misery that made up much of their world—poverty and misery so extreme that one recent historian simply admits of the futility of trying in any general way to convey it to the modern reader.[13]

Along with the thousands of wandering beggars who filled the countryside, the constant companions of any Englishman traveling about in the seventeenth century included the omnipresent specters of disease and starvation. For a century and a half, from the early sixteenth to the mid-seventeenth century, London was free of the bubonic plague for barely a decade. During some years more than one of every six inhabitants of the city died of the scourge. On occasion entire villages were destroyed by it. In one little hamlet in Cheshire in 1625, for example, literally everyone was killed off by an epidemic; and when the last adult came down with it he dug his own grave in his yard and buried himself, apparently because he knew that the only remaining survivors were children, who would have been incapable of removing his body from the house. Physicians were helpless in the face of almost any disease, and before the onslaught of the plague they simply fled. Lesser ills were treated by bloodletting and purging, which doubtless did more to weaken the patient than to cure him; but when the plague struck, as one Englishman of the time described it, "then all friends leave us, then a man or woman sits and lies alone and is a stranger to the breath of his own relations."[14]

The life expectancy at birth of English noblemen of the third quarter of the seventeenth century was less than thirty years. But these were noblemen; unlike many of their less fortunate countrymen, noblemen did not die of starvation. At a time when there simply was not enough food to go around, and that which was available was often sadly lacking in nutritional value, it should not be surprising to discover parish register entries such as the following from Staffordshire in 1674: "John Russel being famished through want of food (Josiah Freeman being overseer), was buried with the solemnity of many tears." For as one writer pointed out in 1631, "the poore of parishes are faine to bee relieved by the Farmer, the Husbandman, and the middle rank, or else they must starve, as many upon my own knowledge did this last Snowie-winter." Even in the worst of years there were, of course, alternatives available, as suggested, for example, by the 1623 report from Lincolnshire that "dog's flesh is a dainty dish, and found . . . in many houses."[15] But even this alternative was not readily available to everyone.

This, then, was the world that gave birth to the Puritan: a world that saw divine perfection, purpose, and design in every detail of nature; a world that accepted the everyday reality of witches and demons and fought back against them with magic and astrology; a world that was helpless before the devastation of disease, starvation, and neglect. It was a world in which the nights were blacker, the days more silent, and the winters more terrifying and cold than most men of the twentieth century can even begin to imagine.

If, as I have suggested, the world in which the Puritan lived was closer in many ways to the Middle Ages than to the twentieth century, it was also quite different in at least one significant respect. This difference was as much the creation of as it was a stimulus for the Puritan movement. It was the Reformist vision of time.

In the Middle Ages men's eyes may often have been trained on heaven, but when they focused on more mundane matters they became preoccupied with the present. Whether in the sphere of finance or social planning, the ideas of medieval men seem to reflect little concern for or trust in the future. Men looked to the future, as one medievalist has recently written, as an extension of the present. The idea of progress was foreign to them, and when guidance was sought or plans were made, the tendency was to look to the lessons of the past rather than to expectations of what was to come.[16] As a result, despite the disorder and anarchism that marked the social movements of the time, the Middle Ages were decidedly nonrevolutionary in an ideological sense and were bereft of both formal social criticism and utopian dreaming. Even the seeming exception of the Peasants' Revolt was marked by short-sightedness on these counts, since it did not lead to the formation of any long-range policies or plans for future practical action. This static quality of life in the Middle Ages, as D. W. Robertson, Jr., has observed, meant that in consequence medieval men "lacked much of our disillusionment, just as they lacked our hope."[17]

The Puritans lacked neither of these qualities, though for a very long while their disillusionment was smothered by the intensity of their hope. And their hope—indeed, their deep-rooted expectation—was for Christ's imminent Second Coming. Human history to the Puritan had been one long descent into ever-deepening depravity ever since the betrayal of Adam and Eve. But Christ's great sacrifice had paved the way for reformation, and they viewed themselves as the vanguard of the movement now afoot in all of Christendom to bring God's kingdom home. The most detailed interpretations of scripture merely confirmed what the evidence all about them suggested: that the millennium was at hand. Thus infused with the dynamic spirit of reform, they ventured out to bring England in under Heaven's wing—just as they closeted themselves in their homes and searched agonizingly for the signs of their own individual deliverance.

The Puritan quest was thus both national and individual, and on both fronts it was carried out with an almost unprecedented zeal. From at least the middle of the sixteenth century God had been ordained an Englishman by that country's most zealous reformers, an attitude that as time went on was hammered home again and again by those who were acquainted with the most popular books in the land: the Bible; John Bunyan's *Pilgrim's Progress,* which construed the sense of quest and destiny in allegorically personal terms; and John Foxe's *Actes and Monuments,* a detailed and vivid description of the lives and deaths of England's Protestant martyrs, and a book that cast those lives and deaths in terms of their meaning for the rapidly unfolding drama of England's emergence as God's "elect nation."[18] By the middle of the seventeenth century Oliver Cromwell had grown fond of reminding his countrymen that they constituted the core of the "new Israel." But the same idea had by then been carried to New England and there transplanted by the shiploads of Puritans who had decided America was now the best refuge for the holiest remnant of God's people. The failure of the Puritans to effect total reformation of the English church had led some of them to believe, in John Winthrop's words, that in the same way that "all other Churches of Europe are brought to desolation . . . our sins . . . doe threatne evill times to be cominge upon us, and whoe knowes, but that God hath provided this place [New England] to be a refuge for many whome he meanes to save out of the general callamity."[19] In the sea of history the Puritans saw themselves riding the crest of the final great tidal wave that was to bring with it the Apocalypse. To the bearers of this sense of destiny, all past history paled in significance. Thus, in 1665 the Reverend Samuel Danforth could soberly interpret for his New England congregation the meaning of a "Late Comet or Blazing Star" that had recently appeared in the heavens, by appealing to history: a comet overhead had preceded the death of Claudius and the succession of "bloody *Nero*"; two comets had presaged the invasion of the world by a "great *Plague*" in *"anno* 729"; and—on the same level of historical importance as these and other instances of heaven-sent devastation—*"Anno* 1652. There appeared a Comet at the beginning of Mr. Cotton's sickness, and disappeared a few days after his death."[20]

But if the Puritans' sense of *national* mission was infused with an overwhelming and single-minded confidence, their sense of *individual* salvation was beset with agonizing insecurity. Ever since the Fall of Adam man had been scarred with a natural depravity so deep and repulsive that no one who subsequently walked the earth was worthy of salvation. But God in His infinite mercy and love had extended a heavenly lifeline, as it were, to a select and predetermined few. Although it was impossible for a man ever to know with confidence that he was among this holy elect—to presume such knowledge would be to presume a godlike omniscience— all Puritans battled fiercely with their consciences as they searched to find among the numberless indications of depravity some signs, at least, that they *might* be among the chosen few. The search for the seeds of grace took the Puritan on a journey of harrowing and tearful introspection that, even if only preliminarily successful, brought with it the most painful recognition of unworthiness and, in Max Weber's words, "unprecedented inner loneliness."[21] "I can compare this sight," wrote Thomas Goodwin, "and the workings of my heart rising from thence, to be as if I had in the heat of summer looked down into the filth of a dungeon, where by a clear light and piercing eye I discerned millions of crawling living things in the midst of that sink and liquid corruption."[22] And it was a never-ending search: to the day he died, no Puritan would ever dare to presume that he had unequivocally discerned God's will.

In March of 1630 a fleet of eleven ships, propelled as much by their passengers' sense of mission as by the wind, set sail from England for the New World. In the most profound ways, things, they assured themselves, would be different there. Almost two hundred miles before landfall, it was said, they would be able to catch in their nostrils the scent of pine emanating from the land they were to settle. It was, they were told, a barbarous and howling wilderness infested with demons and peopled with a mysterious and threatening race of men, a race of men they determined to convert to Christ's ways. It was a place of wondrous plant life, of birds so many in number that flocks of them would occasionally blot out the sun, of bears and lions and "fiery flying serpents," and of animals like the horn snake that hissed like a goose, fought with its spurred tail, and was capable of withering trees as well as killing men at a single blow. If many of the tales the Puritans had been told in advance were apocryphal, others were true; but in any case they had no way of then knowing which were true and which were not.[23]

It was indeed a New World. But these settlers brought much of the Old World with them: their sense of the divine purpose and design of the universe, with the earth at its perfect center; their belief that the earth was occupied by evil spirits as well as evil men; their conviction that the world was now in its waning moments and that the millennium was near at hand; and their desperate, ever-present individual hopes that, although the vast majority of men were destined for a postmortem fate of excruciating and eternal torment in Hell, they *might* be among the very few God had chosen to save from damnation.

All these ideas deeply influenced the way these men and women would deal with the new life that awaited them. But death as well as life awaited them; and the way they would deal with it was no less affected by the world they brought with them than by the world that lay ahead. It is the New England Puritans' experience with and reaction to death, and the intertwining of that experience and reaction with the rise and subsequent fall of Puritan culture, that is the subject of the chapters to follow.

3

Death and Childhood

From time to time in the history of man, a new idea or way of look-
ing at things bursts into the body of ideas of a society with such
force that it virtually reestablishes the terms for all subsequent discussion. The Copernican, Darwinian, and Freudian revolutions—
perhaps, as Freud on occasion noted, the three most destructive
blows human narcissism has had to endure—are, from among the
many, the clearest examples of such intellectual explosions. Others
have been of considerably more limited influence: the concept of
culture in anthropology is one example of this more limited break-
through, the frontier thesis as an explanation for certain developments in American history is another. At still another level is the
seminal study of a particular and more specific problem. An example of this last is Philippe Ariès's monumental study *Centuries of
Childhood,* a work that established much of the currently conventional wisdom on the subject of the family in history, a work so
important that throughout the past decade historians of family life
have conducted much of their work in its shadow.

One of Ariès's most original and influential findings was that
childhood as we know it today did not come into being until the
early modern period. "In medieval society," he observed, ". . . as
soon as the child could live without the constant solicitude of his
mother, his nanny or his cradle-rocker, he belonged to adult so-

ciety."[1] It was not until the sixteenth and seventeenth centuries, and then only among the upper classes, that the modern idea of childhood as a distinct phase of life began to emerge.

The picture Ariès sketched, drawing on such diverse sources as portraiture, literature, games, and dress, was predominantly one of French culture and society; but it was clear that he believed his generalizations would hold true for most of the Western world. Historians of colonial New England have in recent years attempted to reinforce this assumption by extending Ariès's conclusions to life in seventeenth- and eighteenth-century Massachusetts. But the support for this contention is unsteady, based as it is on much less substantive data than that on which Ariès's argument rests. For instance, the clothing of children as adults—only one strand of evidence in Ariès's historical tapestry—has been seized upon by some colonial historians and used as the principal basis for arguing that in seventeenth- and eighteenth-century Massachusetts there was little or no distinction made between children and adults. "If clothes do not make the man," writes Michael Zuckerman in describing what he views as the "scaled-down adults" of Puritan New England, "they do mark social differentiations"; and, adds John Demos, "the fact that children were dressed like adults does seem to imply a whole attitude of mind."[2] The phenomenon that both writers accurately describe, the similarity of dress of children and adults, may well suggest social differentiations and/or imply a whole attitude of mind—but not necessarily the one claimed.

In the first place, to argue in isolation from other data that the *absence* of a distinctive mode of dress for children is a mark of their being viewed as miniature adults is historical presentism at its very worst; one might argue with equal force—again in isolation from other facts—that the absence of beards on men in a particular culture, or the presence of short hair as a fashion shared by men and women, is a mark of that culture's failure to fully distinguish between men and women. In each of these cases there are alternative explanations, explanations that do not presuppose that special clothing for children or beards for men or different hair lengths for adults of different sexes are universally natural and proper cultural traditions. As to the specific matter of dress, children in New England were treated much the same as children in England. Until age six or seven they generally wore long gowns that opened down the front; after that, they were clothed in a manner similar to that of their parents. Rather than this stage marking an abrupt transition from infancy to adulthood, it is more likely, as Alan Macfarlane has pointed out, that the change in attire at this point was merely a sign that children had then reached an age at which sexual differentiation seemed in order.[3]

Second and most important, the supporting evidence that Ariès brings to bear in making his case for the situation in medieval France generally does not exist for colonial New England—and when it does, it makes clear that there was, on the contrary, no confusion or ambiguity in the mind of the adult Puritan as to the differences between him and his children. Puritan journals, autobiographies, and histories are filled with specific references to the differences between children and adults. A wealth of parental-advice literature exists for the seventeenth century, literature that gives evidence of clear distinctions between adults and children well into their teens, and in effect from the earliest years of settlement was a large body of law that established as the norm distinctly different standards of behavior and appropriate punishment for children, postadolescent youths, and adults.[4]

The matter of children's literature is one case in point. Ariès has argued, both in *Centuries of Childhood* and elsewhere, that in France "books addressed to and reserved for children" did not appear until "the end of the 17th century, at the same time as the awareness of childhood." Recently, Marc Soriano has supported Ariès's contention by showing that prior to the stories of Perrault in the 1690s, French literature and folktales were directed "almost entirely" at an adult audience, though of course children were exposed to them as well.[5] The situation was quite different in both old and New England in the seventeenth century, as William Sloane showed almost twenty years ago. Limiting himself to a definition of a child's book as "a book written *only* for children"—a limitation that excludes books which subsequently became children's fare and "works which are the tools of formal instruction"—Sloane compiled an annotated bibliography of 261 children's books published in England and America between 1557 and 1710.[6] It is true that most of the books listed would not meet Zuckerman's definition of a child's book as one that provides "a sequestered simplicity commensurate with a child's capacities," but that is not because children were viewed as synonymous with adults; rather, it is because seventeenth-century New Englanders simply had a view of the nature and capacities of children quite different from that held by Zuckerman or other twentieth-century parents.[7]

The differentness of that view is central to this chapter, and it will be developed at some length. But first we must deal with the fact that there were indeed children at home and in the streets of Puritan New England and that their status as children was recognized—and never questioned—by their parents, ministers, or by other adults in the community. In many ways those children were seen and treated differently from children of today. In many ways they *were* different: to analyze, as this chapter will, the Puritan child's actual and anticipated confrontation with death will be but one of many ways in which to gauge the extent to which that difference made itself felt. But there simply is no real evidence to support the contention that in seventeenth-century New England, as perhaps in fifteenth- and sixteenth-century France, there were few or no distinctions between children and adults.

Probably at no time in modern history have parents in the West agreed on the matter of the correct and proper approach to child-rearing. Certainly this is true of our own time, but it was equally so in the age of the Puritan.

"A child is a man in a small letter," wrote John Earle in 1628,

> yet the best copy of *Adam* before hee tasted of *Eve* or the Apple. . . . Hee is natures fresh picture newly drawne in Oyle, which time and much handling dimmes and defaces. His soule is yet a white paper unscribled with observations of the world, wherewith at length it becomes a blurr'd Notebooke. He is purely happy, because he knowes no evill, nor hath made meanes by sinne, to be acquainted with misery. . . . Nature and his Parents alike dandle him, and tice him on with a bait of Sugar, to a draught of Worme-wood. . . . His father hath writ him as his owne little story, wherein hee reads those dayes of his life that hee cannot remember; and sighes to see what innocence he ha's outliv'd.[8]

In view of this attitude among certain Englishmen of the seventeenth century—an attitude that, it appears, was prevalent in colonial Maryland and Virginia—it should come as no surprise to read in the report of a visiting Frenchman at the end of the century that "in England they show an extraordinary complacency toward young children, always flattering, always caressing, always applauding whatever they do. At least that is how it seems to us French, who correct our children as soon as they are capable of reason." This judgment was echoed a few years later by an Englishman reflecting on the customs of his people: "In the *Education* of *Children,*" wrote Guy Miege in 1707, "the indulgence of Mothers is excessive among the *English;* which proves often fatal to their children, and contributes much to the Corruption of the Age. If these be Heirs to great Honours and Estates, they swell with the Thoughts of it, and at last grow unmanageable." Had Miege been writing a bit later in the century he might have given as evidence for his assertion the life of Charles James Fox, who at age five had been accidentally deprived of the privilege of watching the blowing up of a garden wall; at his insistence his father had the wall rebuilt and blown up again so that the boy might witness it. On another occasion, when the young Charles announced his intention of destroying a watch, his father's reply was: "Well, if you must, I suppose you must."[9]

But neither John Earle in 1628 nor Charles Fox in 1754 was a Puritan; and neither Henri Misson in 1698 nor Guy Miege in 1707 was commenting on Puritan attitudes toward children. Had they been, their reports would have read very differently.

In 1628, the same year that John Earle was rhapsodizing on the innocence and purity of children and on parental accommodation to the young, Puritan John Robinson wrote:

> And surely there is in all children, though not alike, a stubbornness, and stoutness of mind arising from natural pride, which must, in the first place, be broken and beaten down.
> . . . This fruit of natural corruption and root of actual rebellion both against God and man must be destroyed, and no manner of way nourished, except we will plant a nursery of contempt of all good persons and things, and of obstinacy therein. . . . For the beating, and keeping down of this stubbornness parents must provide carefully for two things: first that children's wills and willfulness be restrained and repressed. . . . The second help is an inuring of them from the first, to such a meanness in all things, as may rather pluck them down, than lift them up.[10]

In place of Earle's child, seen as "yet the best copy of Adam before hee tasted of Eve or the Apple," the Puritan child was riddled with sin and corruption, a depraved being polluted with the residue of Adam's sin. If there was any chance of an individual child's salvation, it was not a very good chance—and in any case, ultimate knowledge of who was to be chosen for salvation and who was not was not a matter for earthly minds. Further, only very rarely was an apparent childhood conversion accepted as real by a congregation. Thus, Jonathan Edwards devoted a great deal of attention to youthful conversions during the stormy emotionalism of the Great Awakening, but only after first noting: "It has heretofore been looked on as a strange thing, when any have seemed to be savingly wrought upon, and remarkably changed in their childhood." And even James Janeway, whose *A Token For Children: Being an Exact Assessment of the Conversion, Holy and Exemplary Lives, and Joyful Deaths of Several Young Children* was one of the best-read books of seventeenth- and eighteenth-century Puritans, admitted in a later edition that one of his examples of early spiritual development—that of a child who supposedly began showing signs of salvation between the ages of two and three—seemed to many "scarce credible, and they did fear [it] might somewhat prejudice the authority of the rest."[11]

One need not have been of such a tender age as Janeway's suspect example, however, to be an unlikely candidate for conversion. Throughout the seventeenth and early eighteenth centuries in most New England communities, well under 10 percent of the newly admitted converts were less than twenty years old—and of them all but a handful were at least in their mid- to late teens.[12] Still, even if conversion was unlikely at an early age, it was at least possible. Given the alternative, then, of apathetic acceptance of their children as depraved and damnable creatures, it is hardly surprising that Puritan parents urged on their offspring a religious precocity that some historians have interpreted as tantamount to premature adulthood. "You can't begin with them *Too soon,*" Cotton Mather wrote in 1689.

> They are no sooner *wean'd* but they are to be *taught.* . . .
> Are they *Young?* Yet the *Devil* has been with them already.
> . . . They go astray as soon as they are born. They no
> sooner *step* than they *stray,* they no sooner *lisp* than they *ly.*
> Satan gets them to be proud, profane, reviling and revengeful,
> as *young* as they are. And I pray, why should you not be
> afore-hand with *him?*[13]

Puritan children, even "the very best" of whom had a "Corrupt Nature in them, and . . . an Evil Figment in their Heart," were thus driven at the earliest age possible both to recognize their depravity and to pray for their salvation. In the event that children proved intractable in this regard, the first parental response was to be "what saies the Wise man, *A Rod for the fools back";* but generally more effective—and more insidious—was the advice "to watch when some *Affliction* or some *Amazement* is come upon them: then God opens their ear to Discipline." If Puritan parents carried out these designs with fervor, it was of course out of love and concern for their children. But at least some of the motivation may well have had guilt at its source; as Mather and others were frequently careful to point out, "Your Children are Born Children of Wrath. Tis *through you,* that there is derived unto them the sin which Exposes them to infinite Wrath."[14]

We should not, however, pass too quickly over the matter of the Puritan parent's genuine love for his or her children. Even a casual reading of the most noted Puritan journals and autobiographies— those of Thomas Shepard, Samuel Sewall, or Cotton Mather—demonstrates that a deep-seated parental affection for children was the most common, normal, and expected attitude. The relationship of parents to children was often compared with that of God to his children. "That God is often angry with [his children]," Samuel Willard wrote in 1684, "afflicts them, and withdraws the light of his countenance from them, and puts them to grief, is not because he loves them not, but because it is that which their present condition requires; they are but Children, and childish, and foolish, and if they were not sometimes chastened, they would grow wanton, and careless of duty."[15] Indeed, in the same work in which Cotton Mather referred to children as "proud, profane, reviling and revengeful," he warned parents that *They must give an account of the souls that belong unto their Families.* . . . Behold, thou hast *Lambs* in the *Fold,* Little ones in thy House; God will strain for it, — if wild beasts, and Lusts carry any of them away from the *Service* of God through any neglect of thine thou shalt smart for it in the fiery prison of God's terrible Indignation."[16]

Children, then, were on the one hand deeply loved *"Lambs* in the *Fold*"; as Willard noted, "If others in a Family suffer want, and be pincht with difficulties, yet the Children shall certainly be taken care for, as long as there is anything to be had: they are hard times indeed when Children are denied that which is needful for them."[17] On the other hand, they were depraved and polluted; as Benjamin Wadsworth wrote, "Their Hearts naturally, are a meer nest, root, fountain of Sin, and wickedness." This paradoxical image was perhaps best captured by Samuel Willard when, in 1691, he referred to infants as "innocent vipers."[18]

Of course, none of this is to imply that unconverted infants or children were necessarily to be condemned to damnation. God's design for them was as hidden from human knowledge as were his plans for their parents. But it was this very inscrutability that was to cause so much apprehension on the part of youth and parent alike. As Reverend Willard was to exclaim in his sermon *The Mourners Cordial: "We are apt to say, oh! if we were but sure of their well being, we could then be quiet and contented; but that is to fight against God: it is his pleasure to keep these things secret for the present."* The dying child might be destined for Heaven, but it was just as likely that he might be destined for Hell. And if it were the latter—if the child was in fact one of the large number of acknowledged "reprobate infants"—there was probably not much consolation in the fact that some Puritans, though not all, believed that he or she would at least receive the "easiest room" in that pit of eternal fire and torment.[19]

Not only was the state of a child's spiritual health an extremely worrisome and uncomfortable matter for the Puritan parent, but the state of his physical health was equally troublesome. In recent years historians of colonial New England have shown convincingly that the colonists of certain New England towns in the seventeenth and early eighteenth centuries lived longer and healthier lives than did many of their countrymen in England. This finding—like many others by these new demographic historians—is important to our understanding of life in early New England; but in acknowledging the relative advantages of life in some New England communities compared with parts of England and Europe in the seventeenth century, we should be careful not to blind ourselves to the fact that death was to the colonist, as it was to the Englishman and Frenchman, an ever-present menace—and a menace that struck the children of the community with a particular vengeance.

Philip J. Greven's study of colonial Andover, Massachusetts, is noteworthy both for the skill of the author's analysis and for the stability and healthiness of the families whose lives he studied. As Greven points out, compared with the mortality rate in Boston and other New England communities, Andover's mortality rate was exceptionally low, though it did climb steadily in the eighteenth century. It is worth dwelling briefly on the differences between Boston and Andover, since the power and sophistication of Greven's work may tend to suggest an implicit and erroneous picture of Andover as a representative New England town. It may or may not be representative of a certain type of Puritan community—more collateral studies must be done before this can be determined—but demographically it was vastly different from Boston, the hub of the Holy Commonwealth. Mortality rates in Andover during the early eighteenth century, when those rates were on the increase, fluctuated within a normal annual range of about half those in Boston during the same period—somewhere between fifteen and twenty per thousand in Andover, somewhere between thirty-five and forty per thousand in Boston. Epidemic years are excluded from these calculations in both cases, but it should be noted that Andover's worst epidemic lifted the death rate to seventy-one per thousand while Boston's worst epidemic during the same period pushed the death rate well over one hundred per thousand—thus literally decimating the resident population.[20] In the seventeenth century, the devastating smallpox epidemic of 1677–78, in conjunction with the normal death rate, probably killed off more than one-fifth of Boston's entire population. "Boston burying-places never filled so fast," wrote a young Cotton Mather.

It is easy to tell the time when we did not use to have the bells
tolling for burials on a Sabbath morning by sunrise; to have 7
buried on a Sabbath day night, after Meeting. To have coffins
crossing each other as they have been carried in the street.
. . . To attempt a Bill of Mortality, and number the very
spires of grass in a Burying Place seem to have a parity of
difficulty and in accomplishment.[21]

Indeed, if mortality rates in Andover fare well in comparison
with these same figures for English and European towns, Boston's
do not: it was not at all uncommon for the death rate in Boston to
hover near or even exceed that of English towns like Clayworth,
which have been cited for their exceptionally high mortality rate.[22]

One of the problems with all these figures, however, is their dis-
tortion through the almost inevitable underestimation of infant
mortality; as Greven and other demographic analysts freely acknowledge, most infant deaths were unrecorded and their number
can now only be guessed at. One such guess has been made by
Kenneth A. Lockridge. In a study of Dedham, Massachusetts, in
the seventeenth and early eighteenth centuries, Lockridge found
that an upward adjustment of 1/9 on the town's birth rate would
most likely take account of unrecorded infant deaths. If the same
adjustment is made on the birth rate of colonial Andover, a fairly
accurate comparison of childhood birth and mortality rates can be
made. To be sure, Lockridge's statistical adjustment is little more
than an educated guess that may or may not be relevant to the situation in Andover. Nevertheless, it seems rather safe to employ it
in the Andover context, since it is probably the most conservative
of the various alternatives. Greven himself, while pointing out the
favorable situation in early Andover compared with certain English towns, finds it not unreasonable to estimate a childhood mortality rate of *double* that found in available records, while in Plymouth, John Demos has estimated that a 10 percent infant
mortality rate—though seemingly "surprisingly low"—appears to
be a sensible figure. Further, studies of seventeenth- and eight-

eenth-century Salem indicate fluctuating infant mortality rates
ranging from a low of 105 per thousand for eighteenth-century
male children to a high of 313 per thousand for seventeenth-
century female children. As Maris A. Vinovskis has recently observed, "In other words, ten to thirty percent of the children never
survived the first year of life."[23] In keeping with Andover's almost
uniquely favorable condition, then, the Lockridge adjustment
would seem to provide the most cautious possible method of ac-
counting for unrecorded infant deaths.

Although Greven demonstrates a trend throughout the generations examined showing a steady drop in fertility and life expectancy rates as Andover became consistently more urbanized,
viewing the period as a whole, one can consider the town a good
example of one of the healthier communities in New England. If
we use the Lockridge adjustment to include unrecorded infant
deaths, the average number of children born per family in Andover
throughout the century under discussion was 8.8. Of those, an
average of 5.9 survived to adulthood. In other words, approximately three of the close to nine children born to the average
family would die before reaching their twenty-first birthday. But,
as Greven notes, the most vulnerable period in life was that "beyond infancy but prior to adolescence—the age group which appears to have been most susceptible, among other things, to the
throat distemper prevalent in the mid-1730s." If we again apply
the infant mortality adjustment to Greven's figures, the rate of survival to age ten for all children born between 1640 and 1759 was
approximately 74 percent—with a generational high of 83 percent
and a low of 63 percent, this latter figure of course indicating that
at one point fewer than two out of three infants lived to see their
tenth birthday. During the period as a whole, more than one child
in four failed to survive the first decade of life in a community
with an average births-per-family rate of 8.8.[24]

Thus a young couple embarking on a marriage did so with the
knowledge and expectation that in all probability *two or three* of

the children they might have would die before the age of ten. In certain cases, of course, the number was more than two—Greven discusses instances when parents lost six of eleven children in rapid succession, including four in a single month and four of eight children in less than a year—and this in a town remarkable for the relative health and longevity of its residents. In Boston the rate was much higher, and even the most prominent and well-cared-for residents of that city were constantly reminded of the fragility of life in childhood.

If old England seems to have had more than its share of Alice Thorntons—whose seventeenth century journal is filled with ex-cruciatingly detailed descriptions of the births of her dozen children, only two of whom survived beyond their fifth birthday—the list of similarly afflicted families in New England includes some of the most prominent names in the history of early America. Thomas Shepard, for instance, had seven sons, three of whom died in infancy; the other four outlived their father, but he died at forty-three—having in that short time outlived two wives. Edward Taylor, in his first marriage, had eight children, five of whom died in infancy. And as Joseph E. Illick has recently pointed out, Samuel Sewall and Cotton Mather each fathered fourteen children: "One of Sewall's was stillborn, several died as infants, several more as young adults. Seven Mather babies died shortly after delivery, one died at two years and six survived to adulthood, five of whom died in their twenties. Only two Sewall children outlived their father, while Samuel Mather was the only child to survive Cotton." It is small wonder, then, that Sewall was "much affected" by recurring dreams that his wife or offspring had died or, in the case of his daughter, had mysteriously disappeared after he had taken her "in a little closet to pray with her." Nor is it cause for surprise to find Mather "in a continual Apprehension" over the thought that his son Samuel "(tho a lusty and hearty Infant) will dy in its Infancy."[25] For time after time such dreams and apprehensions turned out to be prophetic.

It is important for us to recognize that conditions for living in colonial New England were sometimes superior to those in seventeenth-century England and Europe. But it is equally important for us not to lose sight of the fact that the Puritan settlements were places where "winter was to be feared," as Kenneth Lockridge has written, where "harvests were a gamble that kept men's minds aware of Providence, plague arose and subsided out of all human control and infants died in numbers that would shock us today." Worthy of particular note in all this is the matter of the Puritans' own assessment of their situation. Far from expressing the sort of indifference to early death that Philippe Ariès found as late as the seventeenth century in France, New Englanders not only appear to have been obsessed with the idea of death but they were also acutely sensitive to its physical presence. As a result, as Maris A. Vinovskis has pointed out, they greatly *over*estimated the presence of mortality in their own society. Death was an ever-threatening, ever-present condition to them—as it was to most of the world's population at the time—and the lives of children were seen as particularly fragile. Indeed, such lives were, as the Puritan poet Ann Bradstreet so beautifully put it, "like as a bubble, or the brittle glass."[26]

It has often been noted by writers on the Puritan family that the prescribed and common personal relationship between parents and children was one of restraint and even aloofness, mixed with—as we have seen—an intense parental effort to impose discipline and encourage spiritual precocity. Parents were reminded to avoid becoming "too fond of your children and too familiar with them" and to be on their guard against "not keeping constantly your due distance."[27] Edmund S. Morgan has shown how this "due distance" worked in both directions, as when Benjamin Colman's daughter Jane wrote to her father requesting forgiveness for the "flow of affections" evident in some of her recent letters. Colman responded by urging her to be "careful against this Error, even when you say your Thoughts of Reverence and Esteem to your Father, or to a Spouse, if ever you should live to have one," and commended her for having "done well to correct yourself for some of your Excursions of this kind toward me."[28] Morgan has also seen the common practice of "putting children out," both to early apprenticeship and simply extended stays with other families, often against the child's will, as linked to the maintenance of the necessary distance between parent and child; "these economically unnecessary removals of children from home," he writes, probably resulted from the fact that "Puritan parents did not trust themselves with their own children, that they were afraid of spoiling them by too great affection."[29]

Morgan's suggested explanation for this practice seems logical and convincing, but there may have been another, deeper source for both this practice and the larger Puritan attitude toward severely restrained displays of fondness between parents and children. For children, despite the natural hold they had on their parents' affection, were a source of great emotional discomfort for them as well, in that there was a very real possibility, if not probability, that parental affection would be rewarded by the death of the child before it even reached puberty. The "due distance" kept by Puritan parents from their children might, at least in part, have been an intuitive response to this possibility, a means of insulating themselves to some extent against the shock that the death of a child might bring. This sort of reaction would rarely, of course, find a consciously articulated outlet. But that it existed is more than speculation. Although he was writing rather late in the day for Puritanism, Thomas Skinner probably spoke for many of his forebears when he warned:

> Remember that although, Parents and Children, Husbands and Wives, Friends and Acquaintance are pleasant, yet they are but uncertain, withering and dying Enjoyments. You are

favoured with them around you to Day, but to morrow they may expire and give up the Ghost, and leave you sighing and disconsolate. . . . In short, The more immoderately you love them, the less Satisfaction, (in all Probability) will they yield you, and the greater will your Smart and Vexation be in parting with them. When a Friend or Relative is taken away, upon whom the Heart and Affections are too eagerly set, how terribly does it disquiet and rack the Man? In a Word, Overmuch to love a Relative is the Way to increase, if not double the Anguish of parting with him.[30]

Of those relationships for which this sort of advice was most persuasive, none was more clear-cut than that between parent and child; for only the very aged—in Andover, those who had passed their seventieth birthday—had a rate of death higher than that of children.

Such a response, whether articulated or not, would seem to be reasonable in any society with a relatively high rate of childhood mortality. But to the Puritan the child was more than a loved one extremely vulnerable to the ravages of the environment; he was also a loved one polluted with sin and natural depravity. In this, of course, he was no different from any other member of the family or community, including those Visible Saints viewed as the most likely candidates for salvation: Original Sin touched everyone, and all were considered polluted and not worthy of excessive affection. What is important here, however, is not that this dictum touched everyone, but that in the process it touched those most emotionally susceptible to its pernicious effects—the children of the zealous and devoted Puritan.

The Puritans of New England held as doctrine the belief that they were involved in a binding contract or "covenant" with God. This belief was complex and multifaceted, but one aspect of it held that the entire community had contracted a "social covenant" with God by which they promised strict obedience to his laws. Failure to obey on the part of any individuals within the com-

munity—even children—could result in the venting of God's wrath
on the entire community. Thus, whenever signs of God's anger
appeared, might they be comets, earthquakes, or the deaths of
eminent men, Puritans searched for the source of the divine displeasure and fearfully awaited future expressions of it.

The depraved and ungodly child was, it is true, in his sinfulness
naturally repellent; but more than that, the activity that might
easily grow out of that sinfulness posed a very real danger to the
well-being of the community. In response, understandably enough,
the Puritan parent strove mightily to effect conversion or at the
least to maintain a strict behavior code, but at the same time—when
combined with the love he felt for his child, the tenuous hold the
child had on life, the natural repulsiveness of sin—he may well
have been driven to find ways of creating emotional distance between his offspring and himself.[31]

Separation, then, may have been emotionally beneficial to the
Puritan parent, but it almost certainly had the precise opposite
effect on the Puritan child. John Demos has recently speculated
on the "profound loss" experienced by many Puritan children in
the second and third years of life due to the fact that they were
likely weaned at the start of the second year and very often witnessed the arrival of a younger brother or sister at the start of the
third.[32] This in itself, it might be argued, does not make Puritan
children unique: the spacing of children at two-year intervals is
common among many of the world's cultures, and weaning at
twelve months is hardly an exceptional custom. But added to these
practices was the conscious effort of Puritan parents to avoid
forming excessively intimate relationships with their children. If
this normal practice of distancing was not enough, Cotton Mather
was probably echoing a fairly common sentiment in viewing as
"the sorest Punishment in the Family" the banishment of the child
from the parents' presence.[33] Separation, however, can be both
real and imagined, can be both present and anticipated. And of
course the ultimate separation is death. This was a fact of which

the Puritan parent was well aware and that the Puritan child—from the earliest age possible—was never allowed to forget.

May of 1678 was a month of great apprehension in Boston. Smallpox had entered the city some months earlier and had begun its relentless slaying of the population. By May hundreds had died and the governments of the colony and the town were hurriedly passing legislation aimed at holding down the spread of the deadly infection—people were directed not to hang out bedding or clothes in their yards or near roadways, and those who had been touched by the disease and had survived were forbidden contact with others for specified periods of time.[34] The worst was yet to come. By the time the siege was over it was as though, proportionate to New York City's current population, an epidemic were to kill over a million and a half of its people in a period of just eighteen months. In but one day, on September 30, 1677, thirty people had died— the proportional equivalent of more than *sixty thousand* New Yorkers today.[35] The city girded for what still awaited it.

Only two years earlier New England had endured the devastation of King Philip's War, in which—not even counting the enormous numbers of Indian dead—greater casualties were inflicted in proportion to the population than would subsequently occur in any future war in American history.[36] Death was everywhere in 1678 when, on May 5, Increase Mather addressed his Boston congregation and prayed "for a Spirit of Converting Grace to be poured out upon the Children and *Rising Generation* in *New England.*"[37] A decade later, Increase's son Cotton would write, as I have noted earlier, that a particularly effective means of disciplining children was "to watch when some *Affliction* or *Amazement* is come upon them: then God opens their ear to Discipline." On May 5, 1678, the then teenaged young man probably witnessed a particularly effective demonstration of this principle as it was directed toward an entire congregation.

In his sermon that day Mather dwelt at some length on the fact that although "the line of election" tended "for the most part [to] run through the loins of goldly Parents," such parents must beware of complacency in this regard. *Truly* concerned and godly parents, he reminded his listeners, would "therefore be stirred up to the more fervency in cries to Heaven, for the blessing promised."[38] But the heightening of parental concern was only part of Mather's purpose. He then turned to the children of the congregation themselves. Addressing the older youth, those of some "discretion and understanding," he mentioned explicitly the "affliction and amazement" that was at hand:

> Young men and young Women, O be in earnest for Converting Grace, before it be too late. It is high time for you to look about you, deceive not yourselves with false Conversions (as many young men do to their eternal ruine) or with gifts instead of Grace. . . . Death waits for you. There is now a Mortal and Contagious Disease in many Houses; the Sword of the Lord is drawn, and young men fall down apace slain under it; do you not see the Arrows of Death come flying over your heads? Why then, Awake, Awake, and turn to God in Jesus Christ whilst it is called today, and know for certain that if you dy in your sins, you will be the most miserable of any poor Creatures in the bottom of Hell.[39]

But Mather's most determined and terrifying words were reserved for the youngest and most vulnerable members of the congregation, as well as for those of more discretion and understanding. It was for this more inclusive group that the specter of parental and ministerial separation and betrayal was merged with the promise of death and damnation. "Beg as for your lives that the God of your Fathers would pour his Spirit upon you," Mather exhorted them.

> Go into secret corners and plead it with God. . . . If you dy and be not first new Creatures, better you had never been born: you will be left without excuse before the Lord, ter-

rible witnesses shall rise up against you at the last day. Your godly Parents will testifie against you before the Son of God at that day: And the Ministers of Christ will also be called in as witnesses against you for your condemnation, if you dy in your sins. As for many of you, I have treated with you privately and personally, I have told you, and I do tell you, and make solemn Protestation before the Lord, that if you dy in a Christless, graceless estate, I will most certainly profess unto Jesus Christ at the day of Judgement, Lord, these are the Children, whom I spake often unto they Name, publickly and privately, and I told them, that if they did not make themselves a new heart, and make sure of an interest in Christ, they should become damned creatures for evermore; and yet they would not repent and believe the Gospel.[40]

If there is one thing on which modern psychologists have agreed concerning the fear of death in young children, it is that such fear is generally rooted in the anticipation of separation from their parents. Time and again experimental studies have shown that, as one writer puts it, "the most persistent of fears associated with death is that of separation—and the one which is most likely to be basic, independent of cultural, religious, or social background." "In children," this writer adds, "dread of separation seems to be basic."[41]

There are, to be sure, ways that children seem to have of defending against separation anxiety resulting from the anticipation of death. One of these—one that has inspired poets down through the ages—is the expectation of reunion in death, a defense that makes separation a temporary matter.[42] But this was a defense denied the Puritan child. As if addressing this question directly, Increase Mather in 1711 remarked on

what a dismal thing it will be when a Child shall see his Father at the right Hand of Christ in the day of Judgment, but himself at His left Hand: And when his Father shall joyn with Christ in passing a Sentence of Eternal Death upon him, saying, Amen O Lord, thou art Righteous in thus *Judging:* And when after the Judgment, children shall see their Father going with Christ to Heaven, but themselves going away into Everlasting Punishment![43]

As Edmund S. Morgan has pointed out, this verbal "picture of parent and child at the Day of Judgment . . . was a favorite with many Puritan ministers, for it made the utmost of filial affection."[44] It did indeed, but it was "filial affection" mixed with a great deal of both guilt and terror, the guilt deriving from the accusation that sinful children were in fact *"Parricides,* or, Parent killers," in Cotton Mather's fearsome words—words expressly addressed to children:

> I must further, and sadly tell you, You are in a fair way to be the *Death* of your poor *Parents,* if you will yet give yourselves up, unto the *Phrensies* of *Ungodliness:* I tell you, You'l make *Them* to Dy *before their Time:* and what are *you* then, but *Wicked Overmuch.* Unworthy Creatures; How can you find in your *Hearts* to shorten the *Lives* of those, through whom you yourselves have Derived your *Lives? . . .* Methinks, I overhear your *Parents* with weeping Eyes, and bleeding Hearts thus calling upon you, O *Unthankful Children, After all that we have done, for you, will you kill us by your Obstinate Ungodliness*[?][45]

Paralleling this theme of guilt was the theme of outright terror— terror deriving, again and again, from the threat of parental separation and betrayal. Still addressing the children of his congregation, Mather warned that "when you come to Ly and Broil in that horrible *Fire* of the wrath of God, all the *Godliness* of your *Parents,* will be but *Oyl* unto the Flame." In addition, "that which will exceedingly Aggravate these *Torments* of your *Damnation,* will be the Encounter which you shall have with your Godly Parents," for on that Day of Judgment such children will see their parents concur in their condemnation and hear them say, "We now know them no more, Let them depart among the Workers of Iniquitie."[46]

It was probably not of much comfort to Puritan children to hear that, if they were to be separated from their parents, they would at least still have the companionship of certain playmates—given the circumstances. For, as Jonathan Edwards put it in one of his sermons specifically addressed to young children: "How dreadful it will be to be all together in misery. Then you wont play together any more but will be damned together, will cry out with weeping and wailing and gnashing of teeth together."[47]

Another common defense against childhood fear of separation and death that is mentioned (though proscribed) in the psychological literature is the parental interjection that only old people die, not children.[48] Puritan children met precisely the opposite advice. The young "may bear and behave themselves as if imagining their hot blood, lusty bodies, activity, beauty, would last alwayes, and their youthful pleasures never be at an end," acknowledged Samuel Wakeman at a young man's funeral in 1673; "but," he warned, *"Childhood and Youth are vanity:* Death may not wait till they be gray-headed; or however, the earliest Morning hastens apace to Noon, and then to Night."[49] From the moment they were old enough to pay attention children were repeatedly instructed regarding the precariousness of their existence. The sermons they listened to, the parents who corrected them, the teachers who instructed them, and eventually the books they read all focused with a particular intensity on the possibility and even the likelihood of their imminent death.

James Janeway's *A Token for Children,* a book designed for reading to and by children, had as its sole purpose to remind children of the ever-nearness of death and its possible consequences. It may have been exceeded in popularity only by the *New England Primer;* but even as they learned the alphabet from this latter book, Puritan children were instructed with such rhymes as: "G—As runs the *Glass* / Mans life doth pass"; "T—*Time* cuts down all / Both great and small"; "X—*Xerxes* the great did die, / And so must you & I"; "Y—*Youth* forward slips / Death soonest nips." And Cotton Mather, once again, in words directed to the "many children: the *Small People*" in his congregation, including both those who had and those who had not achieved a certain "Forwardness at the *Grammar School*," advised that they "Go into *Burying*-Place, CHILDREN; you will there see *Graves* as short as your selves. Yea, you may be at *Play* one Hour; *Dead, Dead* the next." Further, those who died young, it was often noted, died suddenly—"Death is oftentimes as near the young man's back as it is the old man's face," wrote Wakeman—and matter-of-fact repetitions of this ever-present threat joined with burning pictures of Judgment Day to hammer the theme home. "I know you will die in a little time," the esteemed Jonathan Edwards calmly told a group of children, "some sooner than others. 'Tis not likely you will all live to grow up."[50] The fact that Edwards was only speaking the very obvious truth did not help matters any.

Nor did the literalness with which Puritan children must have taken the descriptions of depravity, sin, imminent death, judgment, and Hell offer anything in the way of relief. At least since the early writings of Piaget, psychologists have been familiar with the various stages of the child's sense of causal reality, one central and persistent component of which is termed "realism." Realism, as one writer puts it, "refers to the fact that initially all things are equally real and real in the same sense and on the same plane: pictures, words, people, things, energies, dreams, feelings—all are equally solid or insubstantial and all mingle in a common sphere of experience. . . . Realism does not imply fatalism or passive resignation, but simply a failure [on the part of the young child] to doubt the reality of whatever comes into awareness."[51] The children observed in the psychological experiments that gave rise to the identification of these stages of reality awareness were the children of twentieth-century parents, children living in, if not a secular universe, at least one in which a fundamentalist view of divine creation and judgment is largely absent. Puritan children, however, lived in a world in which their parents—indeed, the greatest scientific minds of the time: Newton, Bacon, Boyle—were certain of the reality of witches and subterranean demons.

As Chadwick Hansen has recently reminded us, the eminence of such great seventeenth-century scientists as these should not obscure the fact that Newton spent much of his time studying the Bible's apocalyptic passages and carefully analyzing the measurements of Solomon's temple in search of the mystic keys to the universe; that "Bacon believed you could cure warts by rubbing them with a rind of bacon and hanging it out of a window that faced south, and that witchcraft may take place 'by a tacit operation of malign spirits' "; and that Boyle, perhaps most famous as the author of *The Skeptical Chymist,* displayed a surprising lack of skepticism when he interviewed English miners in an attempt to find out if they "meet with any subterraneous demons; and if they do, in what shape and manner they appear; what they portend, and what they do." Indeed, in 1674, surprised at Benedict de Spinoza's skepticism regarding spiritual entities, a correspondent of the free-thinking philosopher doubtless spoke for most men of his time—the famed "Age of Reason"—when he replied: "No one of moderns denies specters."[52]

It has long been known, as indicated earlier, that one component of the problem of death in the Middle Ages concerned the fate of the corpse itself, in that it was feared that a fully disintegrated body or one that had been destroyed in war might be unable to be present at the Judgment. It is less well known, or less often acknowledged, that a similar literalism retained a hold on the Puritan mind into the eighteenth century. Thus, in 1692 a highly respected New England minister could effectively deal with questions concerning the Last Judgment in the following manner:

> Where will there be room for such a Vast Multitude as Adam, with all his Children? The whole surface of the earth could not hold them all? Ridiculous exception! Allow that this World should Last no less than *Ten-Thousand* Years, which it *will not;* Allow that there are at once alive a *Thou-*

sand Millions of men, which there *are not;* Allow all these to march off every *Fifty years,* with a New Generation rising up in their stead; and allow each of these Individuals a place *Five Foot* Square to stand upon. I think these are Fair Allowances. I would now pray the Objector, if he have any skill at *Arithmetick,* to Compute, Whether a Spot of Ground, much less than *England,* which contains perhaps about Thirty Millions of Acres, but about a *Thousandth Part* of the Terraqueous Glob, and about the *Three Hundred thirty third* part of the Habitable Earth, would not hold them all.[53]

In a world in which the presence of early death was everywhere and in which the most sophisticated and well-regarded adults expressed such a literal sense of spiritual reality, it is hardly surprising that the children of these adults would respond with a deadly serious mien to reminders of "how filthy, guilty, odious, abominable they are both by nature and practice," to descriptions of parental desertion at the Day of Judgment and of subsequent condemnation to the terrors of Hell where "the Worm dyeth not . . . [and] the Fire is not quenched," and to the exhortations of respected teachers to "remember Death; think much of death; think how it will be on a death bed."[54] In such a world it is far from surprising that a girl of seven should react "with many tears"—and her father with tears of sympathy—to a reading of Isaiah, Chapter 24, in which she would have encountered:

> Therefore hath the curse devoured the earth, and they that dwell therein are desolate: therefore the inhabitants of the earth are burned, and few men left. . . . Fear, and the pit, and the snare, are upon thee, O inhabitant of the earth. And it shall come to pass, that he who fleeth from the noise of the fear shall fall into the pit; and he that cometh up out of the midst of the pit shall be taken in the snare: for the windows on high are opened, and the foundations of the earth do shake.

Nor, in such a world, should we consider it unusual that later in her youth this same girl would again and again "burst out into an amazing cry . . . [because] she was afraid she should goe to Hell," would "read out of Mr. Cotton Mather—why hath Satan filled thy heart, which increas'd her Fear," and would eventually be unable to read the Bible without weeping, fearing as she did "that she was a Reprobat, Loved not God's people as she should."[55]

The case of young Elizabeth Sewall is by no means unique. Puritan diaries and sermons are filled with references to similar childhood responses to the terrors of separation, mortality, and damnation. As we shall see in the next chapter, these fears followed the Puritan child into adulthood and combined there with the disquieting complexities of Puritan theology and Christian tradition to produce a culture permeated by fear and confusion in the face of death. To the adult Puritan the contemplation of death frequently "would make the flesh tremble."[56] To the Puritan child it could do no less.

But we do well to remember that the world of the Puritan—child and adult—was a rational world, in many ways perhaps more rational than our own. It is true that it was a world of witches and demons, and of a just and terrible God who made his presence known in the slightest act of nature. But this was the given reality about which most of the decisions and actions of the age, throughout the entire Western world, revolved. When the Puritan parent urged on his children what we would consider a painfully early awareness of sin and death, it was because the well-being of the child and the community *required* such an early recognition of these matters. It merits little to note that the Puritans (and Bacon, Boyle, and Newton) were mistaken in their beliefs in hobgoblins; the fact is such hobgoblins were *real* to men of the seventeenth century—as real as Ra and his heavenly vessels were to the ancient Egyptians, and at least as real as the unconscious is to devout followers of Freud—and the responses to that reality were as honest and as rational, in the context of the times, as are the responses to reality of any parent today.

If children were frightened, even terrified, by the prospects of life and death conjured up by their parents and ministers, that too was a natural and rational response. As more than one Puritan writer suggested, to fail to be frightened was a sure sign that one was either spiritually lost, or stupid, or both. Death brought with it, to all but a very few, the prospect of the most hideous and excruciating fate imaginable. One necessary—though by itself insufficient—sign of membership in that select company of saints was the taking to heart of the warning to "beware of indulging yourselves in a stupid secure frame."[57] Thus, wrote Samuel Willard with remarkably cool detachment and insight,

> here we see the reason why the People of God are so often doubtful, disquiet, discontent, and afraid to dy (I put things together). The ground of all this is because they do not as yet see clearly what they shall be: It would be a matter of just wonderment to see the Children of God so easily and often shaken, so disturbed and perplexed in hours of Temptation, were it not from the consideration that at present they know so little of themselves or their happiness: Sometimes their sonship itself doth not appear to them, but they are in the dark, at a loss about the evidencing of it to the satisfaction of their own minds, and from hence it is that many doubtings arise, and their souls are disquieted.[58]

Willard knew firsthand of what he spoke. He was often the one chosen to try to calm the fears of those who found the prospect of death too much to bear; in fact, Judge Sewall called him in to help with young Elizabeth's disconsolate weeping. It may be that despite their experience, ministers and parents like Willard were unaware of all the components that went into the making of the Puritan child's fear of death: it was, as we have seen, a complex problem touching on a variety of matters that Puritan children had to face every day of their lives. But they did at least know that when a young Betty or Sam Sewall broke down in tears over the prospects of death and damnation, the children—and they were children, not miniature adults—were most often acting normally, out of their own experience in the world, and in response to their parents' solemn, reasoned warnings.

4

Death and Dying

At the heart of the Puritan's introspective experience—and few other experiences were so important to him—was the matter of the attainment and recognition of saving grace. But "attainment" in this case can be a deceptive word. For although saving grace was essential to the Puritan quest for salvation, it was a gift bestowed by God upon certain of his children without regard to their earthly pleadings or behavior. "The Lord to shew the soveraign freedom of his pleasure," Thomas Hooker wrote, "that he may do with his own what he will, and yet do wrong to none, he denyes pardon and acceptance to those who seek it with some importunity and earnestness . . . and yet bestowes mercy and makes known himself unto some *who never sought him.*" Preparation for salvation, as Norman Pettit has written, "while a necessary prerequisite to the conversion experience, was no guarantee of salvation."[1]

Not only was the divine granting of saving grace a matter beyond man's utmost persuasive powers—indeed, an individual's fate was determined long before his actual arrival in this world—but the Puritans' Calvinistic heritage also clearly included the impossibility of ever fully recognizing oneself as a member of God's small body of the elect or large body of the damned. "Because a small and contemptible number are hidden in a huge multitude," Calvin had written, "and a few grains of wheat are covered by a pile of chaff, we must leave to God alone the knowledge of his church, whose foundation is his secret election." With this as a guiding premise, from the 1580s to the 1660s the Puritans never ceased their stout resistance to a variety of offensive chapters in the Anglican Book of Common Prayer. They even insisted, for example, that at burial services the prescribed words—"we therefore commit his body to the ground in sure and certain hope of resurrection to eternal life"—were contrary to doctrine. After nearly a century of struggle, in 1661 they finally succeeded in having the words "sure and certain" stricken from the pages of the prayer book.[2]

But for the Puritans, if less so for Calvin, there were signs or "marks," indications of God's will, that laymen and ministers alike struggled to detect in their persons and in those of members of the congregation. It was the appearance of these signs within a specifically ordered framework that was recognized as the morphology of conversion: a sequence of introspectively recognized experiences ranging from a deep sense of humiliation to one of eventual spiritual "assurance." If convincingly testified to in the presence of the elders and other members of the church, the Visible Sainthood of an individual might be acknowledged by the congregation, and the individual would thereafter be regarded as one of the probable elect. But assurance, one of the most important steps up this steep ladder of salvation, was a step fraught with particular difficulty and confusion for the devout and conscientious Puritan. "It is a great exercise to some Saints," noted Solomon Stoddard,

> whether they are sincere Saints, they labour in it for many years; and one Minister gives signs, and they try themselves by them, and another gives signs, and they try themselves by them; and sometimes they think they see the signs of Saints, and sometimes the signs of hypocrites: and they dont know what to make of themselves.[3]

Satisfaction on this point, however, still brought little comfort to the newly converted, for even attainment of the level of assurance and recognition by one's earthly peers as a Visible Saint was no guarantee of salvation. Men could both deceive and be deceived, and thus there was always a lingering doubt—indeed, a necessary doubt. "Even after he reached the stage of assurance," Edmund S. Morgan has observed, "his doubts would continue. If they ceased, that would be a sign that he had never had faith to begin with, but had merely deluded himself and had not really entered into the covenant of grace."[4] The cessation of doubt was a sign of "security," of that false assurance of which, in 1629, Arthur Hildersam wrote,

> for one that Sathan hath overthrowne by desperation, there are twenty whom he hath overthrowne with this false assurance. Wee are therefore to be exhorted to examine our assurance. . . . For, as the true assurance of Gods favour is a comfortable thing; so is a false peace and assurance one of the most grievous judgements that can befall a man. . . . Of the two, it were better for a man to be vexed with continuall doubts and feares, than to be lulled asleepe with such an assurance. For, besides that it keepes a man from seeking to God, it will not hold, but faile him, when he shall have most neede of it.[5]

The roots of this necessary doubt were deep, and the effects wide-ranging and persistent. It was "one of the most vexing problems in the Great Awakening," C. C. Goen has noted, referring to the great revival that swept New England over a century after Hildersam's writing. And as the first stirrings of that movement were being felt, Jonathan Edwards observed that "the greater part" of newly converted Saints

> generally have an awful apprehension of the dreadfulness and undoing nature of a false hope; and there has been observable in most a great caution, lest in giving an account of their experiences, they should say too much, and use too strong terms. And many after they have related their experiences, have been greatly afflicted with fears, lest they have played the hypocrite, and used stronger terms than their case

would fairly allow of; and yet could not find how they could correct themselves.[6]

Thus for as long as he lived, even the most apparently obvious candidate for Sainthood did not dare take his election for granted; there was no way in this world of knowing with certainty whether one was saved or not. In other words, the best sign of assurance was to be unsure. As a result, the devout Puritan constantly examined himself and assailed all evidence of impurity, filling journals and diaries with interminable exhortations on the depravity of all men, but most importantly himself. For, as Edwards put it, "there is no man on earth, that is so just, as to have attained to such a degree of righteousness, as not to commit any sin." Wickedness, "if divine grace does not prevent . . . may as truly be said to be the effect which man's natural corruption tend to, as that an acorn in a proper soil, truly tends by its nature to become a great tree."[7] The Puritan faith, then—upon one tenet of which, in 1633, John Preston had pronounced, "this is a very comfortable doctrine, if it be well considered"—was instead a faith marked by a never-ending, excruciating uncertainty. So intense and so demanding of resolution was this uncertainty that on one occasion, as John Winthrop related, "a woman of Boston congregation, having been in much trouble of mind about her spiritual estate, at length grew into utter desperation, and could not endure to hear of any comfort, etc., so as one day she took her little infant and threw it into a well, and then came into the house and said, now she was sure she should be damned, for she had drowned her child."[8]

An equally critical and stress-creating ambivalence was built into the Puritan view of death. On the one hand, life was seen as but a "vapour," a fleeting "pilgrimage"—the latter word apparently taken from the eleventh chapter of Hebrews, where it is applied to Abraham and his descendants.[9] Puritan writing is filled with such references as Increase Mather's mention of "the dayes of my pilgrimage now drawing to their close" and of his wife as "the Dear Companion of my Pilgrimage on Earth," or John Collins's offer of a book to the reader as being "peculiarly suited to the support and consolation of the Saints in this their wayfaring and afflictive pilgrimage." It was in the afterlife that the Saints were to be rewarded and the sinful punished. As Collins wrote: "Death is only sweetened to us as we can look upon it our priviledge; as an out-let from sin and misery, and an in-let to *Glory* both in Holiness and Happiness."[10]

Collins's attitude was neither uncommon nor new. More than a century earlier William Perkins had described death as "a blessing . . . as it were a little wicket or doore whereby we passe out of this world and enter into heaven." Indeed, Increase Mather once wrote, after contemplating the beauty of the soul's flight to heaven, "the thought of this should make the Believer long for death."[11] The desirability of such a longing was, of course, given Biblical justification—most frequently 2 Corinthians 5:6–8: "Being therefore always of good courage, and knowing that, whilst we are at home in the body, we are absent from the Lord (for we walk by faith, not by sight); we are of good courage, I say, and are willing rather to be absent from the body, and to be at home with the Lord."

All this was, to be sure, consistent with the long Christian tradition discussed in a previous chapter. The Bible does, however, have other things to say about death, things present but less emphasized in earlier Christian thought. Among the more important passages is Rom. 5:12: "Therefore, as through one man sin entered into the world, and death through sin; and so death passed unto all men, for that all sinned." The reference to "one man," of course, is to the story of Genesis. The point was not lost on the Puritans. Whenever they listed the "stings of death," as Leonard Hoar did in 1680, the very first was death as punishment for sin. "The first sting of death," Hoar wrote, "is that it came into the world through man's own fault. . . . It is sin brought in death as a curse and punishment. Death comes from God, not as instituting the course of Nature at first; but as revenging sin." Indeed, death,

Hoar writes, "is the greatest evil in the world."[12] Again and again the image of death as a dreadful punishment for the sin of Adam surfaces in Puritan writing, from the simple tombstone carving

> Death which came on man by the fall,
> cuts down father child and all[13]

to the eloquence of Jonathan Edwards:

> For death, with the pains and agonies with which it is usually brought on, is not merely a limiting of existence, but is a most terrible calamity; and to such a creature as man, capable of conceiving of immortality, and made with so earnest a desire after it, and capable of foresight and of reflection on approaching death, and that has such an extreme dread of it, is a calamity above all others terrible, to such as are able to reflect upon it. . . . It is manifest, that mankind were not originally subjected to this calamity. . . . Sin entered into the world, and death by sin, as the apostle says.[14]

The ambivalence inherent in such a dual concept, that death is in a sense both punishment and reward, is evident in virtually every Puritan funeral sermon or other discourse on the subject.[15] Further, death as a phenomenon—whatever the specific image of the moment—seems to have been, as it was in the late Middle Ages, one of the devout Puritan's more important preoccupations. Although he was not exposed to an inordinate amount of premature death when compared with his relatives in England, it was the unquestioned duty of every right-thinking Puritan to keep the thought of death ever on his mind. "A prudent man," Cotton Mather wrote, "will *Dy Daily;* and this is one Thing in our doing too: Tis to *live* Daily under the power of such Impressions, as we shall have upon us, when we come to Dy. . . . Every Time the *Clock* Strikes, it may *Strike* upon our Hearts, to think, *thus I am one Hour nearer to my last!* But, O mark what I say; That *Hour* is probably *Nearer* to None than to such as *Least* Think of it." Later, in *Death Made Easie & Happy,* he urges the reader to remind himself daily "that he is to die shortly. Let us look upon everything as a sort of Death's-Head set before us, with a *Memento mortis* written upon it."[16] As we have seen, this concern left a deep impression on the minds and emotions of Puritan children. One has only to leaf casually through the pages of Samuel Sewall's *Diary* to see repeated examples of this preoccupation in action among adults as well.

But what of it? What do these "ambivalences" and "preoccupations" add up to? What do they mean? Few historians have had anything to say about the Puritan encounter with death, but this should not be surprising: neither has there been, until very recently, much psychoanalytic work on the subject of death in any sense. One psychiatrist who has investigated the subject at some length suggests that "psychiatrists, no less than other mortal men, have a reluctance to consider or study a problem which is so closely and personally indicative of the contingency of the human estate."[17] Whether he is accurate in this assessment and whether it also applies to historians are of minor importance here; what is important is that, for whatever reason, there is a definite paucity of literature on the subject. Nevertheless, from the small amount that does exist one gains the general impression that adult Puritans confronted death optimistically, with neither doubts nor fears. Perry Miller, for example, directs himself to what he terms the "cosmic optimism" of the Puritans in facing all manner of adversity, then notes the relatively "few sermons specifically devoted to immortality compared with the tremendous number drawing out the lessons of depravity or analyzing in minute detail the processes of regeneration. Perhaps the expectation of immortality was so axiomatic," he surmises, "that little discussion was needed, but I am inclined to suspect that because their energies were so intensely concentrated upon the problems in hand they had few left for doubts about those to come." Or, as Allan I. Ludwig has more recently—and somewhat more dramatically—put it: "In the midst of darkness and confusion there was light, the triumph of Death was overcome by eternity. The fear of death gave way to the thrill of spiritual pleasures yet to come as archangels trumpeted the glorious day."[18]

The evidence does not confirm this interpretation. Instead, it suggests that the Puritans were gripped individually and collectively by an intense and unremitting fear of death, while *simultaneously* clinging to the traditional Christian rhetoric of viewing death as a release and relief for the earth-bound soul. Increase Mather provides a clear-cut example of this duality. Mather was fond of the kind of declaration cited earlier, indicating that believers should long for the deliverance of death. Indeed, in one of his sermons published in 1715, he cried, "I know that the time of my departure out of this World is now very near at hand. . . . And now that I am *Preaching Christ,* how glad should I be, if I might dye before I stir out of this pulpit!"[19] But eight years later, when death was in fact near at hand, his reaction was quite different. As his son Cotton relates and explains it:

And in the Minutes of the Darkness wherein he lay thus *feeble and sore broken,* he sometimes let fall expressions of some *Fear* lest he might after all be Deceived in his *Hope* of the *Future Blessedness.* His Holy Ministry having very much insisted on that Point, that *no care could be too much to prevent our being Deceived in that Important Matter;* tis no wonder, that as the *Dark Vapours* which assaulted and fettered his Intellectual Powers, broke in upon him, his Head should run much upon the Horror of being *Deceived at the last.* Yea, had there not been anything at all of a *Natural* Debilitation and Obnubilation in it, yet it were a very Supposeable thing, and not at all to be wondered at, if the *Serpent* be let loose to vex a Servant of GOD in the *Heel* of his Life; and if the *Powers of Darkness,* knowing the *Time to be short,* fall with *Great Wrath* on the Great Opposers of their *Kingdom,* and make a very *Dark Time* for them just before the *Break* of the Eternal Day upon them. And how justly might it awaken the rest of us to *Work out our own Salvation with Fear and Trembling,* when we see such a man as Dr. *Mather,* concerned with so much *Fear and Trembling,* lest he should

> be *Deceived at the Last?* . . . The best Judges of Things
> have agreed in this Judgment; That going to Heaven *in the*
> *way of Repentence,* is much safer and surer than going *in the*
> *way of Extasy.*[20]

Not only does this passage illustrate the difference between Increase's earlier pronouncements and his actual deathbed behavior,
but with equal force it points out the dissonant nature of the
father's experience of death and the son's "rhetorical" interpretation of it. Cotton, after all, remained clearly convinced of his
father's salvation, despite the force of his father's despair.

Increase Mather had an exceptional recording secretary in his
son, and such meticulous descriptive passages are more the exception than the rule among extant materials. Still, the elder Mather's
experience was not unique, nor was it contrary to what was expected of devout Puritans. More than forty years before Increase
Mather's birth, William Perkins had opened one of his works with
a quote from Ecclesiastes—"The day of death is better than the
day that one is borne"—but then proceeded to observe that "not
only wicked and loose persons despaire in death, but also re-
pentant sinners, who oftentimes in their sickness, testifie of themselves that being alive and lying in their beds, they feel themselves
as it were to be in hell, and to apprehend the very pangs and torments thereof."[21]

One of the earliest extant funeral sermons preached in New
England was that of Samuel Wakeman for John Tappin of Boston,
a victim of death at the age of eighteen. That Tappin was a godly
youth is testified to by Wakeman and appears evident from the entire middle section of the sermon, a warning to the "rising generation" to make haste in "setting their hearts seriously God-ward,"
which had been written by the young man for delivery upon his
death. Still, when at the end of the sermon Wakeman describes
Tappin's final moments, he notes that Tappin

> looked upon himself an undone man without an interest in
> Jesus Christ; yet he was not without some hope that he was

at peace with God in him, yet not without fears, bemoaning himself in respect of his hardness of heart and blindness of minde, and that he had been no more thoroughly wrought upon by the Means that he had formerly enjoyed. O Sirs, Dying times are Trying times.[22]

Writing seven years later, Leonard Hoar sounds almost jealous of what he sees as the comparative ease with which too many of the ungodly depart the world:

I acknowledge its an error in the saints and people of God to be so much affrighted at death, and to goe so mournfully out of this world: surely they have not learn'd to look off this world, and to look up to that which is to come; yet I am sure it is a greater error, and a damning error in the wicked and ungodly when they are not afraid of Death at all, when they look upon Death as a common and usual event and have slight thoughts of it, all their complaints are out of sympathy with their friends, or from their bodily pains, or their distracted thoughts about worldly matters, but never consider what a weighty thing it is to dye well, or what a dreadful thing it is to miscarry in their latter end. And O the wretched stupidity of some that can be then most secure, and are even like the beasts which perish, *Psal. 49.12.* O then blame not any that have woeful apprehensions of death, and beware of indulging your selves in a stupid secure frame, for as Solomon saith in another case, *Prov. 23. 32.* It will sting like an Adder and bite like a Serpent.[23]

None of this is to suggest, of course, that *all* New England Puritans faced the ends of their lives in desperate fear and trembling. Many of them did not, and, at least as reported in the didactic postmortem expositions of their ministers, perhaps most even gasped a sigh of personal conviction as their final breath escaped.[24] Still, even those Saints who were most peaceful in their dying hours could never fully avoid the intense emotional oscillation caused by the need to simultaneously accommodate the fear of, in Hoar's words, "indulging . . . in a stupid secure frame," *and* the desire for Paradise and the traditional Christian prescription of a

tranquil passing. The death of Katharin Mather provides an in-
structive example. Katharin's death is clearly one of the most
glorious on record, not only to the historian but to her contemporaries as well. Whereas, as her father readily acknowledged, other
Saints had often faltered at the approach of death—such as the
"worthy Non-Conforming Minister, Mr. Thomas Pyke, [who] as
his Death drew near, said, He found the best Preparations of any
Men living, were little enough, when they came to Dye"—Katharin's tranquility was of such a measure that even "some who had
Read and *Heard* much, said, they never *Saw* till now." But even
this extraordinary young woman was not immune to the fear of
succumbing to security. Her assurance, it was noted, "was not a
Rash Perswasion. She was desirous to have the matter *Disputed*
unto the uttermost. How pathetically would she say, *Oh that my
portion may be among the wise Virgins!* But, in this time, often
she would say unto her Father, *Is my Soul safe? Will my Saviour
accept me?"* Her father's counsel "in such *Agonies,* as might come
upon her" was that God would indeed most likely accept her. But
the battle continued, the battle to overcome with calm "the *Storms,*
which had sometimes disquieted her Soul." And despite her suc-
cesses, "yet these *Triumphs* now and then met with Interruptions."
And then: "On December 12. In the Night she seemed entring
into the last Agonies of *Death.* And felt then some Returns of
Darkness upon her. In which she expressed her self *afraid of
Dying, afraid* whether her *Saviour* would accept of her."[25] In the
end, however, she passed into death in a state of peace and glory
and "good courage"—a state consistent with the recommendatory
rhetoric.

Katharin Mather was, as those who eulogized her agreed, an
exceptional case. But even she could not escape the intense
stresses that worked within the Puritan heart as death drew near.
To many others, as her father was to put it some years later, "if
the *Arrest of Death* were laid upon them, the *Terror of Death*

alone would be enough to kill them! They would *Chatter like a Crane or a Swallow, and mourne like a Dove,* going to be pulled out of their *Nest,* and cry out, *Lord,* This Hour is what I am not ready for!"[26]

Initially then, the reason for such frequent deathbed anxiety among godly Puritans—death itself often being called "the King of Terrors"[27]—seems rooted in a combination of the Puritans' theology and their everyday sense of reality. Their theology taught them of their uttter and total depravity and assured them of their helplessness in securing their own salvation. Reinforcing this pessimistic determinism was the doctrine of assurance: as noted earlier, doubt *of* salvation was essential *to* salvation; that Puritan who—for so long as he breathed—became at any time secure and comfortable in the knowledge of his salvation was surely lost. In addition to the examples already cited, a striking account of the kind of emotional stress created by these beliefs is that of the deathbed scene of that formidable personality John Knox, as related by William Perkins:

> He [Knox] lay on his death bedde silent for the space of four hours, very often giving great sighes, sobbes, and grones, so as the standers by well perceived that he was troubled with some grievous temptation: and when at length he was raised in his bedde, they asked him how he did, to whome he answered thus: that in his life he had indured many combates and conflicts with Satan, but that now most mightily the roaring lyon had assaulted him: often (said he) before he set my sinnes before mine eyes, often he urged me to desperation, often he laboured to intangle me with the delights of the world, but beeing vanquished by the sword of the spirit, which is the word of God, he could not prevaile. But now he assaults me another way: for the wily serpent would perswade me that I shall merit eternall life for my fidelitie in my ministrie. But blessed be God which brought to my minde such Scriptures whereby I might quench the fierie darts of the devill, which were, *What hast thou that thou hast not re-*

ceived: and, *By the grace of God, I am that I am:* and, *not
I but the grace of God in me:* and thus being vanquished he
departed.[28]

A break from the established Christian tradition of dealing with
death can be clearly perceived here. In the *Ars Moriendi* of the
late Middle Ages, for example, the dying man was assaulted by a
variety of demons tempting him with infidelity, despair, impa-
tience, vainglory, and avarice; but the victim, aided by a battery
of saints and angels, attained salvation by resolutely clinging to
his optimistic belief in his own goodness and the justness of God.
Similarly, in the seventeenth century the Jesuit Henry More, re-
porting on the death of Father Jasper Heywood, notes that the assaults of the Devil—assaults involving the threat of damnation "because you have been unorthodox in your teaching"—were met by
the dying priest with such self-righteous confidence in the unde-
niability of his salvation that the Devil soon retired, leaving Father
Heywood to die in peace.[29] Knox, on the other hand, though subject to these same sorts of temptations during his life, was tempted
in precisely the reverse manner when death grew near—tempted,
that is, by *security* founded on the heretical premise of good
works—and seemingly attained salvation by denying it.

In order for the doctrine of assurance to be effective, it was essential that believers have an unquestioning belief in the reality of
the contrastive terrors and bliss of the afterlife. At a time when, as
D. P. Walker has pointed out, the doctrine of eternal torment for
the damned was beginning to come under attack in England and
on the Continent (even as it had fourteen centuries earlier by
Origen and others), among the New England Puritans there remained no plainer reality.[30] And while it is true that in the past
the fire and brimstone nature of the Puritan sermon and tract has
been greatly exaggerated, it is equally true that the New England
ministry did not hesitate to conjure up explicit pictures of the terrors of Hell when it suited them, with the result that, in the words
of Increase Mather's uncommon understatement, "oft times there

were more weepers than sleepers in the Congregation."[31] Thus, "If their Strength were the Strength of Stones," Solomon Stoddard wrote of the unregenerate in 1713,

> or their Flesh of Brass, they could not endure their Misery. They will have *Anguish of Spirit,* not know what in the World to do; there will be dreadful Wailing, Mat. 13.42. They will lament their Sins, they will bewail the loss of Opportunities; they will condemn their Folly, they will curse themselves, they will wish they had never seen such things as now their Hearts dote upon . . . they will wish they had no Senses; their Hearing and Seeing and Feeling will be their Misery, their Memory, their Understanding, their Conscience will be their Torment; they will wish they had no Bodies, and wish they had no Souls, their *Bodies and Souls will be* Vessels of Wrath.[32]

Furthermore, he reminds his audience, all the sufferings of this place where "the Worm dyeth not," where "the Fire is not quenched," are eternal:

> The duration of their Misery cannot be measured: We may measure the breadth of the Earth, and the circuit of the Heaven, but can't measure Eternity. Add thousands to thousands, and multiply Millions by Millions; fill Quires of Paper with numbers, and you can't measure Eternity; It cannot be divided into Days, or Years, or Ages; make never so many Parts of it, one will be Eternal: When Men have suffered never so long, there is an Eternity remaining: it don't grow shorter and shorter. This makes every part of their Misery Infinite, their pain will be Infinite, the Terrour Infinite. If Miseries End, there is an opportunity for Comfort afterwards; but Eternity cuts off opportunities for Comfort: Men may well say, *Who can dwell with* everlasting Burnings?[33]

In the middle of the seventeenth century the Anglican bishop Jeremy Taylor had assured his readers that "God knows that the torments of hell are so horrid, so insupportable a calamity that He is not easy and apt to cast those souls which he hath taken so much care and hath been at so much expense to save, into the eternal,

never-dying flames of hell lightly, for smaller sins, or after a fairly
begun repentance, and in the midst of holy desires to finish it."
And a century later, Marie Huber was writing tracts with a wide
European influence arguing that "the Doctrine of the Eternity of
Hell-Torments was not so incontestable, as not to be called in
question by a great number of judicious men."[34] In contrast, during the same period in which Huber was writing, Jonathan Edwards was traveling about New England, drawing and spellbinding
crowds with such passages as

> how dismal will it be, when you are under these racking tor-
> ments, to know assuredly that you never, never shall be deliv-
> ered from them; to have no hope: when you shall wish that
> you might but be turned into nothing, but shall have no hope
> of it; when you shall wish that you might be turned into a
> toad or a serpent, but shall have no hope of it; when you
> would rejoice, if you might but have any relief, after you
> shall have endured these torments millions of ages, but shall
> have no hope of it; when after you shall have worn out the
> age of the sun, moon, and stars, in your dolorous groans and
> lamentations, without any rest day or night, or one minute's
> ease, yet you shall have no hope of ever being delivered;
> when after you shall have worn out a thousand more such
> ages, yet you shall have no hope, but shall know that you are
> not one whit nearer to the end of your torments; but that still
> there are the same groans, the same shrieks, the same doleful
> cries, incessantly to be made by you, and that the smoke of
> your torment shall still ascent up forever and ever; and that
> your souls, which shall have been agitated with the wrath of
> God all this while, yet will still exist to bear more wrath; your
> bodies, which shall have been burning and roasting all this
> while in these glowing flames, yet shall not have been con-
> sumed, but will remain to roast through an eternity yet, which
> will not have been at all shortened by what shall have been
> past.[35]

Even Charles Chauncy, Edwards's determined Puritan rival and
a well-known religious "liberal," was not outside the mainstream.
As he warned his congregation in the summer of 1741:

There is nothing betwixt you and the place of blackness of darkness, but a poor frail, uncertain life. You hang, as it were, over the bottomless pit, by the slender thread of life, and the moment that snaps asunder, you sink down into perdition. . . . Who has bewitched you, O sinners, that you are thus lost to all sense of your own safety and interest! Be convinc'd of your danger. You are certainly in a state of dreadful and amazing hazard.[36]

In England throughout the seventeenth and into the eighteenth centuries there was brewing what became known as the "mortalist heresy," a belief that the soul dies with the body and is resurrected with it on the Day of Judgment.[37] But, as with other ostensibly liberalizing trends in Christian thought, such as those concerning the mitigation of eternal torment in Hell, mortalism never took hold among New England's Puritans. As the world of their English brethren began losing many of its more extreme trappings of reform, that of the New Englanders seems to have rigidified; at the same time, their anxieties concerning death and damnation became, if anything, more intense.

As death drew near for the Puritan, the tension normally built into the doctrine of assurance was dramatically heightened, for now the time of decision was at hand—the time when the Puritan's sin-riddled soul would be judged and either admitted to Heaven or cast into the fiery pit of Hell. If he or she should not be properly prepared, there was no way out, no such thing as the last-minute sacramental reprieve in which the Catholics and some early Christians had believed. Whereas legend had it that centuries earlier the dying Empress Matilda, a "prudent matron" and mother of the future Henry II, had supposedly "distributed her treasures to widows, orphans, and the poor and so escaped the peril of death," to the Puritan such deathbed gestures of repentance were of little value.[38] "There is no Real Conversion in it," Cotton Mather argued. "Men are then only like Iron softened in the Fire; they soon Return to their former Hardness if God spare them from going down into the *Unquenchable* Fire."³⁹ Thus, at death the Puritan knew there was nothing he could do but wait, hope—and doubt.

It seems hardly surprising, then, that in the earliest New England funeral sermon we have, James Fitch refers to the frequent absence in the Puritan experience of the traditional "sweetness of that unspeakable peace in [one's] dying hour" as the result of the fear of "the misery of falling short, for none can be so sensible of that, as those who know experimentally the preciousness of Christ and heavenly things: and though also many times the very thought, what if deceived? what if fall short at last? that thought would make the flesh tremble."⁴⁰ Or, to cite once again the vivid language of Leonard Hoar, who after recognizing the historical tradition with such a typical phrase as "the day of ones Death is better than the day of ones Birth," and rhetorically describing death as "a loosing from this troublesome Shore," becomes much more specific, much truer to the Puritan vision:

> So it may be said of every inhabitant of this earth when he comes to dye, the weight of sin, the unsupportableness of Gods anger, the terrors of hell, the nearness of the danger, the difficulty of salvation will all appear nakedly to the naked soul. When God makes darkness and it is night, then the beasts of the forest creep forth: every frog will be croaking towards the evening, every puddle will send up a stinking vapor in a foggy night; all the several shadows of things will unite, every [illegible] will concur to make up and compleat the misery of the poor sinner. . . . *Hence learn why men dread and are so afraid of death,* yes there are many causes why a natural man should fear Death, because of the sting that is in it.⁴¹

The acute awareness that man was both powerless to affect the matter of his salvation and morally crippled by his natural depravity caused, Cotton Mather wrote, much distress and retrospective agonizing as death closed in. " 'Tis very certain," he noted in *Thoughts of a Dying Man,* "that *at the Last,* when you are taking your leave of this *World,* you will be full of Disdainful Expressions concerning it, and Express your selves to this purpose: *Vain World! False World! Oh! that I had minded this World Less, and my own Soul more, than I have done!*" Later in the same work Mather warned that when, on your deathbed, you are provided with reminders of your past sinful life, "the sight of them will smite thee with more Horror, than if so many *Rattle Snakes* were then horribly crawling about thee." And still later:

> Tis no rare Thing, for eminent *Saints,* when they lay a *Dying,* to profess, as we find in the History of their *Lives,* that some of them have done; *The Loss of Time, is a Thing, that now Sits heavy on this Poor Soul of mine!* . . . Men ordinarily Dy, with words, like those of that Great Person, Sir Henry Wotten, uttered with Tears, *How much Time have I to Repent of! and how Little Time to do* it in![42]

The New England Puritans, despite their traditional optimistic rhetoric, were possessed of an intense, overt fear of death—the natural consequence of what to them were three patently true and quite rational beliefs: that of their own utter and unalterable depravity; that of the omnipotence, justness, and inscrutability of God; and that of the unspeakable terrors of Hell. Unlike Bacon, they did not fear death merely "as children fear to go in the dark"; they feared it because they knew precisely what to expect from it.

One cannot leaf through Increase Mather's *Remarkable Providences* or Cotton Mather's *Wonders of the Invisible World* without sensing the sober reality of the spiritual world to the devout Puritan. Even John Winthrop, generally acknowledged as among the wisest, most level-headed, and pragmatic of New England's Puritans, often displayed a degree of guilelessness that is jarring to the modern imagination. On one occasion, for example, he soberly related an incident involving the birth of a monster to a heretic—only one among a number of such births—as an example of God's "instruction of the parents":

> It was a woman child, stillborn, about two months before the just time, having life a few hours before; it came hiplings

till she turned it; it was of ordinary bigness; it had a face, but no head, and the ears stood upon the shoulders and were like an ape's; it had no forehead, but over the eyes four horns, hard and sharp; two of them were above one inch long, the other two shorter; the eyes standing out, and the mouth also; the nose hooked upward; all over the breast and back full of sharp pricks and scales, like a thornback; the navel and all the belly, with the distinction of the sex, were where the back should be, and the back and hips before, where the belly should have been; behind, between the shoulders, it had two mouths, and in each of them a piece of red flesh sticking out; it had arms and legs as other children; but, instead of toes, it had on each foot three claws, like a young fowl, with sharp talons.[43]

It is not likely an accident that Winthrop's description is remarkably similar, in even the most minute detail, to descriptions and pictorial representations of Satanic demons dating back well into the Middle Ages. But Winthrop was not conscious of the derivative nature of his words: such monsters were as real to him as the trees in the forests, behind which lurked many more of the Devil's servants. Nor is it therefore surprising to find that Winthrop shared what Sacvan Bercovitch has called "the deathbed scene of many other saints," as later recorded in Cotton Mather's *Magnalia Christi Americana:* "he was buffeted with the disconsolate thoughts of black and sore desertions, wherein he could use that sad representation of his own condition: 'Recently I was a judge, now I am judged; I tremble as I stand before the tribunal, to be judged myself.' "[44]

Given, then, this vision of reality, coupled with the theological dilemmas posed by the doctrines of predestination, human depravity and helplessness, and of the inscrutability of God on the matter of salvation, it is clear that there was nothing extraordinary in the Puritans' emotionally turbulent reaction to death. On the contrary, it was only the extraordinary (and possibly suspect)

Saint who could pass through the throes of death without giving way to bouts of extreme despair.

"The power of religion depends, in the last resort," Peter L. Berger writes, "upon the credibility of the banners it puts in the hands of men as they stand before death, or more accurately, as they walk, inevitably, toward it."[45] If the Puritans often experienced what may seem inordinate difficulty in facing death, it was not entirely because of what we have seen to be the fearful images of irresistible destiny conjured up in their collective mind's eye; nor, certainly, can the answer be found in the continued presence of the rhetoric of Christian optimism, of the *Migratio ad Dominum* theme, in their formal thoughts on the matter. The ultimate difficulty lay rather in the attempt to reconcile the differences represented by these two contradictory "banners" that they carried simultaneously. As Berger's observation would suggest, the enduring discomfort they experienced was principally due to their failure to credibly reconcile the answers they were forced to give to questions concerning the proper way of viewing *death* with those problems imposed by the experience of *dying*. By clinging to the rhetorical tone, style, and ritual of a Christianity equipped with a variety of mechanisms whereby man might affect his fate and secure his own salvation, a Christianity that had little application to their own deterministic concept of reality, the Puritans trapped themselves between conflicting belief systems—more specifically, in this case, between conflicting schemes of what, in an earlier chapter, I have termed *world view* and *ethos*.

The functional effects of such conflicts have long interested theorists in the behavioral sciences. The concept of *anomie* or "normlessness," for example, has had a profound effect on modern sociology and psychology.[46] Although the subject of a great deal of controversy, the term in its simplest sense has generally been recognized as referring to the confusion and apprehension that may result from "a clash between belief-systems or, more precisely, a conflict between the *directives* of belief-systems."[47] Similarly, Leon Festinger's cognitive dissonance theory rests on the assumption that "the human organism tries to establish internal harmony, consistency, or congruity" in its cognitive structure; the loss of such consistency, Festinger argues, results in a state of psychological discomfort (or cognitive dissonance), the intensity of which varies in relation to the importance of the incompatible and competing cognitions.[48]

It is not my intent here to try to pin either of these or any other such specific label on the Puritan handling of the problems of death and dying. Such an exercise would properly be subject to both philosophical and substantive criticisms that are beyond the scope of this study. Nevertheless, what appears to be at work here—the simple fact, as William James once put it, that "we cannot continue to think in two contradictory ways at once"—is a phenomenon so basic that it transcends disciplinary and chronological boundaries.[49]

For at least two thousand years, as G. E. R. Lloyd pointed out a decade ago, it has been recognized that all belief systems contain within themselves the seeds of their own destruction.[50] In recent centuries this notion has received its most significant elaboration in the Hegelian proposition of progress through thesis and antithesis as rival but interdependent phenomena that find their resolution by a process of synthesis that in turn then generates its own antithesis. This is an inevitable and ongoing process, as Hegel put it in his *Science and Logic,* in that "only insofar as something has contradiction in itself does it move, have impulse or activity." Another less formal and more general way of casting this idea is to say that whatever labels we may care to give the activity, virtually all cultures and individuals experience a constant, if generally slight, changing of structure or focus as adjustments are made to new cognitive or conceptual conflicts. But if this progression is inevitable, the activity itself is not universally fluid. Resolution of conflict—for reasons that can probably be infinitely varied—may in certain situations seem for a time irreconcilably blocked. And on those occasions when accommodation does not take place for an extended time—particularly in relatively closed cultures and when the matter at hand is of primary cultural significance—the reverberations of the continuing clash may cause extreme confusion and discomfort to those persons participating in that culture's ongoing social life.

Death and dying were matters of critical importance to the Puritans; indeed, they constantly urged themselves to direct their lives toward that moment when their earthly pilgrimage would end. In this effort they spared no one, not even their children. And, as we have seen, the effects of this concern on the Puritan child had profound consequences. As the child grew to adulthood the focus of his anxiety shifted somewhat from fear of separation from his parents to concern and confusion as to the nature of his spiritual fate. But the adult Puritan's vision of death with its attendant and deserved terrors was at odds with the inherited Christian advocacy of displaying what James Fitch called "the sweetness of that unspeakable peace" when death approached. The result was a kind of "cultural dissonance," an uncomfortable tension, that pressed for resolution. A culture, no less than an individual, cannot long endure such pressure. One of the principal ways of reducing such tension, Festinger and others agree, is "by changing one or more of the elements involved in dissonant relations,"[51] and this, it now seems clear, is what happened in New England in the eighteenth century.

Precisely when such a change took place in Puritan society remains a matter of conjecture. Indeed, as with most important changes in the structure of intellectual and cultural phenomena, it may well be impossible ever to locate exactly a watershed point. But as will be seen in a subsequent chapter, by the latter half of the eighteenth century, when the emerging New England ortho-

doxy was finally of an increasingly liberal bent, the anxiety-riddled tension between death and dying that had so beset devout Puritans a century earlier no longer appears to have been an active force.

This is certainly not to suggest that the Puritans' successors ceased to fear death. They did fear it, and still do; but in ways very different from their ancestors.[52] Just as Christians in the Middle Ages and earlier fitted their fears into a fairly harmonious system of belief, so have most post-Puritan Christians, with the result that the fear is at least tempered by theological rationalization that is tolerably consistent. The Puritans inherited part of that rationalization, that part which counseled a peaceful death for the regenerate, and this advice recurs like an unthinking, though obviously important, slogan throughout their writing; but it was not consistent with their sense of reality. It did not "fit." And so, though the need for such comforting counsel was apparently present, the reassurance it should have afforded the regenerate individual was often denied him, both by the determinism of the faith and by the excruciatingly difficult balance that had to be maintained between the conversion stages of assurance and security. To return to Peter Berger's imagery, there was simply very little real confidence *possible* in the credibility of *either* of the major religious banners the Puritans carried as they walked inevitably toward death. The result was a vision of death and an attitude toward dying that were locked in perpetual conflict, a conflict that had the potential to bring extraordinary discomfort to bear on the life of the devout Puritan, a conflict that could not be indefinitely endured.

Fig. 6. *Opposite page,* A medieval depiction of one of Satan's demons that resembles in several details John Winthrop's description of the monster born to a heretic in the early seventeenth century. The art of the Middle Ages abounded with similar representations. This one is from the studio of Hans Memling and is a detail from a fifteenth century polyptych entitled "Hell", Strasbourg Musee de Beaux Arts.

5

Death and Burial

It has often been said that no one is more English than the Englishman away from home. If, as with all such sayings, there are numerous exceptions to this, the Puritans of New England are not one of these. So concerned were they not to appear to have separated from England and its national church that they repeatedly reminded themselves and those they had left behind that their removal to the New World was a removal in superficial appearances only; they remained Englishmen and members of the Church of England, and they strove mightily to ensure that no mistake ever be made as to their intentions. Even as the first ships sailed toward what was to become the colony of Massachusetts Bay, John Winthrop reminded his fellow passengers—in what has become one of the most quoted and most misunderstood phrases in American history—that their mission was not to erect a permanent, isolated utopia, but rather to build such a community "that wee shall be as a Citty upon a Hill, the eies of all people are uppon us."[1] These were Englishmen who intended when the time was right to return to their homeland in triumph. Far from deserting the land of their fathers, the New Englanders saw as their divinely appointed role, as the Reverend William Hooke so vividly put it, "to lye in wait in the wilderness," and eventually "to come upon the backs of Gods Enemies with deadly Fastings and Prayer, murtherers that will kill point blanke from one end of the world to the other." In Perry Miller's more succinct words: "The migration was no retreat from Europe: it was a flank attack."[2]

But as the settlements took root and the intention to return to England faded, in at least one respect the culture that developed among the Puritans of New England became something of an exaggerated version of the culture they had left behind. The thought and experience of their Puritan forebears had provided the New Englanders with a framework for approaching the problem of death, but never had the concern with death taken on in England the enormous and complex meanings it soon would in those infant settlements across the Atlantic.

We have seen that this was so; what we have yet to learn is *why*. The intricacies of Puritan theology and the entanglement and clashing of that theology with the realities of everyday thought and action only partly explain the Puritan preoccupation with and fear of death. Although there were important, if subtle, theological differences that developed in time between the Puritans on opposite sides of the ocean, in large measure both parties shared common theological doctrines and assumptions concerning the world about them. We must look beyond these matters if we are to understand the extraordinary concern with death of the New England Puritans, compared with that of their Old World brethren.

The disposal of the dead with some measure of ritual and ceremony is, as we have seen, the earliest indication archaeological records evince of social behavior and thought among men. But the specific meaning of burial ritual varies from culture to culture, depending on the specific conceptions of life and the afterlife, and on the nature of the transitional phase occurring between the two. Thus, for example, the vivid Islamic belief in the "Night of Desolation" immediately following one's death and burial, when the

deceased is interrogated by two terrifying angels as to his qualifi-
cations for entering Paradise, is the apparent source for the custom
of "tutoring" the corpse just prior to and after burial so that it
will be fully prepared with the proper answers. On the other hand,
the Navajo of the Southwestern United States have only a vague
and shadowy notion of a rather barren postmortem existence, and
the fact of death carries with it no optimistic hopes or expectations; as a result, the corpse is shunned by all but the closest relatives responsible for burying it—and they in turn dispose of it with
little delay and with accompanying ceremonies designed more to
protect the living from the pollution of death than to assist the deceased in his journey to the afterlife.[3]

The elaborate and theologically crucial funeral ceremonies of
Catholicism from the early Middle Ages onward were doubtless
connected with a variety of beliefs and images, but none was so
central as the conception of Purgatory, where those who had died
in venial sin (mortal sin being sufficient to bring on eternal damnation) were purified through temporary suffering preparatory to
entering heaven. Since it was believed as well that the prayers and
activities of the living could serve to shorten one's term of purgatorial suffering, the ceremonies and rituals surrounding death took
on major cultural significance. But if they were significant—indeed,
largely *because* they were so significant—such rituals were equally
susceptible to abuse.

The idea of Purgatory, of a middle ground that was at the same
time both a modification of Heaven and a mitigation of Hell, addressed so perfectly the great and fearsome chasm between the extremes of salvation and damnation that in time it became the
dominant picture of the fate that awaited almost all Catholics immediately following their deaths. By the time of the Renaissance
the image of purgatorial suffering had replaced the images of
Heaven, Hell, and the awesome Last Judgment that had dominated the art of the Middle Ages. And with this profound change
in the *vision* of the afterlife came an equally profound change in

attitudes toward the afterlife. The major question most, though by no means all, Catholics had to face was no longer that concerning the alternatives of Heaven and Hell; now it had become one of the duration of purgatorial torment that a person could expect. With such a concern now central throughout Christendom, it is hardly surprising that the system of indulgences—the method by which one's designated punishment might be at least partially remitted—readily fell subject to corruption. Nor is it surprising that one of the principle tenets of Catholicism that came under attack during the Reformation was the concept of Purgatory; indeed, Martin Luther's initial public reaction to papal authority was a direct response to the crass selling of indulgences in his beloved Wittenberg.[4]

Concurrent with the Reformers' denigration of the "popish fiction" of Purgatory came their intense support of the idea of predestination. These fundamental alterations of Catholic dogma had many deep and wide-ranging effects, one of which—the one most important for present purposes—was the functional diminution of the need for elaborate funeral ritual. If the fate of the deceased had been determined in advance of his very earthly existence, and if there was nothing that any man or men could do to alter that fate, there was clearly no place for belief in a temporary afterlife state that was a cleansing way station between earthly and heavenly existence. Nor was there a place for the idea that the efforts of an individual, or his family and friends—whether made during his life, at the time of burial, or afterwards—might have any bearing on his ultimate postmortem fate. Instead, as Calvin wrote, an individual's fate was sealed long before his death, so that one's expected postmortem condition involved merely waiting for the formality of Judgment: "The Souls of the faithful, after completing their term of combat and travail, are gathered into rest, where they await with joy the fruition of their promised glory; and thus all things remain in suspense until Jesus Christ appears as the Redeemer." And the unfaithful? "They are chained up like malefactors until the time when they are dragged to the punishment that is appointed for them."[5] As one modern historian has observed: "Whereas medieval Catholics had believed that God would let souls linger in Purgatory if no masses were said for them, Protestant doctrine meant that each generation could be indifferent to the spiritual fate of its predecessor. Every individual was now to keep his own balance-sheet, and a man could no longer atone for his sins by the prayers of his descendants."[6]

Once death had overtaken an individual, there was nothing his family or acquaintances could do but reassure themselves that his spirit was at least in the hands of God. Whereas St. Thomas Aquinas had felt the need to argue vigorously that there is indeed to be an eventual physical resurrection of the body, and a reunion of the "selfsame soul" with the "selfsame body," to the Puritan the soul of the dead person had flown to its appointed fate, and the corpse that remained behind was but a meaningless husk. Or worse. As one noted English Puritan reminded his readers in 1635, "thy body, when the soule is gone, will be an horrour to all that behold it; a most loathsome and abhorred spectacle. Those that loved it most, cannot now finde in their hearts to looke on't, by reason of the griefly deformedness which death will put upon it. Down it must into a pit of carions and confusion, covered with wormes, not able to wag so much as a little finger, to remoove the vermine that feed and gnaw upon its flesh; and so moulder away into rottennesse and dust. . . . [W]hen the soule departs this life, it carries nothing away with it, but grace, Gods favour, and a good conscience."[7]

This is not to say that the Reformer did not believe in ultimate bodily resurrection, but merely that he seemed relatively unconcerned as to the details by which such a process might be effected. "Our faith," John Weever noted, "is not so fraile as to thinke that the ravenous beasts can deprive the body of any part to bee wanting in the resurrection; where not a haire of the head shall be missing; a new restitution of our whole bodies being promised to all of us in a moment, not onely of the earth alone, but even out of the most secret angles of all the other elements, wherein any body is, or can bee possibly included."[8]

Among a people who hold such beliefs as this, there can be no logical justification for embalming or otherwise preserving the dead body, there is no room for the kinds of fear for the ultimate fate of flesh and bone that gripped Catholics in the Middle Ages, and there is no reason to assume that any sort of burial ritual can have any effect at all on the condition of the deceased. As with so many other areas of Puritan concern, if there was no spiritual justification for a ritual its practice was not merely to be ignored—it was to be fiercely stripped away.

By the mid-1640s, in the flush of their apparent triumphs in England, the Puritans had formalized their prescription for the approved approach to funeral ritual. In *A Directory for the Publique Worship of God,* an outcome of the Westminster Convention of 1645, it was ordered that "when any person departeth this life, let the dead body, upon the day of Buriall, be decently attended from the house to the place appointed for publique Buriall, and there immediately interred, without any Ceremony." Traditional Catholic and even most Protestant ceremonies "are in no way beneficiall to the dead," the *Directory* noted, "and have proved many wayes hurtfull to the living."[9]

But the words of the *Directory* were merely the formal seal of approval for behavior at funerals that had long since been the practice in England, not only for Puritans, but for many more orthodox Anglicans as well. Substantially before the turn of the seventeenth century, Englishmen, including the aristocracy, had begun to demand that after they died, their wealth be spent on the living rather than on opulent and elaborate funerals for themselves. Even when Reformed religious attitudes were not put forth as justification for the avoidance of ceremony, more mundane reasons were given. Robert 2nd Earl of Dorset, for example, ordered in his will that he be buried "without any blackes or great solemni-

tie of funerall but in a Christian manner as other persons are of a
meaner sort, because the usuall solemnities of funeralls such as
heraldes sett doune for noble men are only good for the heraldes
and drapers and very prejudiciall to the children, servauntes, and
friendes of the deceassed and to the poore which inhabit there
about, towards all which the deceassed might otherwise be much
more liberall."[10]

One of the early signs of change is evident in the reaction
against embalming that developed in the mid-sixteenth century.
Lawrence Stone cites a number of instances of individuals expressly directing that they not be so "opened" and notes that such
an attitude "automatically made necessary a swifter and therefore
more economical interment."[11] It is not now possible to determine
with any accuracy the extent of the practice of embalming prior
to this time, since according to recent estimates, European embalming techniques remained extremely crude until somewhere
between the 1570s and 1640s. And since these estimates are based
on data from royal funerals, it seems at least probable that any
efforts made at preserving the corpses of lesser beings would have
taken place at a rather primitive level.[12] But in any case, whatever
the state of the art at that time, the negative attitude toward embalming that Stone observes as present in the mid-sixteenth century
remained dominant in England for at least another century and
a half. A book on "the art of embalming" published in 1705 reads
like a tract designed to bring to an ignorant people a precious secret from the long-lost past. "The present Age therefore accounts
the chief Use of this *Art* to be in *Anatomical* Preparations," wrote
Thomas Greenhill, "but I shall shew another more antient and more
general, which is the Preserving of a Human Dead Body entire,
and which is properly term'd *Embalming*." To those who were
then familiar with the practice, Greenhill wrote, "it is by most
despis'd and look'd on meerly as an unnecessary expensive
Trouble"; moreover, together with other related burial customs, it

was then generally regarded as "needless and superstitious," an attitude Greenhill was determined to change.[13]

If interment was speedy, as both doctrine and nature required, the appearance and behavior of those who attended seventeenth-century English burials were consistent with the simplicity such disposal implies. The body of the deceased was most often clothed in a white flannel shift (a custom, suggested a cynical but perhaps not inaccurate Frenchman of the time, designed "for the Encouragement of the Woollen Manufacture"),[14] but no such standardized dress was prescribed for the mourners. The wearing of black was but one of many "artificial formes of sadness," wrote Robert Bolton, and it was a tradition Puritans went out of their way to avoid. So, too, did they seek to do away with excessive displays of sadness or grief. "Many times men are too forward and over-flowing in those tender offices, and last demonstrations of naturall affection," Bolton warned. "And therefore my counsell in such cases is; that we should shew ourselves Christians: and by the sacred rules of Religion ever prevent that unseasonableness and excesse, which many times with a fruitless torture doth tyrannize over the hopelesse hearts of mere naturall men."[15] As to funeral sermons, they were, Bolton noted, "for the living," not the dead. They were not delivered at the time of burial, and were in fact less like funeral sermons in the conventional sense of the term than they were merely sermons that happened to be occasioned by someone's death. Not until well into the latter part of the seventeenth century, when Puritanism in England was a splintered, weakened, and rapidly waning faith, did such sermons partake of any eulogizing at all. Instead, they were characterized almost entirely by theological exegesis, marking them as little different from sermons delivered on other occasions.[16]

Absence of ceremony and restraint of emotion was, in short, the rule and practice at Puritan funerals in seventeenth-century England, a rule and practice that was shared, to a less extreme extent, by non-Puritans as well. In 1634, John Canne summarized the Nonconformist attitude toward funerals, and in so doing, spoke for the practice that was then becoming increasingly prevalent throughout England:

> Concerning burials, this they say: all prayers either over or for the dead, are not only superstitious and vain, but also are idolatry, and against the plain scriptures of God. . . . as for the white or black cross, set upon the dead corpse, and ring- ing a three-fold peal, the practice is popish: mourning in black garments for the dead, if it be not hypocritical, yet it is superstitious and heathenish: funeral sermons, they also ut- terly condemn, because they are put in the place of trentals, and many other superstitious abuses follow thereby. To be brief . . . the Nonconformists will have the dead to be buried in this sort, (holding no other way lawful,) namely, that it be conveyed to the place of burial, with some honest company of the Church, without either singing or reading, yea, without all kind of ceremony heretofore used, other than that the dead be committed to the grave, with such gravity and sobriety as those that be present may seem to fear the judgments of God, and to hate sin, which is the cause of death; and thus do the best and right reformed churches bury their dead, without any ceremonies of praying or preaching at them.[17]

Even while witnessing such simplicity, however, not all English- men felt comfortable with it. In his little encyclopedia of "rare and excellent matters," David Person recounted the emotion- laden burial customs of "even the most barbarous Nations"—the West Indies, "Find-land or Lapland," and "China, Cathay, and Tartarie"—of Greece, "of Old amongst our British, and yet in our Highlands," and of the Church of Rome, which "reapeth great commodity by their funerall ceremonies, as by their bells, Cym- balls, Torches, processions of order and the rest"; in contrast, he castigated the "silent and dumb obsequies" of his contemporary countrymen.[18] A few years earlier, John Weever had similarly

pointed to the elaborate funeral customs of the past, and had then
proceeded to lament:

> These examples considered, I observe that wee, in these days,
> doe not weepe and mourne at the departure of the dead, so
> much, nor so long, as in Christian dutie we ought. . . . [and]
> funerals in any expensive way here with us, are now ac-
> counted but as fruitlesse vanitie, insomuch that almost all the
> ceremoniall rites of obsequies heretofore used, are altogether
> laid aside: for wee see daily that Noblemen, and Gentlemen
> of eminent ranke, office, and qualitie, are either silently bur-
> ied in the night time, with a Torch, a two penie Linke, and a
> Lanterne; or parsimoniously interred in the day-time, by the
> helpe of some ignorant countrey-painter, with out the at-
> tendance of any one of the Officers of Armes, whose chiefest
> support and maintenance, hath ever depended upon the per-
> formance of such funerall rites, and exequies.[19]

While some Englishmen lamented the dour state of their own
funeral customs, non-Englishmen openly mocked and criticized
them. "The Burials now among the Reformed in England, are in
a manner prophane," wrote one N. Strange in the 1640s, "in many
places the dead being throwne into the ground like dogs, and not
a word said."[20] When Pierre Muret's *Ceremonies funebres de
toutes les nations* was translated into English in 1683, the English
translator took the acknowledged liberty of "retrenching one
Chapter of this *Book,* under the Title of [The Funerals of Here-
ticks] as finding the same little less or more, than an Invective
against *Protestants,* in reference to their *Rites* of *Burial.*" What
Muret had done in this chapter was quote the words of some al-
legedly disaffected Protestants. For example:

> Now we pretend to dress very well for the funeral, to show
> joy on our faces, and to know how to make jokes along the
> way. Previously services were held every year for the de-
> parted [All Souls' Day], but now it is not proper to make the
> least mention of them: that savors too much of Papism we
> say: we must leave the dead with the dead, and live with the

living. Previously our burial places were decorated with flowers, now there is nothing so wretched as our tombs. To look at these tombs, it would appear that the carcass of a pig or an ass was to be buried, and not a human body. And to look at those who accompany the body, to see them so immodest and laughing all along the way, it would appear as though they were going to a comedy rather than to a funeral.

Another of Muret's Protestants reports, with bitterness and succinctness: "Among our people, it makes no difference whether we are buried in a cemetery or in the place where asses are flayed."[21]

With the same fervor which they upbraided their countrymen at every sign of a funeral ritual that smacked too much of papism, the Puritans railed against iconographic reminders of the Catholic heresy. William Prynne spoke clearly for the English Reformist spirit when he warned in 1646 that "Popery may creep in at a glasse-window, as well as at a door."[22] But Prynne was only echoing a sentiment that had taken hold in England more than a century earlier and that was to endure well into the second half of the seventeenth century. During a period beginning with Henry VIII's dissolution of the monasteries in 1535 and lasting, with fluctuating degrees of enthusiasm, until the restoration of Charles II, England's immensely rich collection of religious art and symbolism dating from the early Middle Ages fell victim to the Reformist drive to root out heresy and idolatry wherever it appeared. Viewing this artistic heritage as violative of the ancient Hebraic warning against making, bowing down to, or worshiping graven images, the Reformers took it upon themselves to seek out and destroy these symbols of the heretical past; the success of this destructive impulse was probably greater than that of any similar iconoclastic purge in history.[23]

What began as an effort to eliminate specific remnants of papism, however, became in time the justification for a confused and wanton destruction of all "monuments of superstition" or even anything vaguely reminiscent of Roman influence. Among such "monuments" were tombs and grave markers adorned with religious imagery. In an effort to halt the desecration of memorials to the dead, the queen issued a 1560 proclamation against such activities; at the same time, the tombs of the aristocracy took on new and different forms of artistic design: death's-heads, urns, scythes, and doused torches were among the secularized images that were carved in an effort to avoid the Reformers' wrath.[24] Some of these efforts were successful, but many were not. Even the most inoffensive imagery and straightforward plea for mercy were ignored. Carved on a child's tomb just outside Peterborough, for example, are the bust of a little boy and the inscription:

> To the courteous Souldier:
> Noe crucifixe you see, noe Frightfull Brand
> Of superstitions here, Pray let mee stand.
> Grassante bello civili.

But the child's image has been deliberately defaced, and the destruction is clearly centuries old.[25]

It was in reaction to this increasingly indiscriminate iconoclasm that, in the early seventeenth century, John Weever determined to record for posterity the images and inscriptions that marked the relatively few remaining tombs in England. Noting the care with which sepulchral monuments were maintained in most other countries, and observing "how barbarously within these his Majesties Dominions, they are (to the shame of our time) broken downe, and utterly almost all ruinated, their brasen Inscriptions erazed, torne away, and pilfered," Weever wrote, "I determined with my selfe to collect such memorials of the deceased, as were remaining as yet undefaced."[26] More than three-quarters of Weever's 871 pages are devoted to the enumeration and description of such memorials, collected from across the length and breadth of England. Virtually no religious iconography is reported as remaining extant, and there is a similar absence of even ostensibly "acceptable" themes: imps carrying darts of death, skulls and crossbones, death's-heads, or representations of time such as scythes or hour-glasses. When there is mention or reproduction of visual imagery it is almost always an armorial design with perhaps some images of the deceased and occasionally his family.

Even Weever, however, who feared that "nothing will be shortly left to continue the memory of the deceased to posteritie," who lamented that "the Monuments of the dead are daily thus abused," and who warned that the Reformers who choose "rather to exercise their devotions, and publish their erronious doctrines, in some emptie barne, in the woods, or common fields, than in these Churches, which they hold to be polluted with the abomina-tions of the whore of Babylon" should not be permitted to "runne on in their puritanicall opinions"—even he was not totally un-marked by the spirit abroad in his land at the time.[27] Memorials to the dead were important, he argued, but in a little moral tale paraphrasing the parable of Dives and Lazarus, he noted that they should not be accorded more than was due them:

> The familie of the gorgeous rich glutton, prepared him a sumptuous funerall unto the eyes of men, but one farre more sumptuous, did the ministring Angels prepare for the ulcered beggar, in the sight of God. They bare him not into any Sep-ulchre of marble, but placed him in the bosome of *Abraham*.[28]

The Puritans would certainly have agreed with Weever's senti-ments here, but unlike Weever they carried those sentiments to their logical and extreme conclusions. As a result, very few pre-Restoration headstones exist in England today, suggesting that they were made of wood and have perished, that they were de-stroyed by Puritan zeal, or that they were simply never erected in the first place. Those few that do exist are almost uniformly small, simple blocks of stone.[29]

In England, then, the Puritan approach to funeral ceremony and ritual was to avoid and castigate it. When in control of the reins of government, they took pains to see to it that the care and handling of the dead was removed from the religious sphere and placed in the hands of the civic order.

The Puritans who left England to cross the Atlantic in the 1620s and 30's were no less zealous in their beliefs than those of their faith they had left behind; in many ways, as a necessarily tightly knit community, they were more so. It was to be expected that in their approach to death and burial they would have been at least as antagonistic to ritual and iconography as were those Puritans who remained in England. And, indeed, for a time—but only for a time—they were.

The historical sources concerning funeral customs are less extensive for New England than for England during these years, but Thomas Lechford's report on his travels in New England in the late 1630s and early 1640s suggests that during this time the familiar simplicity of burial practice was the rule in these expatriate Puritan communities. "At Burials," he wrote, "nothing is read, nor any Funeral Sermon made, but all the neighborhood, or a good company of them, come together by tolling of the bell, and carry the dead solemnly to his grave, and there stand by him while he is buried." In addition, in their efforts to convert the Indians of New England to Christianity, one of the rules established by the Puritans was the forbidding of excessive mourning. When on one occasion some Indians sought to pattern a funeral after the model set by the Puritans, they succeeded in their austerity on all but one count. Following a very simple burial, "they withdrew a little from that place," reported Thomas Shepard, "and went all together and assembled under a Tree in the Woods, and there they desired one *Tutaswampe* a very hopefull *Indian* to pray with them; now although the *English* do not usually meet in companies to pray together after such sad occasions, yet it seemes God stird up their hearts thus to doe."[30] Although the evidence is largely circumstantial or at best slender on this matter, it does appear that, at least for the first generation of settlers, Puritan funerals closely followed the English model. Coupled with the observations of such people as Lechford and Shepard, there is the admittedly speculative but very suggestive negative evidence: tombstones, eulogistic funeral sermons, tracts, or journal entries suggesting special treatment of the corpse or even mildly elaborate ceremonies are all absent from the historical record for most of the first two decades of settlement.

But in 1649 the Boston Artillery Officers requisitioned "one barrell & a halfe of the countryes store of pouder," the discharge of which was part of the ceremony "to acknowledge Bostons great worthy dew love & respects to the late honnored Gounor which they manifested in solemnizing his funerall."[31] While too much should not be made of this display of ceremony upon the death of John Winthrop—it fell safely within the bounds of the Puritan acceptance of paying "civill respects . . . suitable to the rank and condition of the party deceased"[32]—in a symbolic sense the booming cannons signified the beginning of the end for the drastically subdued funerals of the earliest years of the colony. It may be that earlier in this century Mary Caroline Crawford was exaggerating somewhat in remarking that the Puritans "made festivals of their funerals," but it was an exaggeration easy to make; long before the seventeenth century was to draw to a close the funerals of New England's Puritans would take on trappings expensive and elaborate enough to have shocked and astounded the departed ancestors in the old country.[33]

Throughout the seventeenth century most of New England's dead were buried within two to four days after death, an indication that embalming or temporary preservation was generally not necessary. Occasionally, in fact, a burial schedule was stepped up because a body "could not be kept," as was the case with Peter Bulkley in 1688 and Mary Winthrop in 1690—in Mrs. Winthrop's case "the Heat of the Weather" compelling not only a speedy funeral but also the use of a "double Coffin." To be sure, Lady Andros, the wife of the royal governor, remained unburied for fully nineteen days following her death in early 1688, suggesting that *something* must have been done to preserve her remains; but the Androses were not Puritans and such treatment is singularly exceptional in the existing records.[34] If it is true that few burials were put off as long as Lady Andros's, it is also true, however, that not all burials were as hasty as those for Bulkley and Mrs. Winthrop. A good number of them took place five to eight days after death, and Nathaniel Morton's casual notation in 1659 that the body of Henry Dunster, former president of Harvard College, "was embalmed, and removed unto *Cambridge* aforesaid, and there honourably buried" suggests that in the colonies embalming had few of the negative connotations associated with it in England.[35] Further, Samuel Sewall's comment that his daughter Hannah "desired not to be embowelled," and his mentioning that in any case because of delay following her death and the nature of her distemper, "now she Canot be embowelled," further demonstrates that in New England, not long after Thomas Greenhill's lonely efforts to revive embalming in England, preservation of the corpse was a practice common enough to elicit casual discussion.[36]

Preservation of the dead has two fundamental purposes: the first resides in the belief held by some groups that the physical remains have some ultimate function in a postmortem state; the second, and less exotic, purpose is to allow time for ceremonial preparations to be made and for the resulting funeral ritual to be carried out. The Puritans entertained no illusions as to the postmortem efficacy of one's mortal remains, but they did require time for ceremony.

Undoubtedly some of the Puritan dead were buried with the dispatch and simplicity called for in English tradition and rule, but as the seventeenth century wore on, increasing numbers of Puritan funerals were conducted with an air of elaborate and formal ritual. Immediately following death, the body of the deceased was washed and dressed while preparations were made for the ceremony to come. The corpse was laid out either at home or—not infrequently—in the church of which it had been a member. When the church was selected as the site for this display, regular church business was conducted while the body lay in the midst of the congregation; the body of Jonathan Danforth, for example, in November of 1682, "lay by the Wall" in Nathaniel Gookin's Cambridge church ("having departed on Monday Morn, of a Consumption") while a Wednesday ordination ceremony took place.[37] In the meantime ceremonial preparations progressed, one of the first of which involved the sending of gloves to friends and acquaintances—both men and women—as a gesture of invitation to the funeral. The number of such invitations often ran into the hundreds, with gloves of varying quality and price sometimes indicating the social status of the person being invited. Since ministers were always invited to funerals, most of them acquired enormous quantities of gloves throughout their lives, some of which they saved, some of which they gave away, and others that they sold. Andrew Eliot of North Church reputedly maintained a record of the gloves he was sent, and in thirty-two years had collected close to *three thousand* pair. He finally sold them to some Boston milliners for the equivalent of between six and seven hundred dollars.[38]

On the day of the funeral the community was summoned by the ringing of the church bell—another practice condemned by English Puritans but so common in New England that during epidemics the tolling of bells finally had to be legislated against as a public annoyance—and the funeral procession moved toward the burial ground. Wearing their gloves and, more often than not, scarves, mourning ribbons, mourning cloaks, or other symbols of grief, members of the cortege frequently took turns carrying the coffin to the grave. When this was unnecessary because of the presence of a coach or hearse to bear the coffin, a small group composed of the family and closest associates of the dead person preceded the hearse, the bulk of the mourners following behind. The coffin itself was often made of excellent wood and lined with cloth, sometimes had the year of death inscribed on it with a pattern of small hammered nails, and was covered with a heavy, dark "mort-cloth." The hearse, and the horses that drew it, might—as in the case of Samuel Shrimpton in 1697—be decked out in mourning as well, "Scutcheon on their sides and Deaths heads on their foreheads."[39] The coffin and hearse were most often further bedecked with pinned-on bits of privately composed funeral verse, a custom that in time became so popular that Cotton Mather once referred to them, at the funeral of Nathanael Collins, as "a *Paper* winding sheet to lay him out."[40]

After placing the coffin in its grave or tomb—family tombs were quite common through the seventeenth and early eighteenth centuries—the members of the procession returned to the church or the home of the deceased, where they feasted and were frequently then given funeral rings to mark their attendance. (Rings were also exchanged at weddings, and in both cases the English Reformer would have reacted with shock, such practices being referred to by one Englishman as "pretty juggling trash . . . a popish and idolatrous practice" that makes of such ceremonies "a maygame.") As was the case with the invitational gloves, these items tended to accumulate: Samuel Sewall in time acquired almost threescore of them, and there are numerous references to individuals who left their heirs tankards full of such rings.[41] The rings distributed in this fashion would not easily have been mistaken for ordinary ones; they were fashioned of gold and were often inlaid with delicately carved black enamel death's-heads, skeletons, coffins, and other reminders of the frailty of life. And as with all these aspects of the funeral ritual, they were costly; even in the cases of the wealthiest individuals, it was not uncommon for funeral expenses to consume 20 percent of the deceased's estate. It is hardly surprising, then, that in time a reaction set in against funerary extravagance. Cotton Mather, although a participant in many elaborate funerals—and whose own funeral was far from simple—in 1713 expressed growing unease with the developing na-

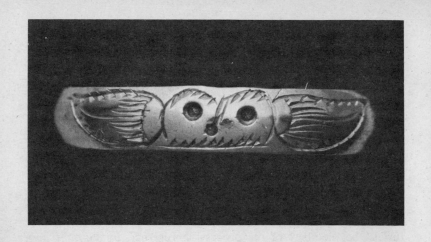

ture of Puritan funerals; and in 1724 the first of a number of acts were passed by the Massachusetts legislature designed "to Retrench the extraordinary Expence at Funerals."[42]

But the opulent nature of many funerals in Puritan New England is only one of the ways such ceremonies diverged from the English model. Even more striking, in contrast to the dictates of the English Puritans, was the involvement of the funeral ritual in the religious sphere of New England life. At the 1685 funeral of William Adams of Roxbury, Judge Sewall reported that "Mr. Williams prayed with the Company before they went to the grave."[43] It is true, as John L. Sibley has noted, that this is perhaps the earliest *evidence* of prayer at a New England funeral, but Sewall's matter-of-fact way of mentioning it—compared, for example, with his frequent expressions of indignation at the growing fashion for the wearing of "Perriwigs"—suggests that it may well not have been offensive or uncommon practice by that time.[44] But whether prayer at funerals was common by then or not, it soon may have become so. Within a year after Adams's funeral, Sewall's diary reports on the burials of several individuals "with the Common-Prayer."[45]

For a time it appears the New Englanders followed the English practice of delivering a funeral sermon some days after the burial of the deceased, but this too changed, at least by the turn of the century. More and more the day of burial became the time for delivering the funeral sermon. And such sermons were by no means limited to scriptural exegesis, as had been the case in England. So

---

Fig. 7. *Opposite page,* Three examples of the mourning rings that were exchanged at Puritan funerals. *Top,* A simple gold band containing an etched death's head with wings; *bottom left,* A gold band inlaid with black enamel and containing a skeleton design in gold on each side of the stone; *bottom right,* A gold and enamel band containing a coffin-shaped, transparent stone, through which can be seen a carved skeleton.

laden with eulogizing were they, in fact, that as early as 1673 one funeral sermon by James Fitch opened on a note of clear disquietude concerning the form such sermons were then frequently taking. "The Abusive, and justly to be Condemned practice of too too many," Fitch wrote, "who in Preaching Funeral Sermons, by mis-representing the Dead, have dangerously misled the living, and by flattering corrupted many, hath occasioned not a few to question (if not conclude against) the lawfulness of Preaching at Such Seasons."[46] Having thus introduced his caveat, Fitch then proceeded to justify in *this* case (the death of Mrs. Anne Mason) the glowing eulogy he eventually delivered.

Although the symbolic representations of death generally avoided, in accordance with Puritan tradition, anything even vaguely suggestive of Rome, this was by no means always the case. The coffin containing the body of James Whetcomb, for example, bore his name, the year of his death, and the image of a cross; whereas in Puritan England this would have been regarded as rank papism, Sewall's response is only mildly quizzical: "with what intent I can't tell" is the extent of his comment on the matter.[47] But whatever the specific imagery of the moment may have been, it is here, in the general area of iconography, that the difference between death in Puritan England and Puritan New England can be seen most clearly. No Frenchman strolling through New England's burial grounds in the seventeenth or early eighteenth century would have thought of comparing them with places "where asses are flayed"—as Pierre Muret's informant did in reflecting on the graveyards of England.

Prior to mid-century, there is no extant evidence of New England's Puritans taking much care at all to even mark the graves of their deceased. While it is possible that some sort of wooden markers may have been employed in the early years,[48] it is a striking phenomenon that only in the mid-1650s did New England's cemeteries begin to become populated not only with bodies, but also with carefully carved stones to indicate the sites of burial.[49] By the

1660s the popularity of this practice was widespread, and the stones themselves had grown increasingly large and the carvings on them more elaborate.[50] Death's-heads, scythes, hourglasses, picks and shovels, and other temporal images dominated the stones of the seventeenth and early eighteenth centuries, but crosses and other religious symbols were not unknown. Not until the eighteenth century is there any evidence that stones were mutilated, but even in these cases the image invariably attacked was that of a soul in Heaven—a representation at last too popish to bear—and the care with which such excisions were carried out suggests that it was not the work of community iconoclasts, but was done prior to the stone's erection by families or stonecarvers who had second thoughts about the symbolic ground being trodden.[51]

The imagery of the tombstone was reflected also on the printed page. The printing of broadside verse celebrating the virtuous and religious nature of the deceased was a major expense at Puritan funerals, and the pages on which such verse was printed were most often covered with intricate woodcut illustrations similar to the images of death carved on gravestones.

In general, then, although the Puritans of New England may well have been at least as zealous as their English brethren concerning most matters of religious custom and doctrine, and although in their intellectual and emotional handling of death they greatly intensified the concerns and fears latent in the Reform tradition, when it came to the ceremonial aspects of death their behavior was extraordinarily different from the model England had provided. In virtually every respect—in the care and handling of the dead, the nature and expense of funeral and burial procedures, the timing and content of the funeral sermon, the intrusion of death into the religious sphere of their lives, and the symbolic and iconographic marking of the individual's mortal remains—the New England Puritans ritualized death as only the most non-Puritan of pre-Restoration Englishmen would have dared do. In meeting death, it seems clear, they encountered something their English

Fig. 8. Examples of developments in gravestone art in Massachusetts from the middle of the seventeenth century to the turn of the eighteenth century. *Opposite page, upper left,* A stone representative of the earliest New England type, the "E.C." stone ("E.C. is the first that we laid hear"), n.d.; *lower right,* The Joseph Tapping stone, 1678; *this page,* The Doctor Palsgrave Wellington stone, 1715.

Fig. 9. Some specific themes that emerged on late seventeenth and early eighteenth century gravestones. *Opposite page*, Suggestions of religious imagery found their way onto the Phebe Tutell stone, 1713. *This page, left*, A demon or imp carrying a dart of death and an hourglass symbolic of the passage of time; a detail of the William Dickson stone, 1692. *Right*, An example of erotic imagery sometimes found in Puritan gravestones; a detail of the Rebeckah Whitmore stone, 1709.

ancestors never had. What they encountered was themselves and their profound sense of tribal vulnerability.

Some years ago the English anthropologist V. Gordon Childe published a summary of results after having analyzed the archaeological evidence concerning funerary practices over a period of fifty thousand years. His treatment was necessarily highly schematic and cannot be regarded as more than suggestive, but his findings for the many cultures so examined were remarkably consistent and unambiguous. As societies become more settled and more culturally and materially stable, he suggested, there is a marked tendency for funeral customs and burial rituals to become less elaborate and less extravagant; conversely, such customs and rituals seem to be most elaborate and most extravagant during periods of social and cultural instability.[52] The same generalization holds true, he argued, concerning sepulchral monuments: they appear most imposing in the least stable societies.

Without doubt there are exceptions to Childe's observation, one of the most obvious being England during the first half of the seventeenth century. But the English exception must be treated with care, since the source of social instability—Puritanism—was at the same time the source most responsible for funerary inhibitions and the destruction of monuments; it was those seeking to restore order by maintaining the social traditions of the past who were most outraged by the Puritan attack on funerary and burial customs. As long as the New Englanders maintained their identities as Englishmen, as long as English Puritanism provided a model and England promised an eventual home for them, as long as they felt themselves part of the forces of history at work in their homeland, the Puritans of New England were culturally and psychologically at one with their relatives and friends on the opposite side of the Atlantic. But once these ties were severed, if not formally at least conceptually, New England's Puritans were on their own. The existence of such a break became apparent within two decades of settlement, by the turn of the 1650s.

Combined with the belief that they would eventually return to England in glorious victory was the conviction of the first Puritan settlers in Massachusetts Bay that Christ's Second Coming was near at hand. Complex and involved analyses of scriptural predictions concerning the Millennium had convinced many of the colony's most respected thinkers that the Apocalypse would occur near the midpoint of the seventeenth century. John Cotton, New England's leading theologian during this period, delivered a series of widely read sermons during the late 1630s and 1640s, predicting the imminence of that great day—even to the extent of pinpointing the date the prophecy would be fulfilled at "about the time 1655." The political rumblings in England during the 1640s only heightened this sense of conviction. Oliver Cromwell had obviously been "raised and improved" by God, wrote John Eliot, "to overthrow Antichrist" as part of the working out of the divine plan now coming to fruition; and Eliot and Cotton were only echoing and further promoting a widely held belief.[53]

As the forces of Puritanism rose to power in the 1640s, there appeared the first signs of the anticipated return exodus of those New Englanders who would be most needed in the Puritan capital. In 1641 alone, over 10 percent of those men in New England with some university training returned to England, and for the next several years the great majority of new graduates from Harvard College eagerly followed them.[54] But it was a stunted and short-lived exodus. The roots that had by then been planted in New England soil surely hindered the actualization of the effort, but events in England provided equally powerful restraints. The eruption of civil war there brought in its wake an official doctrine of religious toleration. Few things were as alien to the Puritan conception of doctrinal righteousness as toleration—the purity and single-mindedness of their enterprise had been the very core and motivation of the New England mission—so that now, with toleration on the ascendancy in England while it remained stoutly resisted in the colonies, New England became, as Perry Miller has put it, "not the vanguard of Protestantism, but an isolated remnant." When more than thirty years later Increase Mather argued that "sinfull Toleration is an evil of exceeding dangerous consequence" and that "the toleration of all Religions and Perswasions, is the way to have no true Religion left," he was speaking for virtually all New England's Puritans—but they were the only ones who were listening.[55]

And instead of abating, the sense of failure and isolation grew. Within three years on either side of 1650, four of the five or six most important men of the first generation died—John Winthrop, Thomas Shepard, John Cotton, and Thomas Hooker. Cut off from the mother country by the apparent betrayal of their now politically victorious brethren, cut off from their hallowed leaders by death, the New Englanders soon suffered a third crucial defeat: the 1650s came and went with nary an apocalyptic whisper. But other things did happen. The population of the colony, after having leveled off in the 1640s as immigration temporarily ground to a halt, was again on the rise. Mercantile interests were now fully entrenched and growing at a rapid pace; the first generation of merchants, like the political and religious leaders before them, succumbed to the ravages of time—seven of Massachusetts Bay's most influential Puritan merchants died between 1652 and 1661[56]— and their places were taken by younger men with bigger economic appetites.

With the passage of mid-century, in short, two major kinds of change were taking place in New England. On the one hand, the development of a bustling, urban commercialism marked the emergence of an increasingly complex society, one that in barely half a century more would give birth to the likes of Benjamin Franklin, and would create a city destined to become one of the major urban centers in the British Empire. On the other hand, the general cultural and intellectual life of that society would for at least the remainder of the century be dominated by individuals who attempted to identify themselves with what they regarded as the values of the earliest settlers. (It is worth remembering that well into the eighteenth century the punishment for blasphemy in Massachusetts included six months' imprisonment, whipping, sitting upon the gallows with a rope about one's neck, and/or having one's tongue bored through with a hot iron.)[57] But, as time and again happened, when these individuals met frustration, compromise, and defeat in the larger social world growing up around them, they responded with increasing rigidity, self-centeredness, and self-righteousness. In a word, what emerged was what Edmund S. Morgan has aptly termed Puritan "tribalism": seeing treachery and adversity all about itself, the still culturally potent but numerically waning Puritan community turned its concerns inward.[58] In 1645, New England divine Thomas Shepard could comfortably write: "The churches are here in peace; the commonwealth is in peace; the ministry in most sweet peace; the magistrates (I should have named first) in peace."[59] Within less than a decade Shepard was dead and fast-day sermons, which had traditionally been delivered in response to externally imposed threats such as storms and crop failures, were beginning to direct themselves to such matters as "the worldly mindedness, oppression, & hardheartedness feard to be amongst us."[60]

An entire literary genre, referred to by Perry Miller as the "jeremiad" because of its intense preoccupation with lamentations and tirades against the perceived spiritual deterioration of the Puritan community, emerged from its beginnings in these fast-day sermons of the 1650s and soon appeared in election-day sermons and even in the directives of the Massachusetts General Court.[61] At the same time that they were tormenting themselves with this intense self-criticism, the Puritans of the later seventeenth century began erecting verbal monuments to the "Golden Age" of the first generation of settlers, and embarked on renewed searches for evidence that the Apocalypse was once again at hand. "Disappointment with Cromwell convinced English millenarians (including the Fifth Monarchists) that the Parousia was far less advanced than previously thought," Sacvan Bercovitch has recently observed, ". . . [but the] New World ministers, already committed to a scheme which could not admit of failure, compensated for their thwarted errand by constructing a legendary past and a prophetic future for the country."[62]

All this, it must be remembered, had its beginnings in the Puritans' perceptions of the rapid collapse of their world in the 1650s. It is no coincidence that at this same time Puritan funeral ritual began diverging from the English model.

In what remains a classic study of cultural attitudes toward death, in 1907 a young student of Emile Durkheim, Robert Hertz, argued that it was a common and serious error for the anthropologist or sociologist to limit his concern with death to the facts of the cessation of bodily life. Every individual in a society, Hertz claimed, possesses as well as a biological being a "social being" that is defined for him and "grafted onto him" by other members of the society. This seemingly elementary proposition was seen by Hertz as a clue to the understanding of different attitudes toward death both within cultures and between them.[63]

Hertz had been struck by the question of why there is a seemingly natural human abhorrence of man's body once death has overtaken it. The obvious explanation—that such horror rests with the physical transformations that set in after death—seemed inadequate to him. If that were so, he asked, how is one to account for the great variety of reactions to the deaths of individuals differently situated in society? For example, in some societies the death of a chief or other individual of high rank can be considered so powerfully contagious that the entire village must be deserted, while the death of a child, a slave, or an outsider will be largely ignored. It seemed clear that it was thus "not as the extinction of an animal life that death occasions social beliefs, sentiments and rites," but as the extinction of a *social* life invested with some meaning and value by the larger society.[64] In losing an individual, a society is reminded of its own temporal tenuousness at the same time that it is, as a society, in fact weakened by the loss. The greater the social importance of the now-dead individual, the greater the damage done to the social fabric—and, as a consequence, the greater the need for ceremony and ritual to come to terms with the individual's absence.

Arnold Van Gennep's *Les Rites de Passage* had not yet been published, but many of the ideas he was to discuss in that work were already under debate in France when Hertz was writing. Seizing upon the principle that all changes of status in an individual's or a society's life history are in fact *rites de passage,* Hertz saw that death—no less than birth, pubertal initiation, or marriage—is almost universally characterized by the same chain of events that surrounds those transitions: the passing of the old status, a period of temporary status suspension (the liminal period), and finally rebirth into a new status. As far as death was concerned, this sequence was most graphically illustrated by the practice in many societies of second burial, a custom characterized by the temporary "storage" of bodies—frequently until they are decomposed, whereupon the bones are picked clean and handled in some ceremonial fashion—and greatly delayed final burial. Although the practice of second burial is by no means universal, its social function is mirrored in analogous ceremonies that are very common throughout the world—from the Kotas of South India, who cremate the body at an initial ceremony known as the Green Funeral and then observe a second or Dry Funeral a year or two later, to the observance of All Souls' Day in much of the Christian world. The liminal period in these cases is the period between the two ceremonies, and it is during this time, Hertz contended, that society is in effect "closing the gap" left by the deceased, without ever having to deal fully with his absence.[65]

Hertz was chiefly concerned with demonstrating the universality of his thesis and with substantiating the connection between the level of individual social status and the subsequent intensity of the societal responses to death. But V. Gordon Childe's later findings, referred to earlier, indicating that the most elaborate funerary customs generally appear when societies are most unsettled and most unstable add a further dimension to Hertz's thesis, though one unrecognized, or at least unarticulated, by Childe.

The reasons for the greater importance of death in unsettled and unstable societies as against older and more settled ones seem remarkably similar to those responsible for its profound effect in relatively primitive and agrarian social units as compared with its limited impact in large, highly diversified technological societies: the loss of an individual is simply much more disruptive to the social order; thus, as Robert Blauner has written, "in simple societies much 'work' must be done to restore the social system's functioning."[66] The "work" in such cases involves the ritualistic and ceremonial treatment of death as the passage from one status to another so that the society can in time come to grips with the loss of a valuable member.

In England during the seventeenth century there was a powerful, successful, and largely Puritan motivated effort to reduce the complexity and significance of funeral ritual. England was by then a long-established, self-confident nation. In New England the same Puritan traditions were at least equally powerful and influential, but within two or three decades after the initial settlement of the colonies the complexity and significance of funeral ritual increased dramatically. It is insufficient, if tempting, to conclude—as a straightforward extension of Childe's thesis—that the Puritan response was in fact only a common response that might be found in all unstable colonial settings. In the first place, this would leave unexplained the reasons why it was only in the 1650s and 60s that death ritual was to become so important to New Englanders. And in the second place, it would not be confirmed by an examination of death customs in other New World colonies. In Virginia, for example, it took nearly a century for funerary ceremonies and monuments to acquire any substantial degree of cultural importance. And in New York during the late seventeenth century, funeral ceremony was so neglected that legislation had to be passed *requiring* that some attention be paid to the dead in order that instances of foul play might be discovered; it was ordered that every time someone in the colony died a delegation of neighbors was to be called to view the body and follow it to an approved grave site to be sure that it in fact arrived there and was properly interred.[67] No such legislation was ever necessary in seventeenth- or early eighteenth-century New England; on the contrary, the only laws concerning funeral ritual in New England during this time were sumptuary laws attempting to restrict funeral expenditures that had grown so out of hand that they were charged with responsibility for the "Impoverishing of many families."[68] What was missing from each of these other colonial settings, but was present in New England, was Puritanism—and Puritanism in conscious but self-lamented retreat.

While, understandably, the embattled Saints never directly perceived the connection between the growth of their introspective tribalism and their heightened concern with funeral ritual, the evidence for such a connection is more than circumstantial. The jeremiadical bemoaning of what they saw as growing worldliness and waning piety all about them coincided chronologically with the Puritans' increasing use of the funeral sermon in ways that would have been condemnable in pre-Restoration England. It was not long before the message of the fast-day and election-day jeremiad became the message of the funeral sermon as well.

The hearers and readers of funeral sermons in the second half of the seventeenth century were repeatedly advised to lament the deaths of members of the Puritan community, "[not] because of their state for they are happy," pointed out James Fitch. "But mourn because they are no longer so helpful to us."[69] This sense of profound social loss became intertwined with intimations of God's disapproval of the state of affairs in New England and gave rise to a combined jeremiad and requiem for the damage done to the Puritan community by the death of one of its Saints. Repeatedly such deaths were referred to as the opening of a gap in the community, or the loss of a pillar. When Jonathan Mitchell died, Increase Mather was to later write, "all New-England shook when that Pillar fell to the ground." And Samuel Willard provided a vivid example of the form the funeral sermon was taking when he wondered, at the death of Thomas Savage:

> When the Pillars are gone, how shall the building stand? When the Watch-men are asleep, who shall descry, and warn us of the enemies approach? When the Wall is pluckt down, and the hedge removed, who shall keep out the Bore of the Wilderness? When the Gap-men are taken away, who shall stand in the breaches? When the lights are put out, who shall direct me in a right way? When the Chariot and Horsemen of *Israel* are removed, who shall defend us from misery and mischief?[70]

On an earlier occasion the same writer mourned the death of one of Massachusetts Bay's last Puritan governors, John Leverett, by describing him as one of those rare men who "stands in the Gap . . . between a sinning people, and a provoked God." Willard urged upon his listeners and readers "the tears of all Israel" as the proper response to the governor's passing; but they were to be tears of lamentation not for Leverett, but for those who survived him. Such deaths were like "wounds," he wrote, "like the cutting off the hands of a people, yea, stopping their breath," and were quite possibly God's signal that his terrible wrath would soon be felt.[71]

The theme was repeated over and over again by Willard and others both before and after the dates of the sermons cited above,[72] and appeared perhaps most dramatically in elegies such as that penned by Urian Oakes for the younger Thomas Shepard in 1677:

What! must we with our God, and Glory part?
Lord: is thy Treaty with *New England* come
Thus to an end? And is War in thy Heart?
That this Ambassadour is called home.
   So Earthly Gods (Kings) when they War intend,
   Call home their Ministers, and Treaties end.[73]

And with typical theatricality, Cotton Mather rendered the impact of the death of Nathanael Collins on the church he left behind by personifying the Middletown congregation as

an *Elect Lady,* There
Grov'ling in Ashes, with dishev'led hair,
Smiting her breast, *black'd* with a *mourning* dress,
Resembling mother *Sion in distress.*[74]

It is a frequently made observation among modern students of survivor behavior that there appears to be a marked ambivalence toward a corpse experienced by close relatives of a recently deceased individual. Such relatives will often shun the corpse as an alien object, yet at the same time act as if it were still alive.[75] Robert Hertz's explanation for the revulsion felt by many in the presence of a corpse has already been discussed. In her more recent and very penetrating study entitled *Purity and Danger,* Mary Douglas has advanced a thesis that along these lines accords well with Hertz's analysis of the initial postmortem period as a liminal phase; she argues that those aspects of social life that are characterized by confusion and ambiguity are most often regarded as ritually "unclean" and thus are shunned and avoided.[76] On the other hand, one recent study of behavior regarding the dead in hospitals notes the common tendency for family members to continue to speak to and caress the recently deceased as a manifestation of their refusal to readily accept the death of one so close; in the same way, nurses who have become friendly with a patient who has died often avoid involvement in the necessities of postmortem treatment because of what is termed a "mystic illusion" that the body is still alive.[77]

This ambivalence regarding reaction to the corpse is bound up with a more general *social* ambivalence concerning the consequences of death for the bereaved and the community of which they are a part. There is a need, it seems, in virtually all human societies both to postpone acceptance of the absence of the deceased and at the same time to take advantage of the reality of death in seeking to renew the survivors' sense of belonging to the larger social whole. It is one of the fundamental purposes of funeral rites to deal with both problems: they at once effect the gradual separation of the deceased from the living and also gradually "aggregate," to use Jack Goody's words, "the bereaved to the community from which they have been temporarily separated."[78] In traditional, tightly knit societies, where each individual is likely to play an important social role and the problem of dealing with separation through death is a community problem, the reaction to the loss of an individual is generally spread out among a large group of mourners; in more urban, diversified societies the community is less often so broadly affected by the death of any individual and thus the family becomes the largest unit among whose members the shock of separation must be borne. The pains of separation, however, are greatly intensified as a consequence of this, since the reaction to death is not "diffused" throughout and shared by the larger community, and in addition the social reintegration of the smaller group of bereaved is more difficult.[79]

The complexities of culture and social structure in any human setting are such that no single explanation can ever suffice in judging *the* cause of major social phenomena, but each of the above generalizations—from those of Childe and Hertz to those of Blauner and Goody—suggest in their different ways at least one fundamental determinant of the Puritans' obsession with death, their fear of death, and their elaborate ritualistic treatment of death. As the

seventeenth century approached its close, and the Puritan community, sensing its growing isolation and powerlessness, turned its
concerns inward, it became—at least in its perception of itself—
increasingly analogous to the isolated modern family. But it was
not merely a family: it was a substantial community within the
structure of New England society that *perceived* and *defined* itself
as a threatened remnant struggling to keep alight God's beacon in
the world.

Thus on the one hand, the Puritans intensely felt the death of a
Saint to be a devastating blow to the dwindling circle of concerned
survivors; on the other hand, this bereaved Puritan "family" resisted reintegration with the larger society, since that larger society
represented all that was wrong with their idealized view of the
world. In short, with the death of one of its members the Puritan
community was beset with the most extreme problems of both the
traditional and the diversified society. But the Puritans' remaining
size, leverage, and influence in the overall society permitted the expression on a large and elaborate scale of funeral ceremonies and
rituals of a relative type only found in simple, closely knit, traditional communities. It was the pessimism with which they now
viewed the state of their holy mission that drove them to respond
to death in ways their spiritual and actual ancestors would have
deemed extraordinarily inappropriate—while at the same time it
was the continued, if diluted, potency of their cultural presence
within New England society that permitted the relatively grandiose
acting out of that response.

As was the case with their fearful emotional response to death,
the Puritans were well aware of the fact that their ceremonial response to it was contrary to the dictates of tradition and doctrine—
the funeral sermons critical of other funeral sermons and the sumptuary laws concerning funerals are among the indications of this
awareness—but as a culture they had no other choice; the day-to-
day world in which they were living imposed on them difficulties

not encountered by their predecessors in England, difficulties that necessitated a different response. In time the problems treated in both this and the preceding chapter would become so overwhelming that Puritan culture would succumb to them. But the tenacity of the Puritan vision was such that it was not to fully yield to such pressures until well into the eighteenth century.

6

Death and Decline

The closing words of the last two chapters have suggested that New England Puritanism—under severe intellectual, cultural, and social strain as the seventeenth century neared its close—managed to maintain a significant, though waning, degree of influence and integrity until well into the eighteenth century. By focusing on the changes in Puritan attitudes toward death by the middle of the eighteenth century, this chapter will seek to etch more clearly the pattern of overall cultural change that in time evolved. But first it should be recognized that the effort to locate and describe the decline of American Puritanism is a task that has a long and controversial history.

At one pole there are the contemporary social critics who have never tired of finding repressed Puritanism still deeply imbedded in the minds of most modern Americans; at the opposite extreme are historians like Charles and Katharine George who deny that Puritanism in fact ever existed at all—insisting that the differences between Anglicans and Puritans are merely the invention of nit-picking and misinformed historians.[1] Between these poles are historical arguments that variously date the beginning of the end for American Puritanism from the docking of the *Arbella* in 1630, the trial of Anne Hutchinson in 1637, the Halfway Covenant of 1662, or the Salem witch trials of the 1690s. Darrett B. Rutman has argued that there never was any such thing as "the Puritan way," while Timothy H. Breen and Stephen Foster have found social cohesion to be the Puritans' "greatest achievement"; Edmund S. Morgan has traced the Puritan ethic to the ideas of the American Revolution, and Sydney E. Ahlstrom has contended that it was deeply involved in the development of the spirit of American democracy.[2]

What makes each of these arguments controversial—and, at the same time, what makes each quite defensible—is the definition each applies to Puritanism. To the social critic Puritanism is merely a shared sense of prudery and repression, and a compulsive, guilt-ridden drive to work. To others its main characteristics have been reduced to a variety of basic schema: a belief in human depravity and predestination; a belief in the need to reorder society and in that group's own unique ability to do so; a belief in a so-called theocratic form of government. And so on.

Given such widespread disagreement, then, I should make clear—albeit perhaps a bit belatedly—what I have meant and will mean when writing of the New England Puritan community. I am writing of those seventeenth- and eighteenth-century New Englanders who generally shared the religious beliefs of their congregational ministers—from John Cotton to Cotton Mather to Jonathan Edwards; who believed in human depravity, predestination, and God's inscrutability; who believed in the divine inspiration for their mission in the New World; and who labored at their earthly tasks with these beliefs ever before them, finding in their experiences portents of God's pleasure or displeasure and indications of his millennial plan. Further, and perhaps most important, they held these beliefs in tandem with a growing sense of unease with, and isolation from, the developing worldliness, liberalism, and secularism of the larger society in which they were living.

There are, of course, many problems with this or any other similar definition. Exceptions can be found that will show it to be both too inclusive in some cases and too exclusive in others. But, exceptions acknowledged, it is the definition with which I have worked. And if, as it does, such a definition defies quantification, it does not deny the cultural artifacts this group of people left behind—one set of which consists of the materials indicating that the people I have called Puritans approached the universal human problem of death in a particular fashion.

It is true, as many historians have argued, that seventeenth- and eighteenth-century New England society was characterized by a good deal of social change. But for the Puritans living in that society such change primarily affected the community's *social structure*—what Clifford Geertz has termed "the ongoing process of interactive behavior." Puritan *culture,* however—in Geertz's words, "the framework of beliefs, expressive symbols, and values in terms of which individuals define their world, express their feelings, and make their judgments"[3]—changed much more slowly; indeed, in reaction to the rapidly changing world about them, the most deeply rooted convictions of the Puritan community rigidified as the remaining members of that community strove to maintain their standards. But culture and social structure are not independent phenomena. They are interdependent entities that require some degree of mutual support. And if in a given situation social structure continues to change without complementary changes in a particular group's cultural life, that group in time becomes anachronistic, its cultural institutions lose their potency, and a sense of profound loss may well set in.[4]

I have argued that there developed in the seventeenth century a tendency for Puritan funeral sermons to sound more and more like the jeremiads of the election- and fast-day sermons. But of equal importance is the fact that at the same time, the election- and fast-day jeremiads began sounding more and more like cries of bereavement.

Modern studies of bereavement have consistently indicated that in an environment in which the impact of death is restricted to a relatively small group of people, the effects on family members are often unusually disturbing. Geoffrey Gorer, for instance, has observed what he terms "unlimited mourning" among numbers of socially isolated individuals in Britain; and Le Roy Bowman has cogently suggested that the frequently bizarre nature of modern American funerals is something of an unconscious protest by the alienated and isolated urban American family that has had to absorb the impact of death on its own.[5] In summarizing such studies, Peter Marris has concluded that bereavement is most commonly characterized by "an inability to surrender the past—expressed, for instance, by brooding over memories, sensing the presence of the dead, clinging to possessions, being unable to comprehend the loss, feelings of unreality; withdrawal into apathy; and hostility against others, against fate, or turned in upon oneself."[6] Further, these same reactions have been observed among people whose "loss" was not of a living family member, but of a home and a sense of community purpose. "It seems quite precise," Marc Fried writes of individuals displaced by urban renewal from their homes in Boston's West End, "to speak of their reactions as expressions of *grief*. These are manifest in the feelings of painful loss, the continued longing, the general depressive tone, frequent symptoms of psychological or social or somatic distress, the active work required in adapting to the altered situation, the sense of helplessness, the occasional expressions of both direct and displaced anger, and the tendencies to idealize the lost place."[7]

In the seventeenth century the increasingly isolated Puritan community of New England turned in its search for meaning to a relationship with the past that was in both form and function one of bereavement. Election sermon after election sermon expressed the same themes: loss, depression, helplessness, guilt and inwardly-turned hostility, idealization of the dead. We are "Sin-Sick Out-Casts," wrote John Norton in 1661; the times are "shaking times, and trying times," lamented John Higginson in 1663; "the crown is fallen from our head," cried Jonathan Mitchell in 1667, as the "Pillars" and "Stakes" and "the breath of our Nostrils" have been taken from us; we were God's "first-born son," wrote William Stoughton in 1668, "we have had *Moses* and *Aaron* to lead us. . . . God sifted a whole Nation that he might send choice Grain over into this wilderness," and "we are grapes of the same vine"—but "the Death and Removal of the Lords eminent Servants in one Rank and in another, this also hath manifested the *Lie* in many of us . . . [and] now that they are dead and gone, Oh how doth the unsoundness, the rottenness and hypocrisie of too many amongst us make itself known"; and in 1670, after reminiscing on the fact that "in our first and best times the Kingdome of Heaven brake in upon us with a holy violence, and every man pressed into it," Samuel Danforth rhetorically wondered: "Seemeth it a small thing unto us, that so many of Gods Prophets (whose Ministry we came into the Wilderness to enjoy) are taken from us in so short a time? Is it not a Sign that God is making a way for his Wrath, when he removes his *Chosen* out of the Gap?"[8]

The melancholic tone of these election sermons from the decade of the 1660s was echoed in the sermons of the 1670s, 80s, and 90s as well. The acme—though not the end—of this response was reached at the turn of the eighteenth century with Cotton Mather's massive *Magnalia Christi Americana, or the Ecclesiastical History of New England.* It may or may not be fair to refer to Mather's efforts in this work, as Peter Gay has done, as the labor of a "pathetic plutarch," but it is certainly true that in his biographical chapters on the earliest settlers—in which John Winthrop, for example, is referred to as *Nehemias Americanus*—Mather carried the postmortem worship of the founding fathers to new and unprecedented hcights; and at the same time it is also true, as Gay writes, that "in an age of Jeremiads the *Magnalia Christi Americana* is the greatest Jeremiad of them all."[9]

But the jeremiad was a complex genre. At the same time that it was a mournful lamentation for an idealized past, it contained within itself the seeds of a rejuvenated sense of mission.[10] In the same sermon in which William Stoughton nostalgically wrote of the Moses and Aaron who had led the first settlers, and in which he decried the "unsoundness, the rottenness and hypocrisie" of the present, he also raised the banner of the millennial promise:

> Antichrist is now displaying his Colours, setting up his Standard, and so is the Lord Jesus Christ, the Anointed *King and Priest and Prophet,* the Fathers *Heir of all things.* The field is large whereinto the Forces on both sides are drawing; but the fight will be very close, and the quarrel in the issue finally decided; there can be no *neutralizing* therefore in this day. . . . It is not *long* before the Lord will *finish his great works in the world: Antichrist* shall be destroyed, Israel shall be saved, *Zion shall be redeemed with judgement, and her converts* with righteousness. . . . *Yet a little while and he that shall come will come, and will not tarry.*"[11]

The justification for this kind of mixed theme in the jeremiad was rooted in the Biblical prophecy that the darkest night would precede the brightest dawn; as Cotton Mather put it in 1692: "The Devil was never more let *Loose* than in our Days; and it proves the *Thousand Years* is not very *Far off.* SHORTLY didst thou say, Dearest Lord!"[12]

However, justification is not explanation. Drawing on studies of social change and revolution from Africa to the United States, Peter Marris has recently fashioned an explanation that, in the abstract, accords well with developments in New England during the seventeenth and eighteenth centuries. Arguing that "revolutionary change—at least when it is internally generated—is a response to loss of meaning as much as a struggle for power," Marris writes:

> The coherence of a social structure begins to disintegrate under the pressure of anomalies and contradictions it cannot assimilate, and as it does so, more and more relationships become confused, irregular and difficult to identify. People experience a sense of loss, and try at once to reassert the past and escape into an idealised, detached vision of the future. Each is an impractical solution to their present distress: but the interaction of these contradictory impulses, like the work-

ing out of grief, gradually abstracts and reformulates from
past experience a viable reconstruction of meaningful relationships. But where society is too fragmented, or its central
authority too severely damaged—often by intrusion from
abroad—tentative reconstructions only weaken still further
the outworn shell of government which tries to incorporate
them. Then only a political revolution can create the framework to contain them—the decisive step in a process of reintegration.[13]

There was, of course, no Puritan revolution in America. But
revolution, as Crane Brinton once observed, is one of the looser
words.[14] The sort of revolution Marris is referring to is one of attempted revival and revitalization of a way of life seemingly on the
verge of extinction. And in that sense there was something of a
Puritan revolution in America; it occurred in the 1730s and 40s
and has become known as the Great Awakening.

On May 14, 1741, Jonathan Parsons delivered an election-day sermon to his congregation in Lyme, Connecticut. His theme was not
an unusual one. Drawing on the Gospel of Matthew, he told his
listeners "that Jesus Christ would certainly come to judge the
World; and that when he did come, he would find it overwhelm'd in
carnal Security." It was, Parsons hoped, a message "proper to
awaken and convince" those who heard him. Awaken and convince it did. As Parsons later recalled:

> Under this Sermon many had their *Countenances changed;*
> their *thot's* seemed to *trouble* them, *so* that the *Joynts* of their
> *Loyns were loosed, and* their *Knees smote one against an-
> other.* Great Numbers cried out aloud in the Anguish of their
> Souls: several stout Men fell as tho' a Cannon had been dis-
> charg'd, and a Ball had made its Way thro' their Hearts.
> Some young Women were thrown into Hysterick Fits. The
> Sight and Noise of Lamentation, seem'd a little Resemblance
> of what we may imagine will be when the great Judge pro-
> nounces the tremendous Sentence of, *Go ye cursed into ever-*

lasting Fire. There were so many in Distress that I could not get a particular Knowledge of the special Reasons at that Time, only as I heard them crying, *Wo is me! What must I do?* And such of short Sentences with bitter Accents.[15]

It was a scene without parallel in seventeenth-century New England, but by the 1730s and 40s it was one that was occurring with increasing frequency. The eighteenth-century descendants of those Puritan men and women who had endured hours of reasoned theological discourse in the seventeenth century, who had most often listened with quiet despair mixed with desperate hope to the jeremiads of that time, now responded with violent emotion to the preachings of their own ministers and turned out by the thousands to hear the words of itinerant preachers such as George Whitefield and Gilbert Tennent, who were then touring the northern colonies. Nathan Cole, a Connecticut farmer, was only one among the multitudes who, upon hearing that Whitefield was to be preaching nearby, literally dropped his farming tools in the fields where he was working and ran with his wife, "as if we was fleeing for our lives," to witness the great event. As he neared the site of the lecture Cole was awestruck by the sight of so many desperate people converging on it from every direction: "it was like a stedy stream of horses & their riders scarcely a horse more then his length behind another all of a lather and fome with swet ther breath rooling out of their noistrils. . . . The banks over the river lookt black with people & horses all along the 12 miles I see no man at work in his field but all seemed to be gone." "It made me trembel to see the Sight," Cole later wrote in his journal, "how the world was in a strugle."[16]

A struggle it was indeed. For the revival that swept New England at this time was by no means popular in every quarter. In his reflections on it in *Some Thoughts Concerning the Present Revival of Religion in New England,* Jonathan Edwards described the controversies surrounding it as involving two armies in battle array, considering it "a more important war" than the one then being waged by England and Spain.[17] It was, at its roots, a war over the nature of true religion, of reason *versus* enthusiasm; but bound up with the religious position of the supporters of the revival was the conviction—once again—that now, at last, the millennium was truly at hand. " 'Tis not unlikely that this work of God's Spirit," wrote Edwards, "that is so extraordinary and wonderful, is the dawning, or at least a prelude, of that glorious work of God, so often foretold in Scripture, which in the progress and issue of it, shall renew the world of mankind. . . . it gives us more abundant reasons to hope that what is now seen in America, and especially in New England, may prove the dawn of that glorious day."[18] And Edwards, compared with many, was conservative in this regard. He was a "postmillennialist," a believer in the idea that the prophesied thousand-year reign would precede rather than follow the Second Coming; others were convinced that the time was imminent when the first would be last, and the last would be first.

It is true, as Perry Miller has observed, that between 1730 and 1760 most of western Europe—and, most strikingly, England—also experienced powerful waves of religious enthusiasm.[19] It is also true that the Great Awakening in New England was only one manifestation of a series of revivals that were then sweeping virtually all the English colonies. But although there may have been elements common to most or all of these spiritual upheavals, it would be a mistake to consider them as one. As to the New England revival, it began long before Whitefield ever set foot in America, and it was marked by a Puritan involvement unlike that found anywhere else. It is this—the *participation* of Puritans in the revival, rather than the revival itself—that is the present concern. For the very fact that not all New Englanders looked favorably on the revival is suggestive of some of its possible underlying dynamics: the great majority, but not all the region's Congregationalists supported the Awakening; Presbyterians and Baptists split on it; only one element was unanimous on the revival, unanimous in *opposition* to it, and that was the area's Anglican community—the symbolic and actual representative of the dominant social order against which the Puritans were so fiercely reacting in their determination to overturn the drift toward worldiness and liberalism.[20]

As I have indicated, the history of the Puritan community in America leading up to and including the Great Awakening bears a striking similarity to the histories of the groups Peter Marris treats in his analysis of cultural disintegration and revolution. It also closely resembles the backgrounds of the several hundred "revitalization movements" Anthony F. C. Wallace analyzed almost twenty years earlier.[21] In his analysis Wallace used certain concepts and terms that need not be uncritically accepted for the general contours of his argument to be found helpful. He employed a rather literal organic analogy, for example, positing a close association between the structures and functions of social and biological entities; taken literally, this conception of society has certain serious limitations—as a good many recent sociologists have pointed out[22]—but the general shape of the idea that societies are composed of individuals with interrelated and interdependent interests tending toward some degree of group stability has not been commonly or convincingly challenged.[23] Similarly, he used the term "mazeway" to describe the individual's "mental image" of society and culture, and of his relationship to these entities—a word that Wallace found helpful, but that is not necessary for understanding the central thrust of the argument.

What Wallace's essay suggests is that a large number of quasi-revolutionary religious movements—from the cargo cults of Melanesia to the Xhosa cattle-killing of South Africa to the Ghost Dance of the Sioux and other Western Indians—have been in large measure attempts to reduce social stress brought on by a particular group's traditional culture having become anachronistic within the larger, rapidly changing social order. One common means of attempting to reduce such stress is through "revivalistic movements [which] emphasize the institution of customs, values, and even aspects of nature which are thought to have been in the mazeway of previous generations but are not now present."[24] Whereas certain individuals and certain cultures find adapting to change relatively easy, many others, for various reasons, do not. Their resistance, which may *seem* revolutionary because it tends so often to focus on overthrowing the new social orthodoxy, is in fact no more than an effort to forestall or at least postpone dealing with the changes taking place around them. But such movements rarely enjoy long-range success. They result from an opposition of the needs of the emerging *social structure* with those of the existing group *culture*—to use the distinctions made by Clifford Geertz in his earlier-cited essay; and when such incongruity is not resolved by effective integration of the two competing elements, it has historically been the almost inevitable fate of the traditional culture to give way to the needs of the ongoing social structure.[25] Viewed in this light, the participation of the New England Puritan community in the revival of the 1730s and 40s seems to have been well characterized by Alan Heimert and Perry Miller as "the dying shudder of a Puritanism that refused to see itself as an anachronism"—although Heimert and Miller, in choosing to see the revival as the awakening of "the spirit of American democracy," were not content with such a terminal diagnosis.[26]

Each of the theoretical models borrowed thus far—from Leon Festinger's theory of cognitive dissonance, to those of Geertz, Marris, and Wallace—clearly suggests at least a partial answer to the problem of locating the time of the "decline of Puritanism." This is not by any means to say that all these models or even any two are in every sense mutually supporting. However, from their various sources of data and their various independent perspectives, they do all indicate that in a good many cases major social and cultural change stems directly from a stress-creating incongruity between the ideal and the real, between traditional culture and society in a state of innovation and change. In the abstract they connote a relationship between the Great Awakening and the final deterioration of a viable Puritan culture; more concretely, this relationship is suggested by the evolving Puritan attitudes toward death.

Up to and into the era of the Great Awakening the Puritan attitudes toward and treatment of death, as described in the preceding pages, remained relatively stable: childhood anxieties persisted; adult fear and confusion continued; and the most graphic evidence, the burial grounds and their headstones, testified to the maintenance of the Puritan traditions. The childhood anxieties had sprung from the perceived realism of orthodox Puritan teachings on depravity, damnation, and parental separation; the adult disquietude had grown out of the merging of these childhood fears with a theological system incapable of supporting the traditional Christian mechanisms for subduing death fear; and the somber, mundane, but carefully wrought and tended gravestones and burial grounds were the product of a culture that was acutely conscious of the precariousness of its very existence and that was shaken to its core with the death of each and every one of its supporting members.

At first sight, the eruption of enthusiasm and the quaking fits of terror at the prospect of damnation that marked the Great Awakening seem a reaffirmation of these traditional Puritan attitudes toward death. But this first sight is a superficial one. In fact, the behavior occasioned by the revival was much closer in content to that later seen in nineteenth-century revivals—the Puritans of an earlier day had expressed their fears not in public displays of tearful distress, but in private, even reluctant admissions of abject despair. Indeed, the tension between rhetoric and reality that made death and dying so troublesome in the seventeenth and early eighteenth centuries was inverted during the Great Awakening: as seen earlier, the paradox of the Puritan vision of death had been rooted in an incongruity between an optimistic rhetorical interpretation of death and a desperate introspective fear of it; conversely, during the Great Awakening much of the rhetorical interpretation was rich with expressions and images of terror, while in private a new optimism was becoming evident. In their enthusiasm to renew

their ties with the hallowed world of the past, the revival's participants had instead evoked a new complex of ideas that would rever-
berate throughout American religion and culture for many years
to come. But by the time the Awakening was over—and, as Edwin
S. Gaustad has observed, like the ebb of a flood it dissipated
quickly in the mid-1740s "because society could not maintain itself in so great a disequilibrium"[27]—the traditional world of the
Puritan was rapidly passing into history. And with it was passing
the Puritan way of death.

While Puritanism was still holding sway in the cultural climate of
New England in the latter part of the seventeenth century, in England the first seeds of sentimentality that would later grow into the
Romantic Era were already germinating. As John W. Draper
showed almost half a century ago, the effects of that early Romantic spirit were deeply and almost immediately seen in certain
aspects of the changing English attitudes toward death.[28] By the
1720s manifestations of that attitude would begin to appear in
New England—though at the time such ideas were still clearly
imports.

Charles Drelincourt's *The Christian's Defence Against the Fears
of Death, With Directions How to Die Well,* had for many years
been enormously popular in England and on the Continent. It was
a book, as its title suggests, intended to allay its reader's fears of
death by making death a state of existence to be longed for rather
than dreaded. Filled with beatific personifications of death as the
blessed "Heavenly Bridegroom"—a far cry from the "King of Terrors"—it attempted to argue its readers out of their fears by such
statements as "there is none but would be glad to lay himself down
to sleep, and pull off his Garments willingly, if he were certain to
be more Healthy, and to find his Garments more beautiful in the
Morning."[29] To the Puritan, of course, no such feelings of certainty concerning postmortem good health could be held. But in

1725 a Boston printer reproduced the book for New England's reading public. Appended to the New England edition, as it had been for some time in England, was Daniel Defoe's little ghost tale, "A True Relation of the Apparition of One Mrs. Veal, the Next Day After Her Death, to one Mrs. Bargrave," an early example of the stories of mysterious conversations with the dead that were to become popular in America in the nineteenth century.

Elizabeth Singer Rowe's *Friendship in Death; in Twenty Letters from the Dead to the Living* was another English book reprinted in eighteenth-century New England that stated well its contents in its title: a series of fictitious letters from the dead to the living giving accounts of their deaths and providing descriptions of the world beyond. Indeed, so popular was Mrs. Rowe's work that soon after her death a biography written by her husband sold well throughout the colonies, as it had in England.[30]

And as for advice on child-rearing, in the midst of the Puritans' soaring rhetoric on damnation and parent/child separation—though still some years before Jonathan Edwards was to warn a group of children that, if they failed to mend their ways, they would "cry out with weeping and wailing and gnashing of teeth together" after having been plunged into Hell "all together in misery"—a revealing little poem was reprinted in Boston and went into several editions. Simply entitled *Health, A Poem,* it was primarily intended to provide straightforward advice on "How to *Procure, Preserve,* and *Restore*" one's health. Most of the advice was purely physiological in nature, but when the text turned to psychological matters the recommendations could well have been directly addressed to the Puritan sermonic tradition:

> But above all, take special Care
> How *Children* you affright and feare,
> In telling stories of things seen,
> *Sprite, Daemon,* and *Hobgoblin;*
> Hence they'l contract such *Cowardice,*
> As ne'er will leave them all their Lives,

And then th' *Idea's* of their Fears
Continued unto riper Years,
Can by no Reason be suppress'd,
But of it they'l be so possess'd,
They sweat and quake, and start and stare,
And meet the Devil ev'ry where.[31]

To be sure, this scattering of imported literary material does not necessarily indicate a major shift in cultural sensibility. But when combined with other evidence, it does suggest that New England's Puritans were at this time living through a period of important cultural transition. For in time the heavy and optimistic sentimentality that pervaded these volumes would come to mark a homegrown variety of American consolation literature, as it would the diaries and funerary art of a later generation. But in the 1720s it was something new. It did not long remain so. The shift in attitudes that took place in New England in the decades following the 1720s—the decades that shook with the powerful reverberations of the Great Awakening—was remarkable. Its dimensions can only be suggested.

In 1717, Benjamin Colman had observed that "Religion adds to the Terrors of Death, shewing it as the righteous and fearful Punishment of Sin, and the dreadful Curse of a Holy God against it." Echoing the fearful obsession of generations of Puritans that had preceded him, he added that "the Change before us is so amazing a One, and our best Preparations are so poor, that no wonder if a sober serious heart be filled with utmost concern and distress."[32] It was with such a sober and serious heart that, in January of 1696, Samuel Sewall's daughter Betty had shown her first signs of terror in the face of death, bursting out into an "amazing cry" because "she was afraid she should goe to Hell, her Sins were not pardon'd." In time, she would be unable to read her Bible because of the horrible implications of damnation that lurked in its pages. But by 1757, Jonathan Edwards's daughter Esther—equally possessed of a sober and serious heart—could exclaim "how good is God!" because he enabled her to "offer up" her dying child to him; indeed, so positive and optimistic were her views on death that "one evening, in talking of the glorious state my dead departed must be in, my soul was carried out in such longing desires after this glorious state, that I was forced to retire from the family to conceal my joy. . . . I cannot help hoping the time is near."[33]

The shift here from fearful anticipation to eager longing for death, though not always so dramatic, runs through virtually all the available materials on death and dying during this period, from poetry to sermons, from journals to sepulchral art. In the seventeenth and early eighteenth centuries, as we have seen, revered ministers like Colman and Samuel Willard went to great lengths to explain, as Willard put it, "the reason why the People of God are so often doubtful, disquiet, discontent, and afraid to dy," usually echoing in their explanations Cotton Mather's assertion that "going to heaven *in the way of Repentance,* is much safer and surer than going *in the way of Extasy."* By the middle of the eighteenth century, however, such apprehension was coming to be regarded, as Jonathan Todd put it, as evidence that in one's dying hour "reason was sometimes affected."[34] It was becoming the norm, the accepted norm, for the godly to die "in Raptures of holy Joy: They wish, and even long for Death, for the sake of that happy state it will carry them into."[35] So carried away, in fact, did Josiah Smith once become with describing the "uninterrupted Flow of Peace" that had characterized Hannah Dart's dying hours, and the "Joy unspeakable" of life after death, that he cautioned himself: "But I must restrain my Pen, and draw the Curtain, lest you cry out; Let us also go that we may die with her!"[36]

This is not to say that the formal doctrines of Puritanism had completely withered by the end of the Great Awakening, but only that a critical change of emphasis had occurred. This is plainly seen in the response of the saintly David Brainerd as death closed in on him in 1747. "I did not want any of the sudden suggestions, with which many are so pleased, *'That Christ and his benefits* are

MINE,' *'That God loves* ME,' in order to give me satisfaction about my state. NO," he wrote, "my soul abhorred those delusions of Satan." This was a reaction that would have found favor with Mather, Willard, Colman, and innumerable other Puritans of an earlier day—if it had been genuine. But there is no indication in the record that Brainerd in fact experienced any of the despair and terror that had marked the passing of so many Puritans of an earlier age. Instead it suggests the merely rhetorical and hollow repetition of phrases that were becoming anachronistic to the generation that was coming into adulthood by the middle of the eighteenth century. For in his actual encounter with death, Brainerd—bolstered by constant self-reassurances that his longing to be in Heaven was based not on selfish premises, but on his desire to continue serving God—betrayed a kind of confidence that his forebears would have viewed with more than a little mistrust. "It is sweet to me to think of eternity: The endlessness of it makes it sweet," he said. "But, Oh, what shall I say to the eternity of the wicked!—I cannot mention it, nor think of it!—The thought is too dreadful!"[37] It was precisely this kind of self-righteousness, which Jonathan Edwards reports with approval, that an earlier generation of Puritans would have seen as those very "delusions of Satan" that Brainerd had claimed to fear.

If, as I have suggested, the Great Awakening brought with it something of an inversion of the elements involved in the traditional Puritan tension between rhetoric and reality in the face of death, by the time the revival had passed, the New England vision of death had come to resemble the attitudes of nineteenth-century Romanticism more than seventeenth-century Puritanism. To be sure, such a change did not come about and could not have come about abruptly. There were, as has been seen, early precursors of it, just as there were later reactions against it. Thus, in 1746, Thomas Skinner lamented the fact that New Englanders were rapidly succumbing to "Stupidity and Insensibility under Bereavements" in that they were failing to "eye, or take any Notice of the

Hand of God that is lift up against them." Instead of seeing in death portents of God's displeasure, his countrymen were tending more and more to glory in the prospect of removal to Paradise. Skinner urged his reader to "examine whether there has not been something amiss in your Heart and Life, and so continued in that God has been provoked thus to chastize and correct you?"[38] But by then most New Englanders were no longer listening; their attention was too intensely trained on what a later generation would call the "Golden Stair" to Heaven.

Modern readers have often, and perhaps too easily, seen in Charles Chauncy's attacks on the enthusiasm of the Great Awakening the beginnings of a liberalizing spirit in New England religious thought. But regardless of how liberal in modern terms Boston's First Church minister may or may not have been, he was clearly in the new mainstream when in 1749 he advised his congregation to face death with optimistic equanimity. "Be not discouraged," he urged, "the Time of your Redemption draweth near. It will not be long before you will arrive at the Place of the *Dead in* CHRIST, where you shall eternally rest from all your Labours and Sorrows."[39] This was the same man who, less than a decade earlier, had warned his flock that they were "in a state of dreadful and amazing hazard," hanging as they were "over the bottomless pit, by the slender thread of life."[40] This was the same man who could trace his spiritual lineage back to a time when Puritan ministers warned of the "wretched stupidity of some that can be then most secure" when death approached; and now, as mid-century drew near, he was instructing his listeners to "look forward" to death, and to "be patient . . . for the coming of the LORD draweth nigh."[41]

If Chauncy's spiritual lineage was an orthodox one, Samuel Mather's biological lineage was at least equally impressive. It is probably just as well, however, that his father was not around in 1753 to hear him speaking of the "calm . . . steady Comfort and supporting and refreshing Joy" of Ellis Gray as he looked into the jaws of death, a comfort and joy resulting from Gray's *"upright Walk before the LORD, and his Consciousness* to it." The message Gray gave Mather to convey to those who survived him, and which Mather took care that it "not slip away from me," was typically charged with the sort of security and confidence that was part of the new orthodoxy, but that earlier generations would have seen as a sure sign of spiritual miscarriage: *"The next Time,* said He, *you see our Brethren; tell them for me to love* GOD *and* CHRIST, *and love one another, and love their Work, and go on steadily in it And then they will have Peace and Comfort, as I have."*[42] Samuel Mather, it seems, inherited his father's preoccupation with italicized prose; but in his vision of death and dying he was much more at home with his contemporaries and with those generations soon to follow. Indeed, he remained close friends with Charles Chauncy until well into the waning years of the eighteenth century when Chauncy supported the publication of John Clarke's *Salvation for All Men,* a book designed to show that the torments of Hell were only temporary and that in time all men would be brought to Heaven's gates. This, it appears, was at last going too far for the tastes of the final remaining member of the Mather dynasty.[43]

A central factor in the change that took place during this time was the undermining of the doctrine of assurance that had been fundamental to the Puritan vision of death and dying. Liberals like Chauncy had begun speaking in favor of a deemphasis of the notion of conversion through stages and were moving to a view of spiritual renewal as something that might well be with the individual from birth. As Norman Pettit has recently shown, this drift is traceable in English theological thought at least to Giles Firmin, who in the latter part of the seventeenth century opposed teachings that required "such strong convictions, such dreadful legal terrors, deep sorrows, and humblings" because they were no help at all in the effort to "ease troubled souls." After returning to England disillusioned by a trip to Massachusetts in the 1660s, Firmin wrote that the New Englanders' stages of conversion were merely "stumbling blocks" in the road to salvation, resulting, in his observations, in the common condition of a people who "could not be resolved that ever their faith was true."[44] It took the better part of a century, but by the time of the Great Awakening the New Englanders themselves were clearing those stumbling blocks away, with Chauncy and the liberals working from one direction and revivalists like Jonathan Edwards from another—the latter contending that the question of spiritual election "may be determined without entering into any controversies about the nature of conversion," since "assurance is not to be obtained so much by self-examination as by active piety."[45] The revivalists had adopted the message brought to New England by the itinerant George Whitefield: that it *was* possible to determine with certainty who was marked for salvation and who was not. The doctrine of assurance had lost its dynamic meaning. And with this prop gone from under the orthodox Puritan edifice, that edifice collapsed and brought down with it the unique Puritan tension between death and dying.

Even the funeral elegy, almost by definition a genre devoted to celebrating both death and the dead, partook of a major change in emphasis. Although there were occasional glimmers of emotionality in the elegies of the seventeenth century, the overwhelming tendency was to resist such sentiments.[46] Thus, for example, Anne Bradstreet's 1653 elegy for her father, in which she announced that she was "By duty bound and not by custom led / To celebrate the praises of the dead," concluded:

> His hoary head in righteousness was found;
> As joy in heaven, no earth let praise resound.
> Forgotten never be his memory,
> His blessing rest on his posterity;
> His pious footsteps, followed by his race,
> At last will bring us to that happy place
> Where we with joy each other's face shall see,
> And parted more by death shall never be.[47]

By comparison with others, Bradstreet was being positively
emotional. Benjamin Tompson, for instance—after opening with
a conventional disclaimer similar to Bradstreet's: "Tis not bare
custom which provokes my Pen / To lisp the praises of this Man
of men"—concluded his 1695 elegy for his elder brother with more
familiar-sounding rhetoric:

> Predictions I effect not, thô I dread
> The places publick peace now he is dead
> Who lov'd and studied Unity so well
> The peace is threatned where this prop is fell.
> Lord grant us Succour to our sinking hearts
> Drop in thy Balsom while we feel thy Darts
> Answer the prayers this Blessed Saint hath made
> Our Soules let Rest with his when we are laid.[48]

The theme of loss, of the community's deprivation, occurs repeatedly in the elegies of this time—as when John Saffin concluded
his elegy for John Hull by writing:

> But tis a woefull and a Gloomy-Day,
> When Righteous men are taken thus away;
> Heaven Speaks aloud to Mortalls, reads ther Doom
> Such are Removed from Dire ills to Come;
> O may not this, this Sad Catastrophe
> Fore run the loss of our Dear Liberty.[49]

By the middle of the eighteenth century a complete reversal had
taken place. The emphasis was now placed heavily on the individual who had been so fortunate as to die, with little said about the
community's loss, and there was a new sense of sentimentality and
urgency in the message conveyed. Thus, the following ode is found
appended to Josiah Smith's 1742 *Doctrine and Glory of the
Saints' Resurrection:*

> Absent from Flesh! O blissful Thought!
> What unknown Joys this Moment brings!
> Free'd from the Mischief sin hath wrought,
> From Pains, and Tears and all their Springs.

> *Absent from Flesh!* Illustrious Day!
> Surprising Scene! Triumphant Stroke!
> That rends the Prison of my Clay,
> And I can feel my Fetters broke![50]

And in the 1749 *Dying Mother's Advice and Farewell* for Mary Williams:

> I long to be within the Veil,
>   And leave this House of Clay;
> Oh for some burning Seraphs Wing;
>   No longer would I stay.
>   . . .
> My willing Mind obeys the Call,
>   And meets Thee with Desire;
> I long, I faint, to be with Thee,
>   How can I longer bear?
>   . . .
> Thus she is gone; her Pulse doth cease;
>   We have her last Farewell;
> Her Glass is run; her Sun is set;
>   In Heav'n she's gone to dwell.
>   . . .
> But shall we mourn? Our Loss is great,
>   Yet greater is her Bliss.
> She's gone to dwell with Jesus Christ,
>   And see him Face to Face![51]

But the most striking evidence of the change in attitudes toward death in this period is provided not by prose or poetry, diaries or sermons, but by the stones New Englanders placed atop the graves of loved ones, and by the conditions of the cemeteries in which those markers were erected. Throughout the late seventeenth and early eighteenth centuries, elaborate Puritan funeral processions entered graveyards filled with traditional reminders of their dominant vision of death: tombstone after tombstone bore one version or another of the familiar death's-head carving, with only a scattered few depicting as the central motif some other more ethereal representation. But by the 1740s this too was rapidly changing.

Tabulations of design changes on tombstones in predominantly Puritan burial grounds have shown the death's-head motif and accompanying epitaphs stressing themes of mortality to have been overwhelmingly preferred, at least until the 1730s. The timing of design changes varies somewhat from cemetery to cemetery, and there is, of course, some overlap, but the general shift is clear: from 1740 to 1760 the death's-head motif and the traditional epitaph steadily gave ground to more optimistic and spiritual representations.[52] Even the work of individual carvers can be seen to have been affected by the changes: death's-heads carved by the same man or members of the same family tended to grow less severe during the early eighteenth century, and by mid-century the grim visage of death had metamorphosed into a pleasant cherubic image.[53]

In Cambridge the death's-head began losing favor by the middle of the eighteenth century as the heavenly cherub image now appeared with increasing frequency. In Plymouth and Concord the change set in earlier, with sharp decreases in death's-head representations occurring in the 1730s—at the same time that the cherubic design emerged. Throughout New England the pattern was the same, and by the close of the century both styles had been replaced by the familiar and full-blow Romantic "urn and willow" motif.[54]

But as cherubs and angels and other heavenly devices appeared with greater frequency on New England gravestones, the cemeteries in which those gravestones were placed began to become overcrowded while simultaneously falling into neglect and disarray. The Puritan community was becoming a relic of history, and the tribal unity that had given meaning to the bones of its ancestors and that had thus necessitated care of those remains was now rapidly dissipating. Eventually it became necessary for a law to be passed, similar to that enacted in New York a century earlier, appointing specific individuals "to attend at Funerals in this Town and carry the Bodies of the Dead to the Graves." Family tombs were replaced by individual graves, and these graves were so neg-

Fig. 10. *This page,* Three typical gravestones from seventeenth and early eighteenth century New England showing the common death's head imagery. *Opposite page,* A series of gravestone details from eighteenth century New England, ranging from 1731 to 1759, showing the metamorphosis away from the death's head image to the beginnings of abstract design and the more romantic and optimistic angel's head motif.

1731

1737

1743

1752

1759

lected that by the 1780s still more legislation was required to see to it that they received at least minimal care. Complaints of the health hazards posed by the cemeteries had become so frequent that in 1786 the Boston Selectmen had to order that coffins be placed a minimum of three feet under the ground, and superintendents were appointed to make sure that the cemetery gates were always locked and that "no Bones or part of Skelletons are suffered to remain on the surface or Tombs & Graves left open to injure the health or the feelings of the Inhabitants, or to offend the Eye of a Stranger who may incline to take a view of our Burial Places."[55]

It was almost a century earlier, in 1689, that Samuel Sewall had observed a similar scene in an English graveyard—"we saw several Graves open and the Bones thick on the Top," he wrote[56]—but New England would have to wait for the passing of Puritanism for its cemeteries to become equally overcrowded and equally neglected. But equally overcrowded and equally neglected they did indeed become. And when, in 1801, Salem's Reverend William Bentley wrote of an "antient" burial ground in New Hampshire that it was "in the greatest confusion and tho' the monuments of the best families are to be found in it they are in the utmost neglect," he could well have been writing of any number of cemeteries throughout New England.[57] As participants in the drama, the Puritans could not have appreciated its irony, but whereas in England Puritanism had been most responsible for the diminished ceremonial importance of death, in New England the process was reversed: only after the decline of Puritanism, only after the self-proclaimed Holy Remnant had lost its hold on New England culture, did ritualistic respect for the dead begin to wane.

At least as far as the problem of death was concerned, the first roots of Romanticism were now firmly planted in New England's soil. Monuments to it were everywhere, from the printed page to the block of carved granite. But something critical had been lost in the process: a sense of driven, purposeful community. It may have been motivated by fear, it may have been motivated by forces that to the twentieth-century mind seem irrational; but it was real. However, by the latter half of the eighteenth century it was largely gone. When Samuel Mather, scion of the famous ministerial elite that had dominated New England religion for so long, finally died in 1785, he was interred—as was his wish—with a total absence of fanfare. In contrast with the opulent Puritan funerals of an earlier day, Mather asked for a simple coffin, "no funeral Encomiums," and "no indulgence to sorrow for me." He requested only that his body "be deposited in the same Tomb with the remains of my honoured Father and Grandfather, and of many other esteemed Relatives, besides my most respected and beloved Wife; I would have only one Bell tolled just before Sun down, and that but for Five Minutes: For I am not willing that sick and infirm Persons should be disturbed with a lengthy Noise at the carrying of the Body of my humiliation to the silent Grave."[58]

In death, as in life, Puritan culture had lost its grip. The elegies and sermons, the journals and wills, the poetry and prose on death all suggest the dramatic changes that overtook the world of the Holy Remnant during the middle of the eighteenth century. But no testimony was more eloquent, incongruous though it may seem, than the unkempt, overgrown, occasionally bone-littered cemeteries of that era, studded with gravestones depicting an optimistic and sentimentalized vision of the afterlife.

April 29, 1695, dawned "warm and Sunshiny" in Boston, but by midafternoon the town was assaulted by a sudden, unexpected hailstorm. The hailstones were "as bigg as pistoll and Musquet Bullets," and they wreaked havoc on many of Boston's homes and public buildings. That evening Cotton Mather and Samuel Sewall dined together. As they stood in Sewall's kitchen discussing the day's storm Mather happened to mention that "more Ministers Houses than others proportionately had been smitten with Lightening." No sooner had he wondered aloud what God had meant by this selective focusing of his destructive powers than "many Hailstones broke throw the Glass and flew to the middle of the Room, or father." Together, the two men burst into prayer "after this awfull Providence."[59]

Rarely was the evidence so vivid and unmistakable, but as the seventeenth century passed into the eighteenth, New England's Puritans recognized the signs everywhere: something was terribly wrong in the Bible Commonwealth, and those who remained in the Puritan fold were aware of little they could do to cope with it. So they prayed.

As Puritan power and influence waned, it did so in a milieu of mounting worldliness and against the background of the rising power and influence of non-Puritan forces. When, in 1724, John Leverett died, having served as president of Harvard College for sixteen years, he left an estate two thousand pounds in arrears. His children, Sarah Wigglesworth and Mary Denison, were driven to sell his house in order to settle his debts. Though bearers of some of the oldest and most revered names in New England's Puritan lineage, these two women were then forced to appeal to the colonial legislature for financial assistance; they were awarded thirty pounds.[60] Not long after this incident, insult was to be added to injury as they witnessed one of the most regal and extravagant funerals in the annals of early New England's history—a state funeral for the colonial governor William Burnet, who had also been governor of New Jersey and New York.[61]

What can be seen in these incidents, writ small, is what was happening on a larger scale throughout New England. The population was growing steadily, doubling every twenty to thirty years, at the same time that it was becoming more concentrated in towns and cities along the Atlantic seaboard. Wealth was also becoming more concentrated as cultivable land grew scarcer and commercialization of the economy intensified; that proportion of the colonial population composed of men regarded as gentlemen, as well as that made up of those accepting poor relief, swelled rapidly between 1720 and 1770.[62] Towns that had traditionally been dominated by a single church now had two or three, or more. And not only were those churches frequently at odds with one another, but their very congregations had begun taking on a new look: as men were drawn into commercial life, religion became the province of women—and throughout the colonies, beginning first at the close of the seventeenth and continuing on into the eighteenth century, the proportion of women to men in church memberships rose to at least two, and often as high as three or four, to one.[63]

Society was changing. The churches were changing. And within that society and those churches new ideas were appearing and spreading rapidly, ideas inspired less by Puritanism than by Enlightenment and early Romantic conceptions of the world and the universe. The faith of the Puritan fathers was under siege as it had never been before.

The Great Awakening was the Puritans' last chance. It was the final opportunity for their apocalyptic dreams to find fulfillment, for the wicked and the worldly to be swept away with a single divine stroke. But Puritanism was by then split and splintered, with much of the theological doctrine of the early church fathers no longer adhered to by any of the parties in the great revivalistic debate. As it had a century earlier, the millennial promise proved to be empty. The disappointments of the 1640s had driven New England Puritanism to isolation and despair; the disappointments of the 1740s marked its demise.

III

Epilogue

7

Toward an American Way of Death

Mary Moody Emerson was born on the eve of the American Revolution. Her life, wrote her nephew Ralph Waldo Emerson, was "a fruit of Calvinism and New England, and marks the precise time when the power of the old creed yielded to the influence of modern science and humanity." Mary Moody Emerson was obsessed with death. She longed for it. "For years," Emerson wrote, "she had her bed made in the form of a coffin; she delighted herself with the discovery of the figure of a coffin made every evening on their sidewalk, by the shadow of a church tower which adjoined the house." Moreover, he noted:

> She made up her shroud, and death still refusing to come, and she thinking it a pity to let it lie idle, wore it as a night-gown, or a day-gown, nay, went out to ride in it, on horseback, in her mountain roads, until it was worn out. Then she had another made up, and as she never traveled without being provided for this dear and indispensable contingency, I believe she wore out a great many.[1]

If Mrs. Emerson was a "fruit of Calvinism," she was, most Puritans would have thought, a very strange fruit indeed. What she was, rather, was a product—a quite extreme product, to be sure—of the romanticization and sentimentalization of death that emerged full-blown in America with the dawning of the nineteenth century. Mrs. Emerson's concern and desire was for her own death, her own "cool, sweet grave";[2] but an equally powerful, obsessive, and more common concern of the time focused on the deaths of loved ones. It is this period in the development of Western attitudes toward death that Philippe Ariès has characterized as the time of *la mort de toi,* as "thy death."[3] It is this period that witnessed the emergence of cults of the dead, of mourning pictures, of prolonged periods of seclusion for the bereaved, of the "rural cemetery" movement—in short, as Ariès puts it, it is during this period that "mourning was unfurled with an uncustomary degree of ostentation."[4]

Ariès's brief survey of changing Western attitudes toward death is profound and insightful, but, as he himself acknowledges, he remains unsure of the role of Puritanism in the development of the American way of death.[5] And on one point he appears to be wrong in detail but correct in substance. That is when he links the American manifestation of "thy death" with earlier American history. As in his previous work, *Centuries of Childhood,* Ariès here too accepts the traditional assumption that the dominant mode of family life until the eighteenth century was the extended family, through which individuals were rapidly socialized as they grew to adulthood; with the eighteenth- and nineteenth-century contraction of this form of organization to the small, tightly knit, and somewhat isolated "modern" or nuclear family, the burden of death fell much more heavily on a smaller, more intimate household, thus giving rise to ostentatious and occasionally hysterical scenes of bereavement. The thesis is compact and persuasive but for one thing: in England and America from the *seventeenth* century onward, the nuclear family, not the extended family, was apparently the norm.[6] This finding of recent demographic historians does not, however, totally compromise Ariès's thesis, since the central idea of his argument is not really dependent upon (though he tends to make it appear so) the changing structure of individual family life. As Philip J. Greven has shown, although the nuclear family was dominant from the earliest years of New England's history, the term itself is of limited meaning in the American colonial setting. The closely knit *inter*-household relationships that existed removed much of the sense of family isolation that is generally associated with the concept of the nuclear family. Thus, as Greven puts it, what is crucial to any analysis of early American social structure "is not the structure of the household (although it could and did vary) but the structure and extent of the extended kin group residing within the community."[7] In sum, Ariès's main argument remains in essence correct: although the extended family was not the norm, the *function* of the extended family was largely carried out by a large network of kin who simply did not happen to live under the same roof.

In addition to these demographic findings, there was another element in Puritan social life that worked to integrate families that otherwise appear to be nuclear and diverse, and that was the Puritans' vision of themselves and their holy mission. From the late Middle Ages onward, Western thought and social organization tended to focus increasingly on the individual and decreasingly on the group. This tendency, which forms much of the basis for Ariès's earlier chapter on what he calls *la mort de soi* or "one's own death," had been previously noted by a number of medieval historians. It can be seen, as D. W. Robertson has shown, in the postmedieval shift away from the view of man as a "moral being," reflecting the character of the group, and toward the modern conception of "personality"; and it also manifests itself, as Henri de Lubac and Colin Morris have shown, in the late-medieval theological movements away from a concern with collective destiny and the destiny of the church, and toward an emphasis on individual salvation.[8] While the New England Puritans did not explicitly reject these developments in Western thought, their conception of themselves as a holy remnant, as the inhabitants of God's New Israel, tended to undercut the individualistic thrust of such thinking. The proclivity, as Roger Bastide has put it, to "think in terms of 'We' rather than 'I,' " is common in colonial settings;[9] the Puritan theological scheme only intensified this inclination toward a communitarian self-definition. Thus, as we have seen, death had a most disturbing impact on the Puritan community—but with the community's absorption of much of this impact it was at least not so intensely focused on the individual survivors. By the turn of the nineteenth century, with the collapse of Puritanism, it was.[10]

But a deteriorated sense of community was only one consequence of the interdependent array of changes thrust upon many Americans at the beginning of the nineteenth century. Equally important, and in different ways related to this deterioration, were such matters as the extraordinary efforts that were then being made to erect institutions that would deal with and "redeem" those deviant individuals who had traditionally been cared for by the community at large; a rising business ethic with a concomitant diversification and specialization of individual tasks; and what Barbara Welter has termed a "feminization" of American religion—a trend that was in fact only a continuation of what we have seen as a phenomenon that emerged in the late seventeenth and early eighteenth centuries.[11] At the same time that penitentiaries, asylums, almshouses, and the like were being built to formally handle what had always been the informal province of the community, a similar formalization and departmentalization of the business world was taking place. The effect was so striking that at least one foreign visitor to the new nation in 1833 noted that American "manners and customs are altogether those of a working, busy society." As Michel Chevalier then wrote:

> The brokers, bankers, and lawyers here have their cells, the merchants their counting rooms; here the banks, insurance offices, and other companies, have their chambers, and other buildings are filled from cellar to garret with articles of merchandise. At any hour, one merchant has but a few steps to go after any other, after a broker or a lawyer.[12]

But other visitors also noticed something else. In 1837 Harriet Martineau observed among Americans a peculiar "devotion of the ladies to the clergy," and criticized what she saw as "the evil of women being driven back upon religion as a resource against vacuity."[13] A few years earlier, Frances Trollope had noted that in America the churches were attended overwhelmingly by women, and had also observed, as Miss Martineau later would, the extraordinary influence that the clergy had on women: on the one hand, she claimed, the clergymen enjoyed a certain social "distinction and preeminence" in female opinion, while on the other hand "it is from the clergy only that the women of America receive that sort of attention which is so dearly valued by every female heart throughout the world." All in all, she concluded, "I never saw, or read of any country where religion had so strong a hold upon the women, or a slighter hold upon the men."[14]

It was into this sort of world, then, that there emerged in the nineteenth century an attitude toward death and dying that was characterized by self-indulgence, sentimentalization, and ostentation—a world rapidly diversifying and compartmentalizing its social and economic spheres, a world in which religion was becoming more and more the chief business of ministers and women, and a world that had lost something that was central to the cohesiveness of Puritan culture: a meaningful and functioning sense of community.

Like the Puritan child, the child of the Romantic and Victorian eras was instructed to spend a good deal of time thinking about death. But the similarity between the Puritan child and the child of the nineteenth century, at least as far as death was concerned, ends there. The child of the Puritan was told to "think how it will be on a deathbed"; to consider the terror of certain separation from, and even betrayal by, parents and loved ones; and to imagine what his well-deserved torments in Hell would be like. The instruc-

Sacred to ye Memory of Mrs
Esther ye Wife of Mr. Edwar
Corwin With her Infant
Who Died August 20th
Aged 71 Years.

Fig. 11. *Opposite page, top,* An early example of the mother and children stone—three stark death's-heads—the Mary Briant and children stone, Norwell, Mass., 1724. By the close of the eighteenth century such stones were incorporating explicit images of maternal intimacy and suggestions of salvation. *Opposite page, bottom,* This can be seen in the right-hand figure (The Esther Corwin and child stone, Franklin, Connecticut, 1797), on which is depicted a mother cradling her child in her left arm as both of them are enclosed in a coffin surrounded by semicircular cloud formations. *This page,* Whereas the Puritans had frequently invoked images of death as a time of parent-child separation, in the nineteenth century the theme was reversed. The inscription on the stone from New Haven's Grove Street Cemetery reads: "Her twin daughters preceded her but a single year; infant son but a few hours. Parting and sorrow they shall know no more."

tion of the nineteenth-century child involved the precise reversal of all this: the child was rarely told to contemplate the physical act of dying, and whenever he was, it was because the transformation thus effected was seen as a peaceful and beautiful deliverance—the releasing of a butterfly from a cocoon; instead of separation from or betrayal by parents and loved ones, eternal and heavenly *reunion* was stressed; and instead of visions of Hell and damnation, the nineteenth-century child was told to contemplate the sweet glory of salvation. Indeed, in place of death a new *life* was emphasized—death as a lonely finality or a grim eternity of torment was simply willed out of existence.

Even in its physical aspects, death to the Romantics, at least as it concerned young women dying of consumption, was often celebrated for its beauty. There is of course a very long historical tradition for viewing death as personified by Harlequin, a dark and mysterious lover. But with the rise of Romanticism this tradition reached new heights. "In fact," notes Mario Praz, "to such an extent were Beauty and Death looked upon as sisters by the Romantics that they became fused into a sort of two-faced herm, filled with corruption and melancholy and fatal in its beauty—a beauty of which, the more bitter the taste, the more abundant the enjoyment." Praz points to Poe and other literary figures as American examples of this association, but the roots were imbedded in American culture even more deeply than that. As a New York state schoolteacher, self-described as a "pennyless unattractive girl," observed in her diary upon the death of her younger sister:

> the broad snowy brow grew more & more fair   her eyes beamed with almost unearthly lustre & the bright crimson spot upon her cheek rendered her even more beautiful than when in her usual health   consumption *seems to delight to deck its victims* just as they are to be hid in the tomb.[15]

In an earlier chapter it was noted that the first New England primers contained numerous references to death, even when the child was simply to be mechanically learning the alphabet. School-books of the nineteenth century also contained frequent references to it—of twenty-nine "Poetical Lessons" in McGuffey's *Fourth Eclectic Reader* at least sixteen involve themes of death—but they were a far cry from the earlier primers' solemn warnings. The following poem, "What is Death?" is a fair example of McGuffey's treatment:

> *Child.* Mother, how still the baby lies!
> I can not hear his breath;
> I can not see his laughing eyes;
> They tell me this is death.
>
> They say that he again will rise,
> More beautiful than now;
> That God will bless him in the skies;
> O mother, tell me how!
>
> *Mother.* Daughter, do you remember, dear,
> The cold, dark thing you brought,
> And laid upon the casement here?
> A withered worm, you thought.
>
> Look at that chrysalis, my love;
> An empty shell it lies;
> Now raise your wondering glance above,
> To where yon insect flies!
>
> *Child.* O mother! now I know full well,
> If God that worm can change,
> And draw it from this broken cell,
> On golden wings to range;
>
> How beautiful will brother be
> When God shall give him wings,
> Above this dying world to flee,
> And live with heavenly things![16]

The same themes can be found over and over again in other school- and popular books, with frequent reference to the child in question as "Little Nellie," "Little William," "Little Georgie," and so on. Little Nellie, for instance, is the focus of attention of "The Golden Stair" in Richard Edwards's *Analytical Fourth Reader:*

> Put away the little playthings
> That the darling used to wear,
> She will need them on earth never,—
> She has climbed the golden stair;
> She is with the happy angels,
> And I long for her sweet kiss,
> Where her little feet are waiting
> In the realm of perfect bliss.
>
> Lay aside her little playthings
> Wet with mother's pearly tears,—
> How we shall miss little Nellie
> All the coming, weary years!
> Fold the dainty little dresses
> That she never more will wear,
> For her little feet are waiting
> Up above the golden stair.
>
> Kiss the little curly tresses
> Cut from her bright, golden hair,—
> Do the angels kiss our darling
> In the realm so bright and fair?
> Oh! we pray to meet our darling
> For a long, long, sweet embrace,
> Where the little feet are waiting—
> And we meet her face to face.[17]

The examples of this treatment of death are legion. In *The Mt. Auburn Memorial* one can read the tale of little Lulu, entitled "Lulu Is Dead!" in which the "baby limbs and features" of the child's corpse are described in great and loving detail, with the exclamatory conclusion: "She was—indeed—too bright, too pure, too beautiful a thing for earth; and so she has gone home to Heaven!" In the same volume, the creator of "Little Charlie—A Lament" weeps over the toys and other earthly traces of the dead child's passing, then closes on a note of romantic denial:

> Within the shrouded room below
> He lies a-cold—and yet we know
> It is *not Charlie* there!
> It is not Charlie cold and white,
> It is the robe, that, in his flight,
> He gently cast aside!
> Our darling hath not died![18]

Published some decades earlier, *The Picturesque Pocket Companion, and Visitor's Guide, Through Mount Auburn* contained the story of one "little William" who misunderstood the minister's words of consolation at his mother's funeral and kept returning to visit her grave because "by and by mammy will come again." When at last instructed that the minister had meant they would be reunited at the time of their *spiritual* resurrection, little William cried: "Let me go, then . . . let me go now, that I may rise with mammy." And such apparently is the power of devotion that within a month the boy did in fact die; "and they opened his mother's grave, and placed his little coffin on hers—it was the only wish the child expressed in dying."[19]

Although verse and prose of this type were widely circulated during the nineteenth century, the fact that they often appear in cemetery literature (as was the case with the last three examples cited above) is of special significance. At the same time that this literary romanticization of death was emerging, the plans for various new "rural" cemeteries were being laid. In place of the dreary, decaying burial grounds that had scarred the landscape after the collapse of Puritanism, the new cemeteries—Boston's Mount Auburn in 1831, Philadelphia's Laurel Hill in 1836, Brooklyn's Greenwood in 1838, and many others to follow—were monuments to a lush and idealized pastoralism; they were, in the words of one popular tract, "Gardens of Graves."[20] In contrast to the locked gates of the late-eighteenth-century burial grounds, the gates to the new cemeteries were kept open from dawn until dusk, and well-behaved visitors, supplied with maps and guidebooks, were invited

Fig. 12. Popular prose and schoolbook verse celebrating and senti-
mentalizing the deaths of little children had their counterparts in the
19th century cemetery. These three examples, from New York's Wood-
lawn and Greenwood cemeteries and the Lowell, Massachusetts ceme
tery, are representative of extremely popular designs.

to wander through them and to contemplate their beauty. They even became the subject of heroic poetry: "Sweet Auburn!" wrote Isaac McLellan in 1843, "o'er thy rolling slopes / The sparkling winter snows are spread; / Fast, fast the feathery flakes descend / O'er these calm dwellings of the dead."[21]

The dead's "calm dwellings" were intended in these cemeteries to be precisely that—dwellings: "perpetual homes" where the community's dead were peacefully gathered. In a world now increasingly marked by social schism and the accelerating pace of cultural change, the cemetery became the place, as John Albro put it in his consecration address for the Cambridge Cemetery, where "all our steps are tending" and where "all our ways, however diverse, and separated by the largest circumference of life, meet at last." At the consecration ceremony for Mount Auburn more than twenty years earlier, Joseph Story had sounded a similar note when he said: "there is nothing which wrings the heart of the dying—aye, and the surviving,—with sharper agony, than the thought, that they are to sleep their last sleep in the land of strangers"; it was the purpose of the new cemetery to provide a "home there with our friends, and to be blest by a communion with them."[22] And the Reverend Theodore Cuyler, author of *The Empty Crib: The Memorial of Little Georgie* and other volumes of popular consolation literature, referred to his son's burial place, Greenwood Cemetery, as "simply a vast and exquisitely beautiful dormitory." It is little wonder, then, that the good reverend and author would, when departing from a visit to Georgie's grave, turn "toward the sacred spot where my precious dead was lying" and bid the boy, "as of old, 'Goodnight!' "[23]

Even the older burial grounds, though not themselves tourist attractions, began sprouting gravestones marked with imagery appropriate to the new national mood: urns and vases and weeping willows appeared at the turn of the century, followed by doves, fingers pointing heavenward, and butterflies emerging from cocoons. Cast as it was against the grim skulls and scythes and hourglasses that were reminders of the Puritan past, this new funerary art was all the more striking. In at least one case a Puritan design was maintained on into the nineteenth century, but with one crucial change. In the seventeenth and early eighteenth centuries, laurel wreaths—symbols of victory—were sometimes found crowning the ominous visage of death; in the nineteenth century the same wreaths could be found encircling upward-pointing fingers and other symbols of the pious "victory" of the soul.

But it is in the newer cemeteries that the social tensions that gave rise to this mood can be most clearly seen. At the same time that the rural cemetery was being celebrated as the eventual home or "dormitory" for everyone, as the epitome of the close community that was but a fast-receding memory of the recent past, the realities of the present were closing in. Such cemeteries were turning out to be enormously profitable investment ventures—the value of the land on which Mount Auburn was situated, for example, increased in value *eighty* times in just a few short years—and more and more they were coming to be the distinctive resting places of the nation's wealthy and rapidly coalescing merchant classes. By the late 1840s so many families had erected iron railings to fence off their plots that people once again began complaining about the appearance of the cemeteries. "The elegant iron rails, which divide the different small lots," wrote two foreign visitors in 1853, "are neither ornamental, nor . . . reverential for the place. Exclusiveness little befits a cemetery; the idea of private property, carried even into the realm of the dead, where no one can own more than he covers, has something unnaturally strange."[24] There was, it seems, a contradictory pull being felt between the individualistic forces of commerce and acquisitiveness and the communitarian forces attempting to find in the graveyard the sense of fraternity and fellowship that had marked the past.

Of course not every American of the time shared the apparent sense of lost fellowship evident in much of the cemetery literature; and of course not every American of the time viewed death in such

Fig. 13. *Opposite page,* The nineteenth century image of the cemetery as the "dwelling place of the dead" is strikingly represented in this example from Springfield Cemetery in Massachusetts. *This page,* Chairs, sofas, and favorite pets became popular in cemetery art as the nineteenth century family drew increasingly inward and separated from the larger community, as illustrated by this example from the Lowell, Massachusetts, cemetery.

a sentimentalized fashion as indicated here. As Lewis O. Saum has recently demonstrated, many of the residents of America's small rural towns approached death in a remarkably *un*sentimental way. In place of the beatific visions of salvation and the idealized verbal pictures of dead children found in the more popular literature, the typical poetic response of what Saum calls the "humble" people was considerably more open and mundane:

> My brothers [and] sister kind & dear
> How soon youve passed away
> Your friendly faces now I hear
> Are mowldren in the clay

So wrote an aspiring Indiana poet in 1851.[25] But such exceptions only seem to prove the rule. The response of such people was the response of those who had no need to revive a sense of community, to give death a richer, deeper meaning; they had in most cases simply not *lost* their fraternal world as their more urban and urbane countrymen had—they had no need to turn to sentimentality. But theirs was a world already shrinking, at least in relative terms: between 1790 and 1860 the rural population of America enjoyed an almost sevenfold increase in size; but during this same period America's urban population experienced a *31*-fold increase. By the closing decade of the nineteenth century the annual rate of expansion of the country's urban population was more than twice that of the rural population—and the rate of urban growth was steadily increasing while the rate of rural growth was decreasing. There is probably no better single illustration of the changes then taking place than that provided by the city of Chicago: in 1832 it did not exist, and on its future site was but a tiny western outpost known as Fort Dearborn; in less than seven decades it had become the world's fifth largest city.

This is not to say, of course, that the dominant American attitude toward death in the nineteenth century, as I have described it, was shared by all urban Americans; nor is it to say that it was *not* shared by many rural Americans. What does seem clear, however, is that in the period from the birth of the new nation at least until the time when Americans were recovering from the Civil War, the overriding national treatment of death was shaped by a reaction to the dual forces of social and commercial expansion and specialization, and cultural romanticism. In large measure, if not entirely in response to the growing individual anonymity brought on by changes in their social world, Americans sought a return to their lost sense of community in the graveyard and the heavenly world of the dead; in the process, paradoxically, they effectively banished the reality of death from their lives by a spiritualistic and sentimentalized embracing of it.

But if the frankness and simplicity of much of rural America's approach to death was increasingly overwhelmed by the romanticization of it in the swelling ranks of the country's urban population, the nature of that romanticization itself would, by the end of the century, be succumbing to still other emerging forces.

In the 1830s John Pierpont had spoken of death in terms characteristic of the times when he wrote: "Death lays his hand upon the burning brow, and it is cool. He touches the aching heart, and its pain is gone; and upon the whole frame that is racked with agony, he sprinkles his cold dew, and all is still." Indeed, so wonderful and desirable was the prospect of death that God had been forced to implant in men a natural fear of it to "keep his children from rushing uncalled into his presence, leaving undone the work which he has given them to do." It would be easy to see such sentiments as—after an extended hiatus under Puritan domination of American culture—a nineteenth-century reemergence of the traditional *contemptus mundi* theme examined in the first chapter of this book. And perhaps in a sense they were. But for a people to logically have contempt for the world they must also hold with conviction a picture of a superior *alternative* to earthly existence. And in the same decade Pierpont was writing, Harriet Martineau, that peripatetic observer of the American scene, after a visit to

Mount Auburn cemetery, insightfully remarked: "It has sometimes occurred to me to wonder where a certain class of persons find sympathy in their feelings about their dead friends, or whether they have to do without it; those, and they are not a few, who are entirely doubtful about a life beyond the grave." Such people may have been more than a few in the 1830s, but their numbers then were as nothing compared with what was to come. As she wrote on, Miss Martineau could very easily have been discussing the intellectual malaise of many twentieth-century men and women:

> Such persons can meet nothing congenial with their emotions in any cemeteries that I know of; and they must feel doubly desolate when, as bereaved mourners, they walk through rows of inscriptions which all breathe more than hope, certainty of renewed life and intercourse, under circumstances which seem to be reckoned on as ascertained. How strange it must be to read of the trumpet and the clouds, of the tribunal and the choirs of the saints, as literal realities, expected like the next morning's sunrise, and awaited as undoubtedly as the stroke of death, while they are sending their thoughts abroad meekly, anxiously, imploringly, through the universe, and diving into the deepest abysses of their own spirits to find a resting-place for their timid hopes! For such there is little sympathy anywhere, and something very like mockery in the language of the tombs.[26]

Both Miss Martineau and the editor of Mount Auburn's *Picturesque Pocket Companion* were living in a time when the romanticization of death and the commercialization of the social order were phenomena still new and on the ascendancy. In her musings on those who did not share all the premises underlying the era's sentimentalized vision of death, Martineau was perhaps unknowingly glimpsing the future. In a more conscious way, so too did the editor of the guide to Mount Auburn. "We are a hard, practical people," he wrote in 1839, "intensely absorbed in business, surrounded by circumstances which accustom us to the livelier kinds of excitement, educated and impelled in every way to lose sight of what may be called the graces of civilization." The new cemeteries, he hoped, would help to revive these graces, these "minor virtues of a community." But he was not optimistic. With Paris's Père Lachaise in mind as a comparison—though it could just as well have been Los Angeles's twentieth-century Forest Lawn—he lamented that "some few ages hence . . . when opulence, and luxury, and fashion, and all the whims of humanity, and all the workings of time, shall have made it more like the great show-place of the gay and vain French Capital," the meaning of Mount Auburn might well simply pass away.[27]

The times changed more rapidly than either writer probably could have imagined. By 1884 the poetry on death that had filled the cemetery and consolation literature of an earlier day, and that was still being reproduced in elementary school readers, was being satirized by Mark Twain in his second "boy's book," *The Adventures of Huckleberry Finn.* Young Emmeline Grangerford, Twain wrote, was an untiring poetic recorder of the deaths of all who passed her way. "She warn't particular," Huck reports, "she could write about anything you choose to give her to write about just so it was sadful. Every time a man died, or a woman died, or a child died, she would be on hand with her 'tribute' before he was cold."[28] The example of her verse "quoted" by Twain—"Ode to Stephen Dowling Bots, Dec'd"—is one of the more humorous passages in the novel to most modern readers; but few modern readers have probably realized how closely the tone and mood of the poem resemble much of the serious verse penned in America only a few years earlier.

At the same time that such sentimentalization was giving way to the cynicism of people like Twain and to the more realistic cultural climate of the late nineteenth century, the ever-rising tide of "progress" and commercialism was working its way into the nation's treatment of death—and in its own way was filling some of the space left behind by the Romantic Era. Embalming of the dead was steadily becoming the norm in postmortem preparations, and even coffin design underwent enormous change. Literally hundreds of patents were taken out between 1850 and 1880 for new and elaborate casings for the dead, as the simple traditional coffin metamorphosed into the more aesthetically pleasing (and expensive) "casket"—the word quite consciously adopted because of its original meaning, a jewel box. By the 1880s the undertaker was becoming a "funeral director" and began joining national professional associations, attending conventions, and reading and contributing to "in-house" publications with names like *Mortuary Management, Sunnyside, Shadyside,* and *The Casket.* If a single example of the change taking place in the new profession can be pointed to as most indicative of the times, perhaps it might be the contest announced in *Sunnyside* in 1885 in which a $1,000 prize was offered for the funeral director exhibiting the "best appearing" corpse after a lapse of sixty days between embalming and examination.[29]

With the dawning of the nineteenth century, then, a number of interconnected developments in American social life—all related in one way or another to a fading sense of community purpose and to changes that had begun to beset the world of the Puritan before the middle of the eighteenth century—contributed to the emergence of new attitudes and responses to death and dying. But by the time the nineteenth century was drawing to a close the speed and force with which these new cultural values were entering the society became more than the structure of Romantic culture could bear: sentimentality began giving way to realism and even secularism. The effects on the American way of death were dramatic.

The Puritan child, we have seen, was immersed in death at the earliest age possible: his spiritual well-being required the contemplation of mortality and the terrifying prospects of separation and damnation. The child of the nineteenth century was also taught about death at virtually every turn, but rather than being taught to fear it, he was instructed to *desire* it, to see death as a glorious removal to a better world and as reunion with departed and soon-to-depart loved ones. These were very different, in fact reverse treatments of the same theme, but in a most basic way they were the same: the child was introduced to death very early in life, was familiarized with it, and was given good reason to believe that he or she could be the victim or beneficiary of it at any moment—children were no more immune to death's sting than was anyone else, including the very old. In the twentieth century this basic assumption has been largely eliminated. In keeping with the demographic revolution of the modern era that has reduced child mortality to an extremely low rate in the context of history, the teaching of children about death—when it is not altogether avoided—commonly excludes them from vulnerability to it. Extensive studies, dating from the 1930s to the present, of children's attitudes toward death indicate that in large measure modern children have accepted their parents' frequent admonitions not to worry about it, since it is something that only afflicts the aged. One boy, in answering a researcher's query "Can a child die?" spoke for entire generations of modern Americans when he replied, "No, boys don't die unless they get run over." In general, as Paul Schilder and David Wechsler have shown, to the child of today, "one's own death is . . . either frankly negated or it appears as such a distant event that one has not to worry about it. Old age, in the minds of most children, is like a far-off land, so remote that even speculation of ever reaching it appears as an idle, useless thought."[30]

As with the children from centuries past, the child of the twentieth century usually grows to adulthood—and so does his attitude toward death. Instead of confusion and terror, however, or even sentimentalization and desire, the twentieth-century American adult moves into a world of death avoidance and denial, a world in which social compartmentalization is so thorough that only the deaths of his very closest loved ones touch him at all. One of the most deeply disturbing facts of modern life—one that poets and novelists and philosophers and theologians never tire of discussing —is the apparent anonymity and simple unimportance of the individual; except in the most intimate of relationships, few men or women can ever regard themselves or anyone else as truly unique and irreplaceable.

This is indeed something new in the history of humankind. In many traditional societies the death of a leader can be so devastating that an entire village will be deserted, while the death of a less important individual can result in the destruction of his property; in Puritan New England the death of a minister or other church member so shook the congregation that it was often regarded as a divine portent of fearsome things to come; in the nineteenth century, when the process of modernization was first setting in, individuals and communities responded by making death meaningful, at least in the spiritual sense. But when, in 1963, the country experienced its most shocking death in a century—the assassination of President Kennedy—millions of Americans, though undeniably upset by the event, were within forty-eight hours glued to their television sets watching professional football games that went on as scheduled; in addition, subsequent public opinion polls indicated that, despite the emotion displayed at the time of the assassination, the basic beliefs and attitudes of most Americans on personal, social, and political matters remained remarkably stable and unchanged by this potentially stunning event.[31]

The development of the hospital as the common ground on which the process of death is carried out has only accelerated the rush toward anonymity and depersonalization. It has been a fact for some years now that the vast majority of Americans die in hospitals, while a good many more spend their dying moments in rest homes: in New York State alone, between the mid-1930s and the mid-1960s, the aged population doubled in size while the number of nursing-home beds increased more than sevenfold—and the size of the average nursing home increased by more than 65 percent. Further, for some years the very process of dying in these institutions has been drastically different from what it was at any other time in human history—it has become a process marked by loneliness, irrelevance, and an absence of awareness.[32]

In much the same way that prisons and asylums began in the nineteenth century to serve as places to which those who proved inconvenient to the larger society were to be removed, the hospital in the twentieth century has become the place to which society sends those about to die. The dying individual—at this particularly crucial point in life—is ejected from his accustomed social milieu and is sent into an environment perhaps more sterile and nonsocial than any he has ever known. Cut off from his social world, often avoided by family and friends who know of his impending death (it is common for hospital personnel to avoid telling relatives of the patient of the seriousness of his illness for fear they will desert him), the individual is faced with a world of doctors and nurses who resort to their own well-planned strategies to avoid "involvement" with him. It is essential to the efficiency of the hospital that death—or, in hospital language, "termination"—have as little impact on the staff as possible. Professional composure must be maintained at all costs. Thus, dying patients are often avoided by doctors and nurses, and when contact cannot be avoided, a frequently used strategy is to deal with the individual in a manner of forced aloofness and detachment. As a result, the patient must resort to counteracting strategies of his own, such as that of one individual observed by Elisabeth Kübler-Ross, who made a practice of taking her telephone off the hook, "just to hear a voice."[33]

All too often, in Ivan Illich's terse phrase, when the hospitalized individual now looks into the eyes of a physician "what he meets is the gaze of biological accountant engaged in input/output calculations," a biological accountant for whom death is simply "that point at which the human organism refuses any further input of treatment."[34] The dying individual who has become inconvenient to society quickly then becomes inconvenient and even something of an affront to the hospital staff as well. But modern medicine has an answer to this problem—sedation. Of the more than two hundred deaths one sociologist observed in hospitals in California and the Midwest in the 1960s all but about a dozen took place while the individual was in a "comatose" state, and none were deaths "of the Hollywood version, wherein the person's last sentence is interrupted by his final breath." The ability to thus reduce the emotionally threatening object—the dying patient—to a socially nonfunctioning state prior to death, and the frequency of such practice, has given rise to the phenomenon of "social death"— "that point," in the words of David Sudnow, "at which socially relevant attributes of the patient begin permanently to cease to be operative as conditions for treating him, and when he is, essentially, regarded as actually dead."[35] At this point the dying individual is conveniently depersonalized, and the nurse can go about her business with a good deal more comfort and equanimity: care may be taken to see that the individual's eyes are "properly" closed for the sake of postmortem convenience; nurses may refer to "riding patients out"—keeping their bodies functioning, at least until the shift change, in order to avoid "the tedious and time-consuming task of postmortem care"; or "soon-to-terminate" bodies may be stored on stretchers in supply rooms overnight so as not to waste clean sheets and a good room on them.[36]

Revelations of this sort of treatment are often, and understandably, greeted with shock—in the same way that reports on the funeral industry's commercialization of death, such as Jessica Mitford's *The American Way of Death,* are greeted with cries for reform. But hospitals and funeral homes do not operate in a social vacuum. The treatment they afford the dead and the dying is quite consistent with the realities of modern America—with the ways, in other words, in which other contemporary institutions treat the living. Whereas in traditional societies the individual is of such importance that his or her life is imaginatively extended either through prolonged mourning or multiple burial rituals, in contemporary America the reverse is true: although the products of medical technology may be exerted in all their gleaming splendor to maintain bodily functioning, the individual is considered to have so little social value that when death draws near, sedation effectively places him in a state of premature social extinction. After all, life—for others—must go on.

It is very easy for the discussion of death in contemporary America to quickly degenerate to either nervous satire or melodrama on the plight of modern man. Both of these responses, however, have a common source, just as does the dual response of denial on a personal level and near obsession on an abstract one; most Americans today, for example, do not see a dead body until well into adulthood, and may *never* witness the actual process of dying—though virtually every day of their lives finds them encountering two-dimensional *representations* of death on television and in the press. It is not really that we have subdued or even cheapened death, but rather that we no longer possess the conceptual resources for giving believable or acceptable meaning to it. As William F. May has cogently put it:

> Our strategies and rites are evasive not because Americans react to death as trivial or incidental, but because they feel an inner sense of bankruptcy before it. The attempts at evasion and concealment are pathetic rather than casual . . . [and] reflect a culture in which men sense their own poverty before the event. . . . Men are tempted simultaneously to conceal death and to hold themselves enthralled before it, because they recognize death as an overmastering power before which other responses seem unavailing.[37]

History has played an ironic trick on modern man. At a time when medical advances have brought about the virtual elimination of the plagues that decimated and crippled untold legions only short decades ago—smallpox, poliomyelitis, even perhaps cancer in the not-too-distant future—death itself has again become a mystery: physicians cannot agree on a simple definition of what death is or when it occurs; theologians cannot agree on what, if anything, death brings in its wake; and laymen, left to sort things out for themselves in this welter of confusion, have no alternative but to cling to life and avoid direct confrontation with the unknown. In a sense we have come full circle. Once again we are faced with the most fundamental of human responses to death, the response that for several millennia has been suppressed by the coercive and imaginative power of religion—the response of bewilderment and fear before the prospect of emptiness.[38]

Death has never been easy for humankind, and probably never will be—but the *style* of unease displayed varies dramatically from culture to culture, depending upon the anticipated meaning of death for both the individual and the society. The tombs of Forest Lawn, with their air conditioning and piped-in music; the "slumber rooms" and "Beautyrama Adjustable Soft-Foam Bed Caskets" of the funeral trade; the recent movement in funerary cryogenics, the freezing of the still-warm corpse in anticipation of medical discoveries that will enable it to be revived at some future date—these are no less indicative of the world view of modern man than are the hospitals that phase out the lonely dying by sedating them into a state of "social death," or the parents who refuse to discuss death with their children as adamantly as previous generations refused to discuss sex.[39]

These are the actions of a people living in a world in which virtually every individual can be replaced with such facility that his absence deeply affects at best only his most intimate relations. In a world bereft of ultimate meaning either in life or in death—in which neither the community of the living nor the vision of a mystical but literal afterlife any longer provides solace—modern man, in the face of death, has been forced to choose between the alternatives of outright avoidance or a secularized masquerade. To be sure, in recent years there has been a vast proliferation of advice literature and of social organizations for the dying and the bereaved, as well as of programs and seminars in hospitals that attempt to come to grips with the modern meaning of death. But admirable and hopeful as much of this activity may be, it is in itself powerful testimony to the fact that death has left modern man reeling in confusion and in need of a third alternative between denial and grotesquerie. And admirable and hopeful as much of this activity may *seem* to be, there are already signs that it is being undercut by the realities of American life: taking their cue from many of these well-meaning efforts to come to terms with death, other organizations are now appearing throughout the country to supply—for an hourly fee—"specially trained companions" to sit with the dying while family and friends go about their everyday business free of the burdens of conscience.

There is, of course, no turning back. In 1839, writing of the future, the editor of Mount Auburn's *Picturesque Pocket Companion* wondered: "Will not the musing moralist of those days, sometimes, weary of sensations and splendor, turn or seek to turn back in imagination to this uncrowded quietude and primitive simplicity . . . this green, fresh beauty of the woods?"[40] Perhaps he will; perhaps he does. But Mount Auburn was the product—the response—of an era just becoming aware of the complexities and anonymity of modern life. We can no more expect to return to it than we can anticipate finding in the pages of our children's schoolbooks poems celebrating the glorious death of Little Nellie.

It may be uncomfortable, it may in many ways be condemnable, but the modern American way of death is a direct response to the modern American way of life. The fact—the sad fact, many would say—is that, to use the terms articulated in an earlier chapter, modern American culture has accommodated itself quite well to modern American social structure. The core of this study has been an examination of a people, the American Puritans, who resisted such accommodation, whose culture was at odds with the larger social world in which they lived, whose world view was inconsistent with the prescribed "way" of dying which they inherited from the Christian past, and whose children had no alternative but to be terrified by the prospect of death. In many ways the Puritans were an anachronism on the stage of world history. And, as I hope has been obvious, this book has not attempted to romanticize or idealize that world of the past. But the very vividness of the Puritan experience can help to highlight our understanding of the interconnecting currents of the problem of death for all mankind— from the very distant past to the present and the future.

If we are to even think of changing our way of death, we will first have to think of changing the very fundamentals of our highly complex and institutionalized way of life. What Simone de Beauvoir has recently said of the prospects for changing our treatment of the aged holds equally true for any efforts that may be made to change our attitudes toward death and the dying: "It is the whole system that is at issue and our claim cannot be otherwise than radical—change life itself."[41] For if there is one simple premise that has been central to this study, one lesson that the Puritan way of death has had to teach us, it is that death cannot be abstracted from life and still retain its meaning.

Notes

Chapter 1

1. Thomas G. Bergin and Max H. Fisch, eds., *The New Science of Giambattista Vico* (Ithaca, N.Y.: Cornell University Press, 1970), p. 53.
2. Sigmund Freud, "Thoughts for the Times on War and Death," in James Strachey, ed., *Standard Edition of the Complete Psychological Works of Sigmund Freud* (London: The Hogarth Press, 1957), vol. 14, p. 289; Miguel de Unamuno, *The Tragic Sense of Life,* trans. J. E. Crawford Flitch (London: Macmillan and Co., 1921), p. 38.
3. C. W. Wahl, "The Fear of Death," in Herman Feifel, ed., *The Meaning of Death* (New York: McGraw-Hill, 1959), p. 23.
4. Johannes Maringer, *The Gods of Prehistoric Man* (New York: Knopf, 1960), p. 37.
5. Grahame Clark, *Aspects of Prehistory* (Berkeley: University of California Press, 1970), pp. 114–115; E. O. James, *Prehistoric Religion* (New York: Praeger, 1957), pp. 23–30. For some suggestive comments on the significance of color symbolism, with some possible application to the practice of coating corpses with red ocher, see Victor W. Turner, "Colour Classification in Ndembu Ritual," in Michael Banton, ed., *Anthropological Approaches to the Study of Religion* (London: Tavistock, 1966), pp. 47–84.
6. V. Gordon Childe, "Directional Changes in Funerary Practices," *Man* 45 (January–February 1945), 13; Andreas Lommel, *Prehistoric and Primitive Man* (New York: McGraw-Hill, 1966), p. 21;

cf. Grahame Clark, *World Prehistory* (Cambridge: Cambridge University Press, 1969), pp. 44–47.

7. James Mellaart, *Earliest Civilizations of the Near East* (New York: McGraw-Hill, 1965), pp. 42–43.

8. Alexander Heidel, *The Gilgamesh Epic and Old Testament Parallels* (Chicago: University of Chicago Press, 1949), pp. 14–16.

9. Ibid., pp. 69, 60, 170.

10. Ibid., p. 70.

11. For a history of this earliest Egyptian literature see the lengthy introduction to E. A. Wallis Budge, *The Book of the Dead* (London: Kegan Paul, Trench, Trübner & Co., 1898), vol. II; cf. the same author's later treatments in *The Literature of the Ancient Egyptians* (London: J. M. Dent & Sons, 1914), chaps. II and IV.

12. S. G. F. Brandon, *The Judgment of the Dead* (London: Weidenfeld and Nicolson, 1967), p. 6. On the matter of the sorts of fate awaiting those mortals not favorably received, see J. Zandee, *Death as an Enemy According to Ancient Egyptian Conceptions* (Leiden: E. J. Brill, 1960), especially pp. 125–160.

13. E. A. Wallis Budge, *Osiris and the Egyptian Resurrection* (London: Philip Lee Warner, 1911), pp. 305–347; cf. Brandon, *Judgment of the Dead*, pp. 28–41.

14. Brandon, *Judgment of the Dead*, p. 41.

15. Hannah Arendt, *Between Past and Future* (New York: Viking, 1961), p. 111.

16. Joseph Campbell, *The Masks of God: Primitive Mythology* (New York: Viking, 1959), pp. 125–26; Arthur Waley, *The Way and Its Power* (New York: Macmillan, 1949), pp. 54–55.

17. Clifford Geertz, "Ethos, World-View and the Analysis of Sacred Symbols," *The Antioch Review* 17 (Winter 1957–58), 421, 422; and Geertz, *Islam Observed: Religious Development in Morocco and Indonesia* (Chicago: University of Chicago Press, 1968), pp. 97–98.

18. Francis Bacon, *The Essays, or Councils, Civil and Moral* (London, 1718), p. 3.

19. E. Rohde, *Psyche, The Cult of Souls and Belief in Immortality Among the Greeks* (New York: Harcourt, Brace, 1925), pp. 19–24, 253–56; Bruno Snell, *The Discovery of the Mind*, trans. T. G. Rosenmeyer (New York: Harper, 1960), pp. 17–18; John 11:25–26; Augustine, *Confessions*, trans. Edward B. Pusey (New York: Modern Library, 1949), p. 190; Ambrose, *De Consolatione Valen-*

tiniani, 45, quoted in Alfred C. Rush, *Death and Burial in Christian Antiquity* (Washington: Catholic University of America Press, 1941), pp. 11–12.

20. St. Thomas Aquinas, *Summa Theologica* (New York: Benziger Brothers, 1948), vol. I, p. 2831. The limits of space and the specific purposes of this chapter do not permit digression on one important point of controversy concerning early Christian attitudes toward death and the afterlife. This is the controversy concerning the origins and implications of, as Oscar Cullmann has phrased it, the contrasting "courageous and joyful primitive Christian hope of the resurrection of the dead and the serene philosophic expectation of the survival of the immortal soul." For those interested in pursuing this matter, Cullmann's famous essay *Immortality of the Soul or Resurrection of the Dead?* (New York: Macmillan, 1958) is the place to begin. Cf. Jaroslav Pelikan, *The Shape of Death: Life, Death, and Immortality in the Early Fathers* (New York: Abingdon Press, 1961); and especially Milton McC. Gatch, *Death: Meaning and Mortality in Christian Thought and Contemporary Culture* (New York: Seabury Press, 1969), pt. II.

21. See Rush, *Death and Burial,* pp. 44–71.

22. For convenient editions of the letters of Ignatius and the main source of Augustine's subsequent condemnation of suicide, see Cyril C. Richardson, ed., *Early Christian Fathers* (Philadelphia: Westminster Press, 1953), pp. 74–120; and Saint Augustine, *The City of God,* trans. Marcus Dods (New York: Modern Library, 1950), pp. 22–32.

23. Theodore Spencer, for example, attributes much of the concentration and consternation concerning death in this period to the development of artistic realism and an attendant rise in emotional identification with the death of Christ—that favorite artistic motif of that and so many other eras. See Spencer, *Death and Elizabethan Tragedy* (Cambridge, Mass.: Harvard University Press, 1936), pp. 15–21.

24. Spencer, *Death and Elizabethan Tragedy,* p. 32; see also Edelgard Dubruck, *The Theme of Death in French Poetry of the Middle Ages and the Renaissance* (The Hague: Mouton, 1964). On the *danse macabre* see Leonard P. Kurtz, *The Dance of Death and the Macabre Spirit in European Literature* (New York: Pub. of the Institute of French Studies, 1934); on the *Ars Moriendi* see Sr. Mary C. O'Connor, *The Art of Dying Well: The Development of*

the Ars Moriendi (New York: Columbia University Press, 1942); on tomb sculpture see Erwin Panofsky, *Tomb Sculpture: Its Changing Aspects from Ancient Egypt to Bernini* (London: Thames and Hudson, 1964), 63–66, and T. S. R. Boase, *Death in the Middle Ages* (London: Thames and Hudson, 1972), pp. 96–103.

25. Johan Huizinga, *The Waning of the Middle Ages* (London: Edward Arnold, 1952), p. 131.

26. François Villon, *The Legacy, The Testament, and Other Poems,* trans. Peter Dale (London: Macmillan, 1973), pp. 60, 61, p. 51.

27. Richard Rolle, *The Pricke of Conscience* [ca. 1340], Richard Morris, ed. (Berlin: A. Asher, 1863), p. 53. It should be noted here that Rolle is no longer considered the author of this work; true authorship has yet to be determined. For relevant passages in *La Lumiere as lais,* see C. V. Langlois, *La Vie en France au Moyen Age* (Paris: Librairie Hachette, 1928), vol. 4, pp. 111–119.

28. O'Connor, *The Art of Dying Well,* p. 5.

29. Huizinga, *Waning of the Middle Ages,* p. 132.

30. Donald R. Howard, "The Contempt of the World: A Study in the Ideology of Latin Christendom With Emphasis on Fourteenth-Century English Literature" (unpublished Ph.D. dissertation, University of Florida, 1954), p. 144.

31. Boase, *Death in the Middle Ages,* p. 106.

32. See Gaby and Michel Vovelle, *Vision de la mort et de l'audelà en Provençe* (Cahiers des Annales 29, 1970). This matter is discussed at somewhat greater length in Chapter 5.

33. Dubruck, *The Theme of Death,* pp. 152, 154.

34. Luise Klein, "Die Bereitung zum Sterben: Studien zu den frühen reformatorischen Sterbebüchern" (unpublished dissertation, Georg-August-Universitat Göttingen, 1958), p. 121. I am indebted to Steven E. Ozment of Yale for calling my attention to this excellent study, and to Robert Kolb of the Center for Reformation Research in St. Louis for generously loaning me his personal microfilm of it.

35. In Henry Harington and Thomas Park, eds., *Nugae Antiquae: A Miscellaneous Collection of Original Papers . . . by Sir John Harington* (London: J. Wright, 1804), vol. II, pp. 332–333.

36. William Drummond, *A Cypress Grove* [1623] (London: Hawthornden Press, 1909), p. 69; Jeremy Taylor, *The Rule and Exercises of Holy Dying* [1651] (New York: Pott and Amery, 1869),

p. 95; Sir Thomas Browne, *Religio Medici* [1643] in *Works,* I, ed. Charles Sayle (Edinburgh: John Grant, 1912), p. 58.

37. For discussion of this phase of Erasmus's life see Howard, "The Contempt of the World," pp. 213–218; and Albert Hyma, *The Youth of Erasmus* (Ann Arbor: University of Michigan Press, 1931), pp. 167–181.

38. H. R. Trevor-Roper, "Religion, The Reformation and Social Change," in G. A. Hayes-McCoy, ed., *Historical Studies, IV: Papers Read Before the Fifth Irish Conference of Historians* (London: Bowes & Bowes, 1963), pp. 30–31.

39. John Calvin, *Commentaries,* trans. and ed. John Pringle (Edinburgh: The Calvin Translation Society, 1851), vol. 42, p. 352.

40. William Perkins, *The Workes of that Famous and Worthy Minister of Christ* (London: I. Legatt, 1626–31), vol. II, pp. 750, 756.

41. Richard Sibbes, *The Saints Cordials* (London, 1637), p. 188.

42. Edward Dering, *A Sermon Preached at the Tower of London* (London, 1597), no pag.

43. Robert Ashton, ed., *The Works of John Robinson, Pastor of the Pilgrim Fathers* (Boston: Doctrinal Tract and Book Society, 1851), vol. I, pp. 258–59.

44. Ernst Troeltsch, *The Social Teaching of the Christian Churches* (London: Allen & Unwin, 1931), vol. II, p. 607.

45. Thomas Cartwright, *A Reply to an Answer Made of Master Doctor Whitgift Agaynst the Admonition to the Parliament* (London, 1572), p. 1.

Chapter 2

1. Robert Bolton, *Mr. Boltons Last and Learned Worke of the Foure Last Things* (London, 1635), p. 12.

2. A. S. P. Woodhouse, *Puritanism and Liberty* (London: J. M. Dent & Sons, 1938), p. xxxvii.

3. Bertrand Russell, "A Free Man's Worship," reprinted in Russell, *Mysticism and Logic* (London: Allen & Unwin, 1917), p. 56.

4. Quoted in E. M. W. Tillyard, *The Elizabethan World Picture* (New York: Macmillan, n.d.), p. 11.

5. Johan Huizinga, *Waning of the Middle Ages* (London: Edward Arnold, 1952), p. 216. The incidents cited just prior to this reference are also from Huizinga, pp. 214–216.

6. Thomas S. Kuhn, *The Copernican Revolution* (New York: Random House, 1959), p. 93. For a general introduction to Puritan ideas about scientific experimentation, see the early work of Samuel Eliot Morison, *The Puritan Pronaos* (1936), reprinted as *The Intellectual Life of Colonial New England* (Ithaca, N.Y.: Cornell University Press, 1956), pp. 241–274. Cf. Robert K. Merton, "Puritanism, Pietism and Science," *Sociological Review* 28 (1936), reprinted in *Social Theory and Social Structure* (New York: Free Press, 3rd ed., enl., 1968), pp. 628–660; and Charles Webster's major new study, *The Great Instauration: Science, Medicine, and Reform, 1626–1660* (London: Duckworth, 1975).

7. David Person, *Varieties: or, A Surveigh of Rare and Excellent Matters* (London, 1635), bk. five, pp. 81–82.

8. Ibid.

9. G. R. Cragg, *From Puritanism to the Age of Reason* (Cambridge: Cambridge University Press, 1966), p. 91.

10. See A. D. J. Macfarlane, *Witchcraft in Tudor and Stuart England* (New York: Harper & Row, 1970), pp. 60–61; H. C. Erik Midelfort, *Witch-Hunting in Southwestern Germany* (Stanford: Stanford University Press, 1972), p. 137; Norman Cohn, *Europe's Inner Demons* (New York: Basic Books, 1975), p. 254.

11. Person, *Varieties*, p. 188.

12. For a superb recent study of popular conceptions of the world in the sixteenth and seventeenth centuries, see Keith Thomas, *Religion and the Decline of Magic: Studies in Popular Beliefs in Sixteenth and Seventeenth Century England* (London: Weidenfeld and Nicolson, 1971).

13. Carl Bridenbaugh, *Vexed and Troubled Englishmen, 1590–1642* (New York: Oxford University Press, 1968), p. 376.

14. This reference is from Thomas, *Religion and the Decline of Magic,* p. 8; other cited references to disease and hunger in sixteenth- and seventeenth-century England can be found in this same work; in Bridenbaugh, *Vexed and Troubled Englishmen;* in Peter Laslett, *The World We Have Lost: England Before the Industrial Age* (New York: Scribner's, 1965); and in J. F. D. Shrewsbury, *A History of Bubonic Plague in the British Isles* (Cambridge: Cambridge University Press, 1970).

15. Laslett, *The World We Have Lost,* p. 117; Bridenbaugh, *Vexed and Troubled Englishmen,* p. 377. P. Bowden, "Agricultural Prices, Farm Profits, and Rents," in Joan Thirsk, ed., *The Agrarian His-*

tory of England and Wales, vol. IV, 1500–1640 (Cambridge: Cambridge University Press, 1967), p. 632. Sorting out deaths from disease from those of starvation has long been recognized as a difficult and controversial historical endeavor. For a recent and important contribution to the debate, see Andrew B. Appleby, "Disease or Famine? Mortality in Cumberland and Westmorland 1580–1640," *Economic History Review,* 2nd series, 26 (1973), 403–431.

16. D. W. Robertson, Jr., *Chaucer's London* (New York: Wiley, 1968), pp. 120–122; cf. Peter Burke, *The Renaissance Sense of the Past* (London: Edward Arnold, 1969), chap. 1; and William J. Brandt, *The Shape of Medieval History: Studies in Modes of Perception.* (New Haven: Yale University Press, 1966), especially pp. 65–80.

17. Robertson, *Chaucer's London,* p. 122. On this matter, it is useful to compare the medieval social movements described and analyzed in Norman Cohn's *The Pursuit of the Millennium: Revolutionary Millenarians and Mystical Anarchists of the Middle Ages* (New York: Oxford University Press, 1970), with Michael Walzer's study of the roots of the Puritan Revolution, *The Revolution of the Saints: A Study in the Origins of Radical Politics* (New York: Atheneum, 1972).

18. See William Haller, *The Elect Nation: The Meaning and Relevance of Foxe's "Book of Martyrs"* (New York: Harper & Row, 1963); cf., for a very brief but insightful discussion, J. H. Plumb, *The Death of the Past* (Boston: Houghton Mifflin, 1971), chap. 2, especially pp. 83–85.

19. *Winthrop Papers* (Boston: Massachusetts Historical Society, 1929–47), vol. II, p. 138.

20. Samuel Danforth, *An Astronomical Description of the Late Comet or Blazing Star . . . Together with a brief Theological Application Thereof* (Boston, 1665), pp. 16–18.

21. Max Weber, *The Protestant Ethic and the Spirit of Capitalism,* trans. Talcott Parsons (New York: Scribner's, 1958), p. 104.

22. *The Works of Thomas Goodwin, D.D.* (Edinburgh: James Nichol, 1861), vol. II, p. lvi.

23. See George H. Williams, *Wilderness and Paradise in Christian Thought* (New York: Harper & Row, 1962), pp. 98ff. For a convenient collection of early travelers' reports on the state of the New World, see Richard M. Dorson, *America Begins* (New York:

Pantheon, 1950). This should be supplemented with the vivid sixteenth- and seventeenth-century pictorial representations of the New World presented in Hugh Honour's magnificent new book, *The New Golden Land* (New York: Pantheon, 1975). The reference to the scent of pine detectable at sea is based on numerous references in the literature of discovery and exploration; for some relatively recent secondary references, cf. Richard Hofstadter, *America at 1750: A Social Portrait* (New York: Knopf, 1971), p. xi; and Annette Kolodny, *The Lay of the Land: Metaphor as Experience in American Life and Letters* (Chapel Hill: University of North Carolina Press, 1975), chap. 2.

Chapter 3

1. Philippe Ariès, *Centuries of Childhood: A Social History of Family Life* (New York: Random House, 1962), p. 128.
2. Michael Zuckerman, *Peaceable Kingdoms: New England Towns in the Eighteenth Century* (New York: Random House, 1970), p. 73; John Demos, *A Little Commonwealth: Family Life in Plymouth Colony* (New York: Oxford University Press, 1970), p. 139.
3. Alan Macfarlane, *The Family Life of Ralph Josselin, A Seventeenth-Century Clergyman* (Cambridge: Cambridge University Press, 1970), pp. 90–91.
4. For a convenient collection of some of this material see Robert H. Bremner, ed., *Children and Youth in America* (Cambridge, Mass.: Harvard University Press, 1970), vol. I, pp. 27–122; cf. Ross W. Beales, Jr., "In Search of the Historical Child: Miniature Adulthood and Youth in Colonial New England," *American Quarterly* 27 (October 1975), 379–398.
5. Philippe Ariès, "At the Point of Origin," in Peter Brooks, ed., *The Child's Part* (Boston: Beacon Press, 1972), p. 15; Marc Soriano, "From Tales of Warning to Formulettes: The Oral Tradition in French Children's Literature," ibid., pp. 24–25.
6. William Sloane, *Children's Books in England and America in the Seventeenth Century* (New York: Columbia University Press, 1955).
7. Zuckerman, *Peaceable Kingdoms,* p. 77. It should be acknowledged that some of Ariès's contentions have been challenged within the French historical setting. On the matter of the presence or absence of an adolescent stage, for example, see the important essay by

Natalie Z. Davis, "The Reasons of Misrule: Youth Groups and Charivaris in Sixteenth-Century France," *Past and Present* 50 (February 1971); an extension of Davis's argument to seventeenth-century London is Steven R. Smith, "The London Apprentice as Seventeenth-Century Adolescent," *Past and Present* 61 (November 1973).

8. John Earle, *Micro-cosmographie or, A Piece of the World Discovered in Essays and Characters* (London, 1628), p. 5.

9. Henri Misson, *Mémoires et Observations Faites par un Voyageur en Angleterre* (Paris, 1698), p. 128; Guy Miege, *The Present State of Great Britain* (London, 1707), p. 222; John Drinkwater, *Charles James Fox* (London: Ernest Benn, 1928), pp. 14–15. On the leniency of parental discipline in some families in the American colonial South, see Edmund S. Morgan, *Virginians at Home* (Charlottesville: University Press of Virginia, 1952), pp. 7–8, where an English traveler is quoted as saying of Maryland and Virginia: "The Youth of these more indulgent Settlements, partake pretty much of the *Petit Maitre* Kind, and are pamper'd much more in Softness and Ease than their Neighbors more Northward."

10. John Robinson, *New Essays: Or, Observations Divine and Moral,* in Robert Ashton, ed., *The Works of John Robinson* (Boston: Doctrinal Tract and Book Society, 1851), vol. I, pp. 246–248.

11. Jonathan Edwards, *A Faithful Narrative of the Surprising Work of God,* in *The Works of Jonathan Edwards,* vol. IV, ed. C. C. Goen (New Haven: Yale University Press, 1972), p. 158; James Janeway, *A Token For Children* . . . [1679] (Boston: Caleb Bingham, 1802), p. 59.

12. See Ross W. Beales, Jr., "Cares for the Rising Generation: Youth and Religion in Colonial New England" (unpublished dissertation, University of California at Davis, 1971); cf. Philip J. Greven, Jr., "Youth, Maturity, and Religious Conversion: A Note on the Ages of Converts in Andover, Massachusetts, 1711–1749," *Essex Institute Historical Collections* 108 (1972), 119–34.

13. Cotton Mather, *Small Offers Towards the Service of the Tabernacle in this Wilderness* (Boston, 1689), p. 59.

14. Cotton Mather, *The Young Mans Preservative* (Boston, 1701), p. 4; Cotton Mather, *Small Offers* . . . , p. 62; Cotton Mather, *Cares About the Nurseries* (Boston, 1702), p. 32.

15. Samuel Willard, *The Child's Portion* (Boston, 1684), p. 31.

16. Cotton Mather, *Small Offers* . . . , pp. 18–19.

17. Willard, *The Child's Portion,* p. 16.
18. Benjamin Wadsworth, "The Nature of Early Piety as it Respects God," in *A Course of Sermons on Early Piety* (Boston, 1721), p. 10; Samuel Willard, *The Mourners Cordial Against Excessive Sorrows* (Boston, 1691), p. 77.
19. Willard, *The Mourners Cordial,* p. 74; Michael Wigglesworth, *The Day of Doom* (London, 1687), stanza 181. See also the statement on infant damnation rendered by a body of Boston clergymen, *The Principles of the Protestant Religion Maintained* (Boston, 1690), especially pp. 78–79. The matter of infant damnation in the Calvinist tradition has recently been examined by Gerhard T. Alexis in "Wigglesworth's 'Easiest Room,'" *New England Quarterly* 42 (1969), 573–583. A forthcoming study by Peter Gregg Slater treats the problem in greater depth and complexity.
20. Philip J. Greven, Jr., *Four Generations: Population, Land, and Family in Colonial Andover, Massachusetts* (Ithaca, N.Y.: Cornell University Press, 1970). For Greven's brief specific comparison of Andover and Boston, see pp. 196–197, fn. 14; detailed information on Boston can be found in John B. Blake, *Public Health in the Town of Boston,* 1630–1822 (Cambridge, Mass.: Harvard University Press, 1959), app. II; an excellent recent study is E. S. Dethlefsen, "Life and Death in Colonial New England" (unpublished Ph.D. dissertation, Harvard University, 1972).
21. Cotton Mather to John Cotton, November 1678, in Massachusetts Historical Society Collections, 4th series, VIII (1868), 383–384; contemporary estimates of the toll of the epidemic were made by John Foster and Increase Mather in Thomas Thatcher, *A Brief Rule to Guide the Common People* (Boston, 1678). See Blake, *Public Health,* p. 20; for the population of Boston at the time and an estimate of the death toll of the disease, see Carl Bridenbaugh, *Cities in the Wilderness: Urban Life in America, 1625–1742* (New York: Capricorn Books, 1964 [orig. pub. 1936]), pp. 6, 87.
22. Peter Laslett, *The World We Have Lost: England Before the Industrial Age* (New York: Scribner's, 1965), pp. 146–147.
23. Kenneth A. Lockridge, "The Population of Dedham, Massachusetts, 1636–1736," *Economic History Review* XIX (1966), 329; Greven, *Four Generations,* p. 25; Demos, *Little Commonwealth,* pp. 131–132; James K. Somerville, "A Demographic Profile of the Salem Family, 1660–1770," unpublished paper read at the Confer-

ence on Social History, Stony Brook, New York, October 25, 1969; Maris A. Vinovskis, "Mortality Rates and Trends in Massachusetts Before 1830," *The Journal of Economic History* XXXII (1972), 195–201; and Maris A. Vinovskis, "Angels' Heads and Weeping Willows: Death in Early America," unpublished paper read at the American Antiquarian Society, April 1974, p. 9.

24. Greven, *Four Generations*, pp. 188–203.

25. *Journal of Alice Thornton*, ms. Yale University Library; Joseph E. Illick, "Child Rearing in Seventeenth-Century England and America," in Lloyd de Mause, ed., *The History of Childhood* (New York: The Psychohistory Press, 1974), p. 325; *The Diary of Samuel Sewall, 1674–1729,* ed. M. Halsey Thomas (New York: Farrar, Straus & Giroux, 1973), vol. I, p. 592; "Diary of Cotton Mather," Massachusetts Historical Society Collections, 7th series (Boston, 1911), VII, 380–82.

26. Lockridge, "Population of Dedham," 343; Ariès, *Centuries of Childhood,* pp. 38–39; Vinovskis, "Angels' Heads and Weeping Willows," *passim;* Jeanine Hensley, ed., *The Works of Ann Bradstreet* (Cambridge: Harvard University Press, 1967), p. 236.

27. Thomas Cobbett, *A Fruitfull and Usefull Discourse . . .* (London, 1656), p. 96.

28. Edmund S. Morgan, *The Puritan Family* (New York: Harper & Row, 1966), p. 107.

29. Ibid., p. 77; cf. Demos, *A Little Commonwealth,* p. 74.

30. Thomas Skinner, *The Mourner Admonished* (Boston, 1746), p. 28.

31. There is a large body of psychological and anthropological literature on related phenomena, and it has been helpful in formulating some of the ideas in this chapter. On the effects of pollution fear see Mary Douglas, *Purity and Danger: An Analysis of Concepts of Pollution and Taboo* (London: Routledge & Kegan Paul, 1966); on the psychological problem of "approach-avoidance conflict," see, among many relevant monographs, W. N. Schoenfeld, "An Experimental Approach to Anxiety, Escape, and Avoidance Behavior," in P. H. Hoch and J. Zubin, eds., *Anxiety* (New York: Grune & Stratton, 1950), pp. 70–99; and Murray Sidman, "Avoidance Behavior," in W. K. Honig, ed., *Operant Behavior* (New York: Appleton-Century Crofts, 1966), pp. 448–498.

32. Demos, *A Little Commonwealth,* p. 136.

33. Cotton Mather, "Diary," VII, p. 535.

34. Boston Record Commissioners, *Report*, VII, 119. Cited in Blake, *Public Health*, p. 19; see also Bridenbaugh, *Cities in the Wilderness*, p. 87.

35. Ola E. Winslow, *A Destroying Angel: The Conquest of Smallpox in Colonial Boston* (Boston: Houghton Mifflin, 1974), p. 26.

36. See Douglas Edward Leach, *Flintlock and Tomahawk: New England in King Philip's War* (New York: Norton, 1958), p. 243. On the matter of Indian casualties, it has recently been estimated that between 1620 and 1720 the Indian tribes of New England lost more than 25 percent of their total populations in wars with the white settlers: Sherburne F. Cook, "Interracial Warfare and Population Decline Among the New England Indians," *Ethnohistory* 20 (1973), 1–24.

37. Increase Mather, *Pray for the Rising Generation* (Boston, 1678).

38. Ibid., p. 12.

39. Ibid., p. 22.

40. Ibid.

41. Marjorie Editha Mitchell, *The Child's Attitude To Death* (London: Barrie & Rockliff, 1966), p. 100; cf. Sylvia Anthony, *The Discovery of Death in Childhood and After* (London: Allen Lane, 1971), especially chap. 8; Roslyn P. Ross, "Separation Fear and the Fear of Death in Children" (unpublished Ph.D. dissertation, New York University, 1966); Eugenia H. Waechter, "Death Anxiety in Children With Fatal Illness" (unpublished Ph.D. dissertation, Stanford University, 1968); and the now almost classic studies of J. Bowlby, especially "Separation Anxiety," *International Journal of Psychoanalysis and Psychiatry*, vols. 41 and 42 (1961), and "Childhood Mourning and Its Implications for Psychiatry," *American Journal of Psychiatry*, vol. 118 (1961).

42. Anthony, *Discovery of Death*, p. 151.

43. Increase Mather, *An Earnest Exhortation to the Children of New England to Exalt the God of their Fathers* (Boston, 1711), p. 35.

44. Morgan, *Puritan Family*, pp. 178–179; cf. Emory Elliott, *Power and the Pulpit in Puritan New England* (Princeton: Princeton University Press, 1975), especially pp. 65–69, for additional references.

45. Cotton Mather, *Help for Distressed Parents* (Boston, 1695), pp. 45, 47.

46. Ibid., pp. 53–55.

47. Jonathan Edwards, unpublished sermon in Edwards's manuscripts in Yale University Library. Quoted in Sanford Fleming, *Children*

and Puritanism (New Haven: Yale University Press, 1933), p. 100.

48. Anthony, *Discovery of Death,* p. 153.

49. Samuel Wakeman, *A Young Man's Legacy* (Boston, 1673), p. 6.

50. *The New England Primer* [1727] (New York: Columbia University Press, 1962); Cotton Mather, *Perswasions from the Terror of the Lord* (Boston, 1711), pp. 31, 36, 35; Wakeman, *Young Man's Legacy,* p. 41; Edwards quoted in Fleming, *Children and Puritanism,* p. 100.

51. Joseph Church, *Language and the Discovery of Reality* (New York: Random House, 1961), pp. 15–16. For full discussion of this and other stages see Jean Piaget, *The Construction of Reality in the Child* (New York: Basic Books, 1954), and *The Child's Conception of Physical Causality* (Totawa, N.J.: Little, Adams & Co., 1966), especially pp. 237–258.

52. Chadwick Hansen, *Witchcraft at Salem* (New York: Braziller, 1969), p. 7; on the belief of seventeenth-century scientists in general in the reality of the invisible world, see Lynn Thorndike, *A History of Magic and Experimental Science* (New York: Columbia University Press, 1958), vols. VII and VIII. The reference to Spinoza is from vol. VIII, p. 570.

53. Samuel Lee, *The Great Day of Judgment* (Boston, 1692), pp. 19–20.

54. Benjamin Wadsworth, "The Nature of Early Piety," p. 15; Solomon Stoddard, *The Efficacy of the Fear of Hell to Restrain Men From Sin* (Boston, 1713), p. 24; Joseph Green, *The Commonplace Book of Joseph Green* (1696), ed. Samuel Eliot Morison, Colonial Society of Massachusetts Publications 34 (1943), 204.

55. *Diary of Samuel Sewall,* vol. I, pp. 249, 345–346, 349. See also the terrified reaction of Sewall's young son Sam to the death of a companion and his father's reminding him of the "need to prepare for Death," ibid., p. 249.

56. James Fitch, *Peace the End of the Perfect and Upright* (Boston, 1673), p. 6.

57. Leonard Hoar, *The Sting of Death* (Boston, 1680), pp. 11–12.

58. Willard, *The Child's Portion,* p. 67.

Chapter 4

1. Thomas Hooker, *The Application of Redemption* (London, 1657), p. 299; Norman Pettit, *The Heart Prepared: Grace and Conversion*

in Puritan Spiritual Life (New Haven: Yale University Press, 1966), p. 19.

2. John Calvin, *Institutes of the Christian Religion,* ed. John T. McNeill (Philadelphia: Westminster Press, 1960), vol. 2, p. 1013. On the efforts to reform the wording of the Book of Common Prayer, see John Strype, *The Life and Acts of . . . John Whitgift* (London, 1718), especially p. 136, and appropriate appendix; and "The Exceptions Against the Book of Common Prayer" [1661] in Peter Bayne, ed., *Documents Relating to the Settlement of the Church of England* (London: W. Kent and Co., 1862), especially pp. 143, 176.

3. Solomon Stoddard, *The Tryal of Assurance* (Boston, 1699), p. 17.

4. Edmund S. Morgan, *Visible Saints* (Ithaca, N.Y.: Cornell University Press, 1963), p. 69.

5. Arthur Hildersam, *Lectures upon the Fourth of John* (London, 1629), p. 311.

6. Jonathan Edwards, *A Faithful Narrative* [1737], reprinted in C. C. Goen, ed., *The Works of Jonathan Edwards,* vol. IV (New Haven: Yale University Press, 1972), p. 186. The Goen quote is from ibid., p. 47; but see also his *Revivalism and Separatism in New England, 1740–1800* (New Haven: Yale University Press, 1969), pp. 44–54.

7. Jonathan Edwards, *Original Sin,* in *Works,* vol. II (New York: Robert Carter, 1881), p. 328.

8. John Preston, *The New Creature* (London, 1633), p. 23; John Winthrop, *History of New England,* ed. James Savage (Boston: Little, Brown, 1853), vol. I, pp. 281–282.

9. For a full discussion of the term, see the research of Albert Mathews in Colonial Society of Massachusetts Publications, XVII (1915), 300–392.

10. Increase Mather, *The Mystery of Christ Opened and Applyed* (Boston, 1686), p. 2; Mather, *A Sermon Concerning Obedience & Resignation to the Will of God* (Boston, 1714), p. 38; John Collins, "To the Reader," in Jonathan Mitchel, *A Discourse of the Glory* (Boston, 1721), pp. 2, 4–5.

11. William Perkins, *Salve for a Sicke Man* (London, 1597), p. 5; Increase Mather, "Preface," in Mitchel, *A Discourse of the Glory,* p. iv.

12. Leonard Hoar, *The Sting of Death* (Boston, 1680), pp. 4, 3.

13. Epitaph from the Hull stone, Cheshire, Connecticut. Cited in

Allan I. Ludwig, *Graven Images* (Middletown, Conn.: Wesleyan University Press, 1966), p. 88.

14. Edwards, *Original Sin*, p. 372.
15. For a particularly clear example of the confusion wrought by this ambivalence, see Urian Oakes's long poem *An Elegie Upon the Death of the Reverend Mr. Thomas Shepard* (Boston, 1677).
16. Cotton Mather, *The Thoughts of a Dying Man* (Boston, 1697), pp. 38–39; see also his *Awakening Thoughts on the Sleep of Death* (Boston, 1712), pp. 16ff., for similar thoughts and phrasing; Mather, *Death Made Easie & Happy* (London, 1701), p. 94.
17. C. W. Wahl, "The Fear of Death," in Herman Feifel, ed., *The Meaning of Death* (New York: McGraw-Hill, 1959), p. 19.
18. Perry Miller, *The New England Mind: The Seventeenth Century* (Boston: Beacon Press, 1961), pp. 37–38; Ludwig, *Graven Images*, p. 108.
19. Increase Mather, *Several Sermons* (Boston, 1715), pp. 59–60.
20. Cotton Mather, *Parentator* (Boston, 1724), pp. 207–208.
21. Perkins, *Salve for a Sicke Man*, p. 6.
22. Samuel Wakeman, *A Young Man's Legacy to the Rising Generation* (Boston, 1673), p. 45.
23. Hoar, *The Sting of Death*, pp. 11–12.
24. Even Increase Mather, after repeated pressing on the matter of his probable salvation—"Do you believe it, Syr, and rejoice in the Views and Hopes of it?" his son demanded—cried "I do! I do! I do!" as he died in Cotton's arms. Cotton Mather, *Parentator*, p. 210.
25. Cotton Mather, *Victorina* (Boston, 1717), pp. 73–78. (Although the title sermon was written by Mather, the pages cited are from "An Account of Mrs. Katharin Mather, By Another Hand.") For still another example in the Mather family of death-related anxieties throughout youth and young adulthood (when he did in fact die), see the biography of Nathaniel Mather in his brother Cotton's *Magnalia Christi Americana* [1702] (Hartford, Conn.: Silas Andrys and Sons, 1853), vol. II, pp. 157–159.
26. Cotton Mather, *Euthanasia* (Boston, 1723), p. 5.
27. See, for example, Samuel Willard, *A Compleat Body of Divinity* (Boston, 1726), p. 234. From Sermon LXVI, October 31, 1693; and Cotton Mather, *Euthanasia*, p. 7.
28. Perkins, *Salve for a Sicke Man*, p. 55.
29. *Ars Moriendi* [ca. 1450] (London: The Holbein Society, 1881);

Henry More, S.J., *Historia Provinciae Anglicanae Societatis Jesu* (1660), lib. iv, S. XI, p. 134, quoted in Philip Caraman, ed., *William Weston: The Autobiography of an Elizabethan* (London: Longmans, Green, 1955), p. 147.

30. D. P. Walker, *The Decline of Hell* (Chicago: University of Chicago Press, 1964).

31. In Mitchel, *A Discourse of the Glory*, p. viii. Mather is here specifically referring to Mitchel's ministry.

32. Solomon Stoddard, *The Efficacy of the Fear of Hell to Restrain Men From Sin* (Boston, 1713), p. 24.

33. Ibid., p. 26.

34. Jeremy Taylor, *The Rule and Exercises of Holy Dying* [1651] (New York: Pott and Amery, 1869), p. 85; Marie Huber, *The World Unmask'd* (London, 1736), p. 262.

35. Jonathan Edwards, "The Eternity of Hell Torments," Sermon XI, vol. IV (New York: Leavitt & Allen, 1843), p. 278.

36. Charles Chauncy, *The New Creature Describ'd* (Boston, 1741), p. 20. For a thorough, if somewhat more pedestrian, summing up of the Puritan view of Hell, see John Bunyan, *Sighs From Hell or Groans of a Damned Soul* (Boston, 1708).

37. See Norman T. Burns, *Christian Mortalism from Tyndale to Milton* (Cambridge: Harvard University Press, 1972); and Harold Fisch, *Richard Overton: Mans Mortalitie* (Liverpool: Liverpool University Press, 1968), pp. xvii–xxv.

38. Quoted in T. S. R. Boase, *Death in the Middle Ages* (London: Thames and Hudson, 1972), p. 124.

39. Cotton Mather, *Thoughts of a Dying Man*, pp. 40–41.

40. James Fitch, *Peace the End of the Perfect and Upright* (Boston, 1673), p. 6.

41. Hoar, *The Sting of Death*, pp. 10–11.

42. Cotton Mather, *Thoughts of a Dying Man*, pp. 9, 15–16, 27–28.

43. John Winthrop, *Journal*, vol. I (New York: Scribner's, 1908), p. 267; on another occasion Winthrop reflected on Anne Hutchinson's supposed delivery of thirty monsters at one time: "And see how the wisdom of God fitted this judgment to her sinne every way, for looke as she had vented mishapen opinions, so she must bring forth deformed monsters; and as about 30. Opinions in number, so many monsters." John Winthrop, "A Short Story," in David D. Hall, ed., *The Antinomian Controversy, 1636–1638* (Middletown, Conn.: Wesleyan University Press, 1968), p. 214.

44. Sacvan Bercovitch, *The Puritan Origins of the American Self* (New Haven: Yale University Press, 1975), pp. 32, 204.
45. Peter L. Berger, *The Sacred Canopy: Elements of a Sociological Theory of Religion* (Garden City, N.Y.: Doubleday Anchor, 1969), p. 51.
46. For a concise discussion of both the sociological and psychological uses of the term, see Robert K. Merton, *Social Theory and Social Structure* (New York: Free Press, 3rd ed., enl., 1968), pp. 215–218.
47. Sebastian De Grazia, *The Political Community: A Study of Anomie* (Chicago: University of Chicago Press, 1948), p. 72.
48. Leon Festinger, *A Theory of Cognitive Dissonance* (Evanston: Row, Peterson, 1957), p. 260.
49. William James, *The Principles of Psychology* (New York: Henry Holt, 1890), vol. II, p. 290.
50. G. E. R. Lloyd, *Polarity and Analogy* (Cambridge: Cambridge University Press, 1966).
51. Ibid., p. 264.
52. For a brief summary of recent thought on the contemporary relationship between death and religion, see Irving E. Alexander and Arthur M. Adlerstein, "Death and Religion," in Feifel, *Meaning of Death*, pp. 271–283. Cf. many of the articles in Hendrik M. Ruitenbeek, ed., *Death: Interpretations* (New York: Delta Books, 1969), and a sweeping criticism of most such studies to date: Barbara Chasin, "Neglected Variables in the Study of Death Attitudes," *Sociological Quarterly* 12 (1971), 107–13.

Chapter 5

1. *Winthrop Papers* (Boston: Massachusetts Historical Society, 1929–47), vol. II, p. 295.
2. William Hooke, *New-Englands Sence of Old-Englands and Irelands Sorrowes* (London, 1645), reproduced in Samuel Hopkins Emery, *The Ministry of Taunton* (Boston: J. P. Jewett & Co., 1853), vol. I, pp. 116–117; Perry Miller, *The New England Mind: From Colony to Province* (Boston: Beacon Press, 1961), p. 5.
3. On the Islamic customs, see S. G. F. Brandon, *The Judgment of the Dead: The Idea of Life After Death in the Major Religions* (New York: Scribner's, 1967), pp. 136–148; and D. Sourdel, "Le jugement des morts dans l'Islam," *Sources Orientales* 4 (1961).

On the Navajo, see Clyde Kluckhohn, "Conceptions of Death Among the Southwestern Indians," Divinity School Bulletin, Harvard University, 1948; and Gladys A. Reichard, *Social Life of the Navajo Indians* (New York: Columbia University Press, 1928), pp. 141–143.

4. On one development of the idea of Purgatory and its great significance for major aspects of Christian thought, see Gaby and Michel Vovelle, *Vision de la mort et de l'audelà en Provençe* (Cahiers des Annales 29, 1970). Cf. Brandon, *The Judgment of the Dead*, pp. 112–118, 131–132; D. P. Walker, *The Decline of Hell: Seventeenth-Century Discussions of Eternal Torment* (Chicago: University of Chicago Press, 1964), pp. 59–60; and Lauran Paine, *The Hierarchy of Hell* (New York: Hippocrene Books, 1972), pp. 107–108.

5. Quoted in Brandon, *Judgment of the Dead*, p. 132.

6. Keith Thomas, *Religion and the Decline of Magic* (London: Weidenfeld and Nicolson, 1971), p. 603.

7. Robert Bolton, *Mr. Boltons Last and Learned Worke of the Foure Last Things* (London, 1635), pp. 82–83; for Aquinas on the body, the soul, and resurrection, see St. Thomas Aquinas, *Summa Theologica* (New York: Benziger Brothers, 1948), vol. III, pp. 2894–2931.

8. John Weever, *Ancient Funeral Monuments* (London, 1631), p. 31.

9. *A Directory For the Publique Worship of God* (London, 1646), p. 35.

10. Quoted in Lawrence Stone, *The Crisis of the Aristocracy* (Oxford: Clarendon Press, 1965), p. 577. As Stone points out, changing attitudes among the aristocracy regarding funerals were part of a broader sphere of changes in aristocratic social life. For an incisive analysis of some of these developing patterns as early as the mid-sixteenth century, see M. E. James, "Two Tudor Funerals," *Transactions of the Cumberland and Westmoreland Antiquarian and Archaeological Society* 66 (1966), 165–178.

11. Stone, *Crisis of the Aristocracy*, p. 579.

12. See Ralph E. Giesey, *The Royal Funeral Ceremony in Renaissance France* (Geneva: Librairie E. Droz, 1960), pp. 27–28.

13. Thomas Greenhill, *NEKPOKHΔEIA: or, The Art of Embalming* (London, 1705), pp. 4–5.

14. M. Misson, *Memoirs and Observations in His Travels Over England* [1698] (London, 1719), p. 89.

15. Bolton, *Mr. Boltons Last and Learned Worke,* pp. 152, 159.
16. Ibid. For a survey and analysis of the content of such sermons, see Selmer N. Westby, "The Puritan Funeral Sermon in Seventeenth-Century England" (unpublished Ph.D. dissertation, University of Southern California, 1970). Another characteristic of English funerals during this period that receives only passing mention in the literature, making it impossible to tell how widespread a custom it was, was the practice of limiting attendance at funerals to family and friends of the same sex as the deceased. See Misson, *Memoirs and Observations,* p. 91. However, for evidence of a similar practice in the United States two centuries later, see Carroll Smith-Rosenberg, "The Female World of Love and Ritual: Relations Between Women in Nineteenth–Century America," *Signs: Journal of Women in Culture and Society* 1 (1975), 24.
17. John Canne, *A Necessitie of Separation from the Church of England* [London, 1634] (London: J. Haddon, 1849), pp. 112–113.
18. David Person, *Varieties: or, A Surveigh of Rare and Excellent Matters* (London, 1635), pp. 159–165.
19. Weever, *Ancient Funeral Monuments,* pp. 17–18.
20. "To the Reader," in Benjamin Carier, *A Missive to His Majesty of Great Britain . . . By Doctor Carier, Conteining the Motives of his Conversion to Catholike Religion* (Paris, 1649) [reprint of an earlier, undated edition].
21. Pierre Muret, *Rites of Funeral, Ancient and Modern,* trans. P. Lorrain (London, 1683), Translator's Introduction (no pag.); Pierre Muret, *Ceremonies funebres de toutes les nations* (Paris, 1679), p. 221.
22. William Prynne, *Canterburies Doome, or the First Part of a Compleat History of the Commitment, Charge, Tryall, Condemnation, Execution of William Laud* (London, 1646), p. 466.
23. A recent and superb study of this iconoclastic movement is John Phillips, *The Reformation of Images: Destruction of Art in England, 1535–1660* (Berkeley: University of California Press, 1973).
24. Ibid., pp. 117–119.
25. Katharine A. Esdaile, *English Monumental Sculpture Since the Renaissance* (New York: Macmillan, 1927), p. 59.
26. Weever, *Ancient Funeral Monuments,* "The Author to the Reader" (unpaginated).
27. Ibid., pp. 18, 54–55.
28. Ibid., p. 31.

29. Frederick Burgess, *English Churchyard Memorials* (London: Lutterworth Press, 1963), pp. 116–118.

30. Thomas Lechford, *Plain Dealing: or, Newes from New England* [London, 1642] (Boston: Wiggin & Lunt, 1867), pp. 87–88; Thomas Shepard, *The Clear Sun-shine of the Gospel Breaking Forth Upon the Indians in New England* (London, 1648), pp. 5, 36.

31. Nathaniel B. Shurtleff, ed., *The Records of the Colony of Massachusetts Bay in New England* (Boston: William White, 1853–54), vol. 3, p. 162.

32. *A Directory For the Publique Worship of God*, p. 35.

33. Mary Caroline Crawford, *Social Life in Old New England* (Boston: Little, Brown, 1914), p. 453.

34. See Samuel Sewall, *The Diary of Samuel Sewall, 1674–1729*, ed. M. Halsey Thomas (New York: Farrar, Straus & Giroux, 1973), vol. I, pp. 168, 260–261, 159–160.

35. Nathaniel Morton, *New Englands Memoriall* (Cambridge, 1669), p. 158.

36. Sewall, *Diary*, vol. II, pp. 1020–1021.

37. Ibid., vol. I, p. 54. Many of the generalizations made in the following few paragraphs are drawn from Sewall's detailed reports on the hundreds of funerals he attended during his life. Except where specific examples are cited, I will not clutter the page with references to all the sources for the behavior described.

38. See Alice Morse Earle, *Customs and Fashions in Old New England* (New York: Scribner's, 1893), pp. 374–375.

39. Sewall, *Diary*, vol. I, p. 387. On the practice of bell-ringing at funerals in England and New England, cf. Canne, *A Necessitie of Separation*, p. 113; and *Acts & Resolves of the Province of Massachusetts Bay* (Boston, 1720–26), vol. 10, app. 5, p. 114.

40. Cotton Mather, *An Elegy on . . . the Reverend Mr. Nathanael Collins* (Boston, 1685), p. 2.

41. Earle, *Customs and Fashions*, p. 376; on the English Nonconformists' attitudes see Canne, *A Necessitie of Separation*, p. 112.

42. Cotton Mather, *A Christian Funeral* (Boston, 1713); *Acts & Laws, of His Majesty's Province of the Massachusetts-Bay in New England* (Boston, 1726), p. 309.

43. Sewall, *Diary*, vol. I, p. 74.

44. John L. Sibley, *Biographical Sketches of the Graduates of Harvard University* (Cambridge: C. W. Sever, 1873–85), vol. II, p. 384.

45. Sewall, *Diary,* vol. I, pp. 119, 125.
46. James Fitch, *Peace the End of the Perfect and Upright* (Boston, 1673), p. 1.
47. Sewall, *Diary,* vol. I, p. 126.
48. See Benno M. Forman, "A New Light on Early Grave Markers," *Essex Institute Historical Collections* 104 (1968), 127–129; and Peter Benes, "Additional Light on Wooden Grave Markers," ibid. 111 (1975), 53–64.
49. Cf. Harriette M. Forbes, *Gravestones of Early New England and the Men Who Made Them* (Boston: Houghton Mifflin, 1927), p. 22; and Allan I. Ludwig, *Graven Images: New England Stonecarving and Its Symbols, 1650–1815* (Middletown, Conn.: Wesleyan University Press, 1966), pp. 283–287.
50. See Dickran and Ann Tashjian, *Memorials for Children of Change: The Art of Early New England Stonecarving* (Middletown, Conn.: Wesleyan University Press, 1974), p. 24.
51. Ludwig, *Graven Images,* pp. 234–236.
52. V. Gordon Childe, "Directional Changes in Funerary Practices During 50,000 Years," *Man* 45 (1945), especially pp. 16–18.
53. John Cotton, *An Exposition Upon the Thirteenth Chapter of the Revelation* (London, 1655), p. 93. [This sermon, according to a preface to the printed volume, was first delivered in either late 1639 or early 1640.] John Eliot and Thomas Mayhew, Jr., *Tears of Repentance* (London, 1653), "To His Excellency," unpaginated. On Cotton's millennial teachings, see Everett H. Emerson, *John Cotton* (New York: Twayne, 1965), pp. 95–101; and Larzer Ziff, *The Career of John Cotton* (Princeton: Princeton University Press, 1962), pp. 170–202. On the millennial impulse of New England's Puritans in general, see A. J. B. Gilsdorf, "The Puritan Apocalypse: New England Eschatology in the Seventeenth Century" (unpublished dissertation, Yale University, 1964); and the very fine recent essay by J. F. Maclear, "New England and the Fifth Monarchy: The Quest for the Millennium in Early American Puritanism," *William and Mary Quarterly,* 3rd series, 32 (1975), 223–260.
54. See Edmund S. Morgan, *The Puritan Dilemma: The Story of John Winthrop* (Boston: Little, Brown, 1958), p. 178; and William L. Sachse, *The Colonial American in Britain* (Madison: University of Wisconsin, 1956).
55. Miller, *The New England Mind: From Colony to Province,* p. 9;

Increase Mather, *A Discourse Concerning the Danger of Apostasy* (Boston, 1679), p. 76.

56. Bernard Bailyn, *The New England Merchants in the Seventeenth Century* (New York: Harper & Row, 1964), p. 110.

57. *Acts and Laws of His Majesties Province of the Massachusetts Bay in New England* (Boston, 1699), p. 99.

58. Edmund S. Morgan, *The Puritan Family* (New York: Harper & Row, 1966), pp. 161–186.

59. Thomas Shepard, *New Englands Lamentations for Old Englands Present Errours* (London, 1645), p. 4.

60. Shurtleff, *Records of the Colony of Massachusetts Bay,* vol. 3, p. 287; cf. Perry Miller, "Declension in a Bible Commonwealth," *American Antiquarian Society Proceedings,* new series, vol. 51 (1941), pp. 49–50.

61. See, for example, Shurtleff, *Records of the Colony of Massachusetts Bay,* vol. I, pp. 59–63.

62. Sacvan Bercovitch, "Horologicals to Chronometricals: the Rhetoric of the Jeremiad," *Literary Monographs* 3 (Madison: University of Wisconsin Press, 1970), pp. 42–43.

63. Robert Hertz, "The Collective Representation of Death" [1907] in Hertz, *Death and the Right Hand,* trans. R. and C. Needham (Glencoe, Ill.: Free Press, 1960).

64. Ibid., p. 76.

65. For more recent treatments, see W. Lloyd Warner, *The Family of God: A Symbolic Study of Christian Life in America* (New Haven: Yale University Press, 1961), pt. III; and Victor Turner, "Betwixt and Between: The Liminal Period in *Rites de Passage,*" in Turner, *The Forest of Symbols: Aspects of Ndembu Ritual* (Ithaca, N.Y.: Cornell University Press, 1967), pp. 93–111. On the Kota of South India, and for some very perceptive comments on funerals in general, see David G. Mandelbaum, "Social Uses of Funeral Rites," in Herman Feifel, ed., *The Meaning of Death* (New York: McGraw-Hill, 1959), pp. 189–217.

66. Robert Blauner, "Death and Social Structure," *Psychiatry* 29 (1966), 387.

67. Patrick H. Butler, III, "Death, the Individual and Society in Colonial Tidewater Virginia" (unpublished Ph.D. dissertation, The Johns Hopkins University, forthcoming); *The Colonial Laws of New York From the Year 1664 to the Revolution* (Albany, N.Y.: J. B. Lyon, 1894), vol. I, pp. 152–153. For some perceptive comments

on other aspects of death in early Virginia, see Darrett B. Rutman and Anita H. Rutman, "Of Agues and Fevers: Malaria in the Early Chesapeake," *William and Mary Quarterly,* 3rd series, 33 (1976), 31–60; and Edmund S. Morgan, *American Slavery, American Freedom: The Ordeal of Colonial Virginia* (New York: Norton, 1975), chap. 8.

68. *Acts and Laws . . . of Massachusetts Bay,* p. 309.

69. Fitch, *Peace the End of the Perfect and Upright,* p. 9.

70. Samuel Willard, *The Righteous Man's Death* (Boston, 1684), p. 160; Increase Mather, *A Call From Heaven* (Boston, 1679), "To the Reader," unpaginated.

71. Samuel Willard, *A Sermon Preached Upon Ezek . . . Occasioned by the Death of . . . John Leveret, Esq.* (Boston, 1679), pp. 5, 10–12. It is worth noting here that since lamentations of this sort were generally reserved for those members of the community deemed most crucial to its survival, virtually all of these vivid expressions of loss were reserved for *male* Saints—except insofar as the loss was described as affecting the family. See Lonna M. Malmsheimer, "New England Funeral Sermons and Changing Attitudes Toward Women, 1672–1792" (unpublished dissertation, University of Minnesota, 1973), especially pp. 149–151. I am grateful to Nancy F. Cott and Kathryn Sklar for bringing this study to my attention.

72. See, for example, Benjamin Tompson's sermon and elegy for John Winthrop, Jr., *New Englands Tears For Her Present Miseries* (Boston, 1676).

73. Urian Oakes, *An Elegie Upon the Death of the Reverend Mr. Thomas Shepard* (Boston, 1677), p. 7.

74. Cotton Mather, *An Elegy . . . on . . . Nathanael Collins,* p. 2.

75. E.g., Blauner, "Death and Social Structure," p. 387; Elisabeth Kübler-Ross, *On Death and Dying* (New York: Macmillan, 1969), pp. 177–179; and Franz Borkenau, "The Concept of Death," in Robert Fulton, ed., *Death and Identity* (New York: Wiley), pp. 42–56. Cf. Bronislaw Malinowski, *Magic, Science, and Religion and Other Essays* (Glencoe, Ill.: Free Press, 1948), p. 30.

76. Mary Douglas, *Purity and Danger: An Analysis of Concepts of Pollution and Taboo* (London: Routledge & Kegan Paul, 1966); cf. Turner, "Betwixt and Between."

77. Barney G. Glaser and Anselm L. Strauss, *Awareness of Dying* (Chicago: Aldine, 1965), pp. 113–115.

78. Jack Goody, *Death, Property and the Ancestors* (Stanford: Stanford University Press, 1962), p. 46.
79. An especially penetrating analysis of this problem is found in Blauner, "Death and Social Structure," pp. 387–389; cf. Geoffrey Gorer, *Death, Grief, and Mourning* (Garden City, N.Y.: Doubleday, 1965), especially pp. 83–91.

Chapter 6

1. Charles and Katharine George, *The Protestant Mind of the English Reformation* (Princeton: Princeton University Press, 1961); for an explicit rejoinder to the Georges, see John F. H. New, *Anglican and Puritan: The Basis of Their Opposition, 1558–1640* (Stanford: Stanford University Press, 1964). An important recent addition to the literature is J. Sears McGee, *The Godly Man in Stuart England: Anglicans, Puritans, and the Two Tables, 1620–1670* (New Haven: Yale University Press, 1976).
2. Darrett B. Rutman, *Winthrop's Boston* (New York: Norton, 1972), especially pp. 274–79; and "The Mirror of Puritan Authority," in George A. Billias, ed., *Law and Authority in Colonial America* (Barre, Mass.: Barre Publishers, 1965), pp. 149–167; Timothy H. Breen and Stephen Foster, "The Puritans' Greatest Achievement: A Study of Social Cohesion in Seventeenth-Century Massachusetts," *The Journal of American History* 60 (1973), 5–22; Edmund S. Morgan, "The Puritan Ethic and the American Revolution," *William and Mary Quarterly*, 3rd series, 24 (1967), 3–43; Sydney E. Ahlstrom, "The Puritan Ethic and the Spirit of American Democracy," in George L. Hunt, ed., *Calvinism and the Political Order* (Philadelphia: Westminster Press, 1965), pp. 88–107.
3. Clifford Geertz, "Ritual and Social Change: A Javanese Example," *American Anthropologist* 59 (1957), 33.
4. See Geertz, ibid., 32–54, for a penetrating study of a people who experienced these difficulties when a particular cultural institution —in this case a funeral ceremony—failed to keep pace with social changes in the larger society.

   Note: It is important here to distinguish between the "world view/ethos" tension (which existed entirely *within* the religiocultural network) and this "culture/social structure" tension (which involved the religiocultural network interacting with the larger so-

NOTES TO PAGES 138-140

ciety in which it was contained). In both cases I am contending there was a need for substantial agreement between the two phenomena for the belief system to "work"—but these are two very different problems. Puritanism, I am arguing, was by the turn of the eighteenth century struggling with discontinuity in both areas.

5. Geoffrey Gorer, *Death, Grief, and Mourning* (Garden City, N.Y.: Doubleday, 1965), pp. 83–91; Le Roy Bowman, *The American Funeral: A Study in Guilt, Extravagance, and Sublimity* (Washington: Public Affairs Press, 1959), pp. 8–10, 112–128. Cf. Vanderlyn R. Pine and Derek L. Phillips, "The Cost of Dying: A Sociological Analysis of Funeral Expenditures," *Social Problems* 17 (1970), 405–417.

6. Peter Marris, *Loss and Change* (New York: Pantheon, 1974), p. 26.

7. Marc Fried, "Grieving for a Lost Home," in Leonard Duhl, ed., *The Urban Condition* (New York: Basic Books, 1963), p. 151; cf. Marris, *Loss and Change,* chap. III.

8. John Norton, *Three Choice and Profitable Sermons* [1661] (Boston, 1664); John Higginson, *The Cause of God and His People in New England* (Boston, 1663), p. 18; Jonathan Mitchell, *Nehemiah on the Wall in Troublesome Times* (Boston, 1667), Preface; William Stoughton, *New England's True Interest* (Boston, 1668), pp. 8, 18, 19, 21, 24; Samuel Danforth, *A Brief Recognition of New Englands Errand into the Wilderness* (Boston, 1670), pp. 10, 19.

9. Peter Gay, *A Loss of Mastery: Puritan Historians in Colonial America* (New York: Random House, 1968), p. 65.

10. For a particularly cogent discussion of this aspect of the jeremiad, see Sacvan Bercovitch, "Horologicals to Chronometricals: The Rhetoric of the Jeremiad," *Literary Monographs* 3 (Madison: University of Wisconsin Press, 1970), pp. 3–124; cf. the same author's " 'Nehemias Americanus': Cotton Mather and the Concept of the Representative American," *Early American Literature* 8 (1974), 220–238; his further elaborations in *The Puritan Origins of the American Self* (New Haven: Yale University Press, 1975); and David Minter's earlier examination of the same theme in his excellent chapter on the jeremiad in *The Interpreted Design as a Structural Principle in American Prose* (New Haven: Yale University Press, 1969), pp. 50–66.

11. Stoughton, *New England's True Interest,* pp. 24, 32.

12. Cotton Mather, *A Midnight Cry, An Essay for our Awakening out of a Sinful Sleep* (Boston, 1692), p. 59.
13. Marris, *Loss and Change,* pp. 151, 166.
14. Crane Brinton, *The Anatomy of Revolution* (New York: Vintage Books, 1965), p. 3.
15. Jonathan Parsons, "Account of the Revival of Religion in the West Parish of Lyme in Connecticut," *The Christian History for the Year 1744* (Boston: Kneeland and Green, 1745), p. 136.
16. Quoted in George L. Walker, *Some Aspects of the Religious Life of New England* (New York: Silver, Burdett, 1897), pp. 89–92.
17. Jonathan Edwards, *Some Thoughts Concerning the Present Revival of Religion in New England* [1742], in C. C. Goen, ed., *The Works of Jonathan Edwards,* vol. 4 (New Haven: Yale University Press, 1972), p. 291.
18. Ibid., pp. 353, 358.
19. Perry Miller, "Jonathan Edwards and the Great Awakening," reprinted in Miller, *Errand Into the Wilderness* (Cambridge: Harvard University Press, 1956), pp. 156–157.
20. See Edwin S. Gaustad, "Society and the Great Awakening in New England," *William and Mary Quarterly,* 3rd series, 2 (1954), 576; cf. Gaustad, *The Great Awakening in New England* (New York: Harper, 1957), pp. 116–125.
21. Anthony F. C. Wallace, "Revitalization Movements," *American Anthropologist* 58 (1956), 264–281.
22. See, for example, Ralf Dahrendorf, "Out of Utopia: Toward a Reorientation of Sociological Analysis," *American Journal of Sociology* 64 (1958), 115–127. Cf. Pierre L. van den Berghe, "Dialectic and Functionalism: Toward a Theoretical Synthesis," *American Sociological Review* 28 (1963), 695–705; and Jonathan H. Turner, "From Utopia to Where?: A Strategy for Reformulating the Dahrendorf Conflict Model," *Social Forces* 52 (1973), 236–244.
23. A now-classic statement on this, and one that deals explicitly with the failings of the cruder forms of organic analogy, is Robert K. Merton, "Manifest and Latent Functions," in Merton, *Social Theory and Social Structure,* rev. ed. (New York: Free Press, 1968), pp. 73–138; for further discussion, cf. Ernest Nagel, "A Formalization of Functionalism," in Nagel, *Logic Without Metaphysics* (Glencoe, Ill.: Free Press, 1956), pp. 247–283.
24. Wallace, "Revitalization Movements," p. 267.

25. There is a very large body of literature on this and related general phenomena. I have chosen Wallace's essay for illustrative purposes because it is a synthesis rather than a study of a particular culture or society. For a more detailed introduction to the problems involved, see the following: Sylvia L. Thrupp, ed., *Millennial Dreams in Action* (The Hague: Mouton, 1962); Vittorio Lanternari, *The Religions of the Oppressed: A Study of Modern Messianic Cults* (New York: Knopf, 1963); I. C. Jarvie, *The Revolution in Anthropology* (London: Routledge & Kegan Paul, 1967), pp. 47–169, 225–242; Michael Barkun, *Disaster and the Millennium* (New Haven: Yale University Press, 1974); Bryan R. Wilson, *Magic and the Milennium* (London: Heinemann, 1973); and David E. Stannard, "Time and the Millennium: On the Religious Experience of the American Slave," in Jack Salzman, ed., *Prospects: An Annual Journal of American Cultural Studies,* vol. 2 (New York: Burt Franklin & Co., 1976).

26. Alan Heimert and Perry Miller, eds., *The Great Awakening* (New York: Bobbs-Merrill, 1967), pp. xiii–xiv, lxi.

27. Gaustad, *The Great Awakening in New England,* p. 62.

28. John W. Draper, *The Funeral Elegy and the Rise of English Romanticism* (New York: New York University Press, 1929).

29. Charles Drelincourt, *The Christian's Defence Against the Fears of Death, With Directions How to Die Well,* trans. J. Spavan (Boston, 1744), p. 127. In noting the shift from the King of Terrors to the Heavenly Bridegroom imagery I do not mean to imply more than a relative shift in emphasis. The personification of death as a lover long predates the advent of Puritanism and, as David C. McClelland has pointed out, remains an element in certain modern pathological fantasies. [See David C. McClelland, "The Harlequin Complex," in Robert W. White, ed., *The Study of Lives* (Chicago: Aldine-Atherton, 1963), pp. 95–119.] Among seventeenth-century Puritans the image, though less common than that of the King of Terrors, occurs most notably in the poetry of Edward Taylor.

30. Theophilus Rowe, *The Life of Mrs. Elizabeth Rowe* (Boston, 1747).

31. Darby Dawne, M.D., *Health, A Poem* (Boston, 1724), second section, "The Doctor's Decade," p. 14.

32. Benjamin Colman, *A Holy Walk With God* (Boston, 1717), pp. 23–24.

33. Letter from Esther Burr to Jonathan Edwards, November 2, 1757, ms., Burr Family Papers, Yale University. For the reference to Betty Sewall's outcry, see chap. I, fn. 55.

34. Samuel Willard, *The Child's Portion* (Boston, 1684), p. 67; Cotton Mather, *Parentator* (Boston, 1724), p. 208; Jonathan Todd, *Be Followers of the Saints* (New London, Conn., 1743), p. 45.

35. William Thompson, *The Duty of a People Respecting Their Deceased Ministers* (Boston, 1743), p. 22.

36. Josiah Smith, *The Doctrine and Glory of the Saints' Resurrection* (Boston, 1742), pp. 12–13.

37. Quotes from Brainerd and his diary in Jonathan Edwards, "A Sermon Preached at the Funeral of the Rev. David Brainerd," [1747] in *The Works of President Edwards* (New York: S. Converse, 1829), vol. 10, pp. 477, 482.

38. Thomas Skinner, *The Mourner Admonished* (Boston, 1746), pp. 20–22.

39. Charles Chauncy, *The Blessedness of the Dead Who Die in the Lord* (Boston, 1749), p. 23.

40. Charles Chauncy, *The New Creature Describ'd* (Boston, 1741), p. 20.

41. Leonard Hoar, *The Sting of Death* (Boston, 1680), p. 12; Charles Chauncy, *Blessedness of the Dead* . . . , p. 23.

42. Samuel Mather, *The Walk of the Upright, With its Comfort* (Boston, 1753), p. 32.

43. For a brief but lucid biographical treatment of Samuel Mather, see Clifford K. Shipton, ed., *Sibley's Harvard Graduates* (Boston: Massachusetts Historical Society, 1945), vol. VII, 216–238.

44. See Norman Pettit, "Hooker's Doctrine of Assurance: A Critical Phase in New England Spiritual Thought," *New England Quarterly* 47 (1974), 518–534; cf. Giles Firmin, *The Real Christian* (London, 1670), especially "Introduction" and "To the Christian Reader."

45. Jonathan Edwards, *An Humble Inquiry* (Boston, 1749), pp. 7, 36.

46. See Robert Henson, "Form and Content in the Puritan Funeral Elegy," *American Literature* 32 (1960–61), 11–27.

47. Jeannine Hensley, ed., *The Works of Anne Bradstreet* (Cambridge: Harvard University Press, 1967), pp. 201–203.

48. Howard Judson Hall, ed., *Benjamin Tompson, 1642–1714; First Native-Born Poet of America* (Boston: Houghton Mifflin, 1924), pp. 137–140.

49. *John Saffin: His Book, 1665–1708,* introduction by Caroline Hazard (New York: Harbor Press, 1928), pp. 117–118.
50. Josiah Smith, *Doctrine and Glory of the Saints' Resurrection,* p. 14.
51. Excerpts from *The Dying Mother's Advice and Farewell* (New London, 1749).
52. See Edwin Dethlefsen and James Deetz, "Death's Heads, Cherubs, and Willow Trees: Experimental Archaeology in Colonial Cemeteries," *American Antiquity* 31 (1966), 502–510. Cf. the less exhaustive, but suggestive, study by Roberta Chin, "English Tombstones: An Attempt to Trace Their Relationship to Social Attitudes and to the Tombstone Trends of Colonial New England," unpublished manuscript, Peabody Museum, Harvard University; and the more cautious remarks of Dickran and Ann Tashjian, *Memorials for Children of Change: The Art of Early New England Stonecarving* (Middletown, Conn.: Wesleyan University Press, 1974), pp. 57–59. The above studies have generally focused on Massachusetts burial grounds, but a personal survey of a number of early Connecticut cemeteries supports these major generalizations.
53. Allan I. Ludwig, *Graven Images: New England Stonecarving and its Symbols, 1650–1815* (Middletown, Conn.: Wesleyan University Press, 1966), pp. 67–77, 389–401.
54. Dethlefsen and Deetz, "Death's Heads, Cherubs, and Willow Trees," p. 505.
55. Boston Record Commissioners, *Report* (Boston: Rockwell & Churchill, 1894), vol. 25, pp. 149, 268, 305–306. For the colonial New York legislation referred to, see chap. 5, fn. 67.
56. Samuel Sewall, *The Diary of Samuel Sewall, 1674–1729,* ed. M. Halsey Thomas (New York: Farrar, Straus & Giroux, 1973), vol. I, p. 227.
57. William Bentley, *The Diary of William Bentley, D.D.* (Salem, Mass.: The Essex Institute, 1907), vol. II, pp. 389–390.
58. Suffolk County (Mass.) Probate Records 84 (1785), p. 452.
59. Sewall, *Diary,* vol. I, pp. 330–331.
60. *Acts and Resolves . . . of the Province of the Massachusetts Bay* (Boston: Wright and Potter, 1903), vol. II, p. 86.
61. Ibid., pp. 431–432.
62. See Kenneth A. Lockridge, "Social Change and the Meaning of the American Revolution," *Journal of Social History* 6 (1973), 403–439.

63. Edmund S. Morgan, *The Gentle Puritan: A Life of Ezra Stiles, 1727–1795* (New Haven: Yale University Press, 1962), p. 188; and Edmund S. Morgan, "New England Puritanism: Another Approach," *William and Mary Quarterly*, 3rd series, 18 (1961), 236–242. For more general confirming evidence see Robert Pope, *The Half-Way Covenant: Church Membership in Puritan New England* (Princeton: Princeton University Press, 1969), pp. 213–214, 217–218, 225. These findings have been supported by a number of subsequent studies of individual New England communities during these critical years. See, for example, Gerald F. Moran, "Conditions of Religious Conversion in the First Society of Norwich, Connecticut, 1718–1744," *Journal of Social History* 5 (1972), especially 332–333.

Chapter 7

1. Ralph Waldo Emerson, "Mary Moody Emerson," in Mark Van Doren, ed., *The Portable Emerson* (New York: Viking, 1946), pp. 544, 563.
2. Ibid., p. 564.
3. See Philippe Ariès, *Western Attitudes Toward Death From the Middle Ages to the Present,* trans. Patricia M. Ranum (Baltimore: The Johns Hopkins University Press, 1974), pp. 55–82.
4. Ibid., p. 67.
5. Ibid., pp. 95–96; cf. Ariès, "The Reversal of Death," trans. Valerie M. Stannard, *American Quarterly* 26 (1974), 536–560.
6. See, for example, Peter Laslett, *The World We Have Lost: England Before the Industrial Age* (New York: Scribner's, 1965), pp. 89–92; and John Demos, *A Little Commonwealth: Family Life in Plymouth Colony* (New York: Oxford University Press, 1970), pp. 62–68.
7. Philip J. Greven, Jr., *Four Generations: Population, Land, and Family in Colonial Andover, Massachusetts* (Ithaca, N.Y.: Cornell University Press, 1970), pp. 15–16. Cf. Demos, *A Little Commonwealth,* chap. 8.
8. D. W. Robertson, *Chaucer's London* (New York: Wiley, 1968), chap. One; Henri de Lubac, *Corpus Mysticum* (Paris: Aubier, 1949), pt. II, chap. II; and Colin Morris, *The Discovery of the Individual, 1050–1200* (New York: Harper & Row, 1972), especially chap. 7. Cf. William J. Brandt, *The Shape of Medieval His-*

tory: Studies in Modes of Perception (New Haven: Yale University Press, 1966).

9. Roger Bastide, "Messianism and Social and Economic Development," in Immanuel Wallerstein, ed., *Social Change: The Colonial Situation* (New York: Wiley, 1966), p. 470.

10. It may well be, as Sacvan Bercovitch has argued, that the legacy of the Puritan mission—specifically as seen in the optimistic side of the jeremiad—can be seen in the development of the "American Dream"; but such a diffusion of the concept would clearly have eliminated its importance in the present context. See Bercovitch, "Horologicals to Chronometricals: The Rhetoric of the Jeremiad," *Literary Monographs* 3 (Madison: University of Wisconsin Press, 1970), pp. 74–90. For a recent study of changes in the American sense of community from Puritanism to the present, see Wilson Carey McWilliams, *The Idea of Fraternity in America* (Berkeley: University of California Press, 1973).

11. On the rise of institutions for deviant individuals, see David J. Rothman, *The Discovery of the Asylum: Social Order and Disorder in the New Republic* (Boston: Little, Brown, 1971); a recent brief but insightful treatment of the "business revolution" and the era of economic and occupational specialization that coincided with the Industrial Revolution of the early nineteenth century, is Thomas C. Cochran, "The Business Revolution," *The American Historical Review* 79 (1974), 1449–1466; the reference to Barbara Welter's work is her essay "The Feminization of American Religion: 1800–1860," in William L. O'Neill, ed., *Insights and Parallels: Problems and Issues in American Social History* (Minneapolis: Burgess Publishing Company, 1973), pp. 305–332.

12. Michel Chevalier, *Society, Manners and Politics in the United States: Being a Series of Letters on North America*, trans. T. G. Bradford (Boston: Weeks, Jordan and Company, 1839), p. 282.

13. Harriett Martineau, *Society in America* (New York: Saunders and Otley, 1837), vol. II, p. 363.

14. Mrs. Trollope, *Domestic Manners of the Americans* (London: Whittaker, Treacher, & Co., 1832), pp. 74–75.

15. The history of death personified as Harlequin is given brief but insightful treatment in David C. McClelland's psychological essay "The Harlequin Complex," in Robert W. White, ed., *The Study of Lives* (Chicago: Aldine-Atherton, 1963), pp. 95–119; Mario

Praz, *The Romantic Agony* (London: Oxford University Press, 2nd ed., 1970), pp. 25–33; Amelia J. Akehurst Diary, 1851 (Akehurst-Lines Collection, University of Georgia), quoted in an unpublished paper by Lewis O. Saum delivered to the American Studies Association conference, San Francisco, November 1973.

16. Excerpts from "What Is Death?" in McGuffey's *New Fourth Eclectic Reader* (Cincinnati: Wilson, Hinkle & Co., 1866), pp. 109–110.

17. W. H. Smith, "The Golden Stair," in Richard Edwards, *Analytical Fourth Reader* (Chicago: Geo. & C. W. Sherwood, 1868), pp. 244–245.

18. *The Mt. Auburn Memorial* (Boston: Safford, Brown & Co., 1861), pp. 61–62, 64–65.

19. J. R. Chandler, "A Mother's Monument," in *The Picturesque Pocket Companion, and Visitor's Guide, Through Mount Auburn* (Boston: Otis, Broaders and Co., 1839), pp. 246–250.

20. John Pierpont, *The Garden of Graves* (Dedham, Mass.: H. Mann, 1841). Originally published in 1832, this little book was reissued in 1841 "for the Benefit of the Ladies' Charity Fair" in Dedham, Massachusetts.

21. Isaac McLellan, Jr., *Mount Auburn, and Other Poems* (Boston: William D. Ticknor, 1843), p. 11.

22. John A. Albro, *An Address Delivered at the Consecration of the Cambridge Cemetery* (Cambridge: Metcalf and Company, 1854), p. 17; "Judge Story's Address," in *Picturesque Pocket Companion*, pp. 67–68.

23. Theodore Cuyler, *The Empty Crib: The Memorial of Little Georgie* (New York: R. Carter and Brothers, 1868), pp. 173, 158. Quoted in Ann Douglas, "Heaven Our Home: Consolation Literature in the Northern United States, 1830–1880" in David E. Stannard, ed., *Death in America* (Philadelphia: University of Pennsylvania Press, 1975), p. 61.

24. Francis and Theresa Pulszky, *White, Red, Black: Sketches of Society in America* [1853] (New York: Negro Universities Press, 1968), vol. III, pp. 98–99; quoted in Stanley French, "The Cemetery as Cultural Institution: The Establishment of Mount Auburn and the 'Rural Cemetery' Movement," in Stannard, *Death in America*, p. 83; Peter Dobkin Hall, "The Cemetery of Mount Auburn: A Mirror of Brahmin Culture" (unpublished paper, Institution for Social and Policy Studies, Yale University, 1975).

25. Lewis O. Saum, "Death in the Popular Mind of Pre–Civil War America," in Stannard, *Death in America*, p. 33.
26. Pierpont, *Garden of Graves*, pp. 9, 7; Harriet Martineau, *Retrospect of Western Travel* (New York: Harper & Brothers, 1838), p. 229.
27. *Picturesque Pocket Companion* . . . , pp. 193–194, 208.
28. Mark Twain, *The Adventures of Huckleberry Finn* (Baltimore: Penguin Books, 1966), p. 162. It should be noted that Philippe Ariès refers to this same incident in his study (*Western Attitudes Toward Death*, pp. 60–61), but cites Twain's satire as an example of what Ariès sees as the continuing vitality of the sentimentalized vision; I would contend that it is evidence of an approach to death already on the wane.
29. Cited in Jessica Mitford, *The American Way of Death* (New York: Simon & Schuster, 1963), p. 222; cf. Barbara Jones, *Design for Death* (Indianapolis: Bobbs-Merrill, 1967); and Robert W. Habenstein and William M. Lamers, *The History of American Funeral Directing* (Milwaukee: National Funeral Directors Association, 1955).
30. Paul Schilder and David Wechsler, "The Attitudes of Children Towards Death," *Journal of Genetic Psychology* 45 (1934), 421. For more recent and more conveniently available comments, see Maria H. Nagy, "The Child's View of Death," in Herman Feifel, ed., *The Meaning of Death* (New York: McGraw-Hill, 1959), pp. 79–93; and Sylvia Anthony, *The Discovery of Death in Childhood and After* (London: Allen Lane, 1971).
31. See Paul B. Sheatsley and Jacob J. Feldman, "A National Survey on Public Reactions and Behavior," in Bradley S. Greenberg and Edwin B. Parker, eds., *The Kennedy Assassination and the American Public* (Stanford: Stanford University Press, 1965), pp. 149–177.
32. Figures computed from various tables in William C. Thomas, Jr., *Nursing Homes and Public Policy* (Ithaca, N.Y.: Cornell University Press, 1969). For some discussion of the effects on the individual of the rising rate of hospital deaths see Robert L. Fulton, "Death and the Self," *Journal of Religion and Health* 3 (1964), 359–368.
33. Elisabeth Kübler-Ross, *On Death and Dying* (New York: Macmillan, 1969), p. 44. An early statement on the avoidance of death by physicians is August M. Kasper's "The Doctor and Death," in

Feifel, *The Meaning of Death,* pp. 259–270. On the various strategies employed by doctors and nurses for maintaining distance and composure, see Barney G. Glaser and Anselm L. Strauss, *Awareness of Dying* (Chicago: Aldine, 1965), pp. 326–356; and Jeanne C. Quint, *The Nurse and the Dying Patient* (New York: Macmillan, 1967), 173–180. On family rejection and desertion of the dying—particularly the elderly—see Rose L. Coser, *Life in the Ward* (East Lansing: Michigan State University Press, 1962), pp. 119–124; and David Sudnow, *Passing On: The Social Organization of Dying* (Englewood Cliffs, N.J.: Prentice-Hall, 1967), p. 97.

34. Ivan Illich, *Medical Nemesis: The Expropriation of Health* (New York: Pantheon, 1976), pp. 170, 206.

35. Sudnow, *Passing On,* pp. 88–90, 74.

36. These and other practices are described in most of the literature on the subject. For the specific practices cited above, see Sudnow, *Passing On,* pp. 74, 83; and Quint, *The Nurse and the Dying Patient,* p. 34.

37. William F. May, "The Sacral Power of Death in Contemporary Experience," *Social Research* 39 (1972), 469, 470–471.

38. It is an unargued assumption here that religion has lost much of its power to either comfort or frighten the modern individual contemplating the meaning of death. I am aware, however, that debate has taken place on this matter; although there is no room for treatment of that debate here, the fact that my assumption is at least not an arbitrary one is testified to by the admission of those who hold contrary views that they are dissenting from the opinions of the overwhelming majority of contemporary philosophers, theologians, and social scientists. See, for example, Andrew M. Greeley, *Unsecular Man: The Persistence of Religion* (New York: Schocken Books, 1972); and Russell Aldwinckle, *Death in the Secular City: Life After Death in Contemporary Theology and Philosophy* (London: George Allen & Unwin, 1972). One of the most important writers representing a different (though his work is too subtle to call it a "contrary") position is Peter Berger. See especially *The Sacred Canopy: Elements of a Sociological Theory of Religion* (Garden City, N.Y.: Doubleday, 1967), where he argues that "religious traditions have lost their character as overarching symbols for the society at large, which must find its integrating symbolism elsewhere" (p. 153), one implication of which is that in much of the contemporary West death no longer "makes sense"—that is, it

is no longer susceptible to plausible or convincing "interpretation" by appeal to a life-transcendent authority.

39. On this last matter, it is worth pointing out that although children's literature on death has become almost nonexistent today, one of the few important and most highly regarded exceptions that does exist—Joan Fassler's *My Grandpa Died Today* (New York: Behavioral Publications, 1971)—both reinforces the idea that death is something that only happens to the very old, and contains not a hint of a religious message: the boy's consolation in the story is based on his grandfather's words, shortly before dying, that he is not afraid to die because the boy "is not afraid to live."

40. *Picturesque Pocket Companion* . . . , p. 208.

41. Simone de Beauvoir, *The Coming of Age* (New York: Putnam's, 1972), p. 807.

Index

Adams, William, 115
Ahlstrom, Sydney E., 136
Albro, John, 180
Ambrose, Saint, 11
Andros, Lady, 110–11
Aquinas, Saint Thomas, 11, 17, 100
Arbella, 135
Arendt, Hannah, 8
Ariès, Philippe, 44–46, 57, 168–69
Ars Moriendi, 15, 19–20, 22, 84
Augustine, Saint, 11, 13

Bacon, Francis, 10, 67
Bastide, Roger, 169–70
Beauvoir, Simone de, 196
Bentley, William, 160
Bercovitch, Sacvan, 90, 126
Bereavement, 131–33, 137–39
Berger, Peter L., 91, 95
Blauner, Robert, 128, 132
Boase, T. S. R., 21
Bolton, Robert, 103
Bowman, Le Roy, 138
Boyle, Robert, 67, 69
Bradstreet, Ann, 57, 154–55
Brainerd, David, 150–51
Brandon, S. G. F., 8
Breen, Timothy H., 136
Brinton, Crane, 141
Browne, Sir Thomas, 23, 28
Bulkley, Peter, 110–11
Bunyan, John, 40

Burial practices. *See* Funeral ritual
Burnet, William, 162
Burr, Esther, 149–50

Calvin, John, 25–26, 72–73, 99–100
Campbell, Joseph, 9
Canne, John, 104
Cartwright, Thomas, 28
Cemeteries, 104–108, 116–17, 129, 156–61, 177–87
Charles II, 106
Chartier, Alain, 34
Chauncy, Charles, 86–87, 152
Chevalier, Michel, 170
Childe, V. Gordon, 122, 128, 132
Childhood: Puritan attitudes toward, 45–52; mortality, 52–57; fear of death, 61–71; nineteenth-century sentimentality, 171–80; twentieth-century denial of death, 188–89
Clarke, John, 153
Cole, Nathan, 142
Collins, John, 75–76
Collins, Nathanael, 113, 131
Colman, Benjamin, 57, 149
Colman, Jane, 57
Contemptus mundi, 19, 21–23, 26–27, 185
Cotton, John, 123–24
Cragg, G. R., 35
Crawford, Mary Caroline, 110
Cromwell, Oliver, 40, 123, 126

233

Raleigh, Sir Walter, 33
René of Chalons, 22
Resurrection, problem of body, 17–
19, 67–68, 100–101
Robert 2nd Earl of Dorset, 101–2
Robertson, D. W., Jr., 39, 169
Robinson, John, 26, 49
Rowe, Elizabeth Singer, 148
Russell, Bertrand, 33
Rutman, Darrett B., 135

Saffin, John, 155
Saum, Lewis O., 184
Savage, Thomas, 130
Schilder, Paul, 189
Separation anxiety, 57–65, 93
Sewall, Elizabeth, 68–70, 149
Sewall, Hannah, 111
Sewall, Samuel, 51, 56, 111, 113–
16, 160–62
Sewall, Samuel, Jr., 56, 70
Shepard, Thomas, 51, 56, 109–10,
124–25
Shepard, Thomas, Jr., 130
Shrimpton, Samuel, 113
Sibbes, Richard, 26
Sibley, John L., 115
Skinner, Thomas, 58–59, 151–52
Sloane, William, 47
Smith, Josiah, 150, 155–56
Soriano, Marc, 46
Spencer, Theodore, 15
Spinoza, Benedict de, 67
Stoddard, Solomon, 73, 85
Stone, Lawrence, 102
Story, Joseph, 180
Stoughton, William, 139
Strange, N., 105
Sudnow, David, 192

Tappin, John, 80
Taylor, Edward, 56

Taylor, Jeremy, 23, 28, 85–86
Tennent, Gilbert, 142
Thornton, Alice, 56
Tocqueville, Alexis de, vii–ix
Todd, Jonathan, 150
Tompson, Benjamin, 155
Trevor-Roper, H. R., 25
Troeltsch, Ernst, 27
Trollope, Frances, 171
Twain, Mark, 187

Unamuno, Miguel de, 4

Van Gennep, Arnold, 127
Vico, Giambattista, 3
Villon, François, 15, 17, 19
Vinovskis, Maris A., 55, 57

Wadsworth, Benjamin, 52
Wakeman, Samuel, 65–66, 80
Walker, D. P., 84
Wallace, Anthony F. C., 144–45
Wechsler, David, 189
Weever, John, 100–101, 104–5,
107–8
Welter, Barbara, 170
Whetcomb, James, 116
Whitefield, George, 142–43
Wigglesworth, Sarah, 162
Willard, Samuel, 51–52, 70
Williams, Mary, 156
Winthrop, John, 40, 75, 89–90, 96,
110, 124, 139
Winthrop, Mary, 110–11
Witches and demons, 36, 38, 42, 67,
69, 89–90
Woodhouse, A. S. P., 32

Zuckerman, Michael, 45, 47